WOMAN IN THE WHEELHOUSE

NANCY TAYLOR ROBSON

Tidewater Publishers, Centreville, Maryland

WOMAN *in the* WHEELHOUSE

Library of Congress Cataloging in Publication Data

Robson, Nancy Taylor, 1951-
      Woman in the wheelhouse.

      1. Robson, Nancy Taylor, 1951-
2. Seafaring life.   3. Tugboats.   I. Title.
G540.R563   1985   910.4'5   84-40824
ISBN 0-87033-331-3

Title page photograph by Charlton A. Gunter
Manufactured in the United States of America
First edition

ACKNOWLEDGMENTS

I WOULD LIKE TO THANK Gary, and Barbara and Bill Starkey, whose editing suggestions, time, and support were so generously given. All were invaluable.

I would also like to thank Charlton A. (Bert) Gunter, The Strand, Oxford, Maryland, for the use of his photographs. He has sensitively and skillfully captured the feeling as well as the detail.

LIST OF ILLUSTRATIONS

WOMAN IN THE WHEELHOUSE

GARY AND I were married in the first week of October, 1975, two weeks after he had been made captain on the tug, *Progress*. He had only been running on tugs a year, but already he was talking of buying our own tug and living aboard her, something that made me shudder each time he mentioned the idea. I had been around the water all my life, as had Gary. We had both sailed pleasure boats since our childhood, and each loved the water in his own way, but the notion of leaving a dry, comfortable home behind to move onto a rusting, rolling tugboat was less than appealing to me. However, I seemed to be the only one who felt that way.

Even my mother, who is anything but an old salt, confided to me that at one time she had considered living on a barge to be the ideal domestic arrangement. Another friend, who had tried unsuccessfully to move into Baltimore Lighthouse for a summer, fairly gushed at the thought of living in such a romantic setting. Men friends grew misty-eyed and waxed poetic while discussing their visions of the life of a tugboat captain. I seemed to be the only one who was not enthralled with the prospect. Also, unlike all these people, I had been aboard an oceangoing tug.

The *Progress* had been tied up at Fredericktown on the Sassafras River, Maryland, for some haphazard repairs in between jobs, and I had been invited to dinner one steamy August evening. It had seemed to me at the time that tugs were greasy,

3

inhospitable mountains of metal. My legs stuck to the vinyl of the galley seat. Flies buzzed through the holes in the screening and clustered around the pots on the stove. Everyone was bathed in perspiration. I could not imagine calling this home.

Still, Gary appeared to love it. He ushered me aboard with all the pride of a new father, and sat me down in the sweltering galley before an enormous meal of roast pork, biscuits, potatoes, vegetables, and dessert. The crew were welcoming and friendly, but I felt suffocated and itched to escape.

The thought of becoming part of the crew horrified me. I wondered how our marriage would survive confinement for weeks on end on that obdurate beast without even the illusion of privacy, sharing our meals, our work, our free moments with three other people. I had begun to feel as though I were drowning in marriage, that the whole thing might have been a vast mistake. The thought of submerging my life so completely in Gary's, in his ambitions and desires, was the realization of my greatest fear, the justification for my original resolve never to marry. Now, I was not only married, but to a man who worked in a profession which had been a bastion of male supremacy for thousands of years, a woman aboard regarded as at best a nuisance, at worst, a jinx. I was a twentieth century woman, who was being transported into a nineteenth century life, and I was trapped.

Gary was due home the day before Thanksgiving that first year, in plenty of time to help me ready the house for the roast goose dinner we planned to serve the family. By suppertime on Wednesday, there was still no word. At about nine that night, Chris Berg, one of the owners of the *Progress*, phoned and said that the tug was coming in to let off all of the crew save Gary.

"I'm getting on," Chris told me, "and we're going to drop the barge in Port Deposit, then come on upriver here tomorrow morning and tie up. Gary wants to know if you want to come."

"Sure, I'd love to," I said, wondering how our dinner would work into this schedule.

This was only the overture to a symphony of last-minute schedule changes and broken plans that were to be littered through our lives like so much flotsam.

4

"Can you come down here and get Curl's car? Then you can follow me down to Betterton," he continued.

"Sure. Fine."

"Eyeah. Well, get down here about eleven-thirty."

Chris is not one to allow thirty minutes where ten will do, and I found myself clinging to the steering wheel of Curl's car, careening over the rough country roads in an attempt to keep up with the dimly receding taillights of the Volvo. We came pelting over the crest of the last hill to make a screeching right-hand turn into the slim parking lot before the pier. Chris jumped out and strode down the old dock, formerly a part of the amusement park, now a half-forgotten relic, its few slips occupied by a handful of small fishing boats.

As they rounded Howell Point, the tug's lights came into view, making the tug and tow look like a glistening Christmas ornament, silhouetted against a black velvet sky. When they drew toward the dock, the searchlight snapped on and swept the face of the pier, touching Chris as he waved one lean arm, then passing on to pick out the pilings. By the time I came up behind Chris, he was perched on the eastern end of the pier, ready to catch a line. Several men stood on the foredeck of the tug, their bags lined up behind the forward ladder. Clarky pitched one of the thick deck lines at the piling in front of Chris, lassoing it with confident skill and making it fast over the quarter bitts.

"Give her some power, Gary!" Chris shouted. "Get her in here!"

I later learned that he had been anxious to get the crew off before midnight in order to save paying them for the extra day. Gary eased the throttle down, increasing speed gradually. The mooring line pulled taut, and held. He worked the speed up, and the barge began to edge across the face of the breeze. The dock shuddered, then groaned. A series of sharp cracks beneath the boards sent me scurrying back toward the shore as the underpinnings stretched and snapped with the strain.

"Come on! Come on!" Chris cried as the barge inched its way alongside the face of the pier.

Finally, the massive grey lump lay against the pilings, and Chris was tying a bow line. Immediately the tug was close enough, bags began to fly up onto the dock, followed in short order by the men. Silently, they trooped up the pier to the two cars and left. Meanwhile, Chris had taken the forward ladder steps two at a time to the wheelhouse and sent Gary below to deck.

"Glad to see you, Babe," Gary said as he kissed me hastily and then scampered over the side to throw off lines.

Once free, Chris turned the tow, which was held tight against the tug's bow with two heavy wires called pushing cables, to slide up toward the looming black hillside of Grove Point before cutting north in a wide arc toward the Susquehanna Flats. The water was calm, broken only by tiny ripples. I had stayed below with Gary, watching in silence as he coiled lines, and feeling the pulse of the engines throb through the metal deck beneath my feet.

After pouring inky coffee into three mugs, we climbed the ladder to sit with Chris as he negotiated the curving, shoal channel toward Port Deposit, Maryland. The two men exchanged questions and answers about the tug and barge, about the trip, and the general maintenance, talking in a shorthand I could only imperfectly decipher. Then there was silence. Gary checked the chart periodically, watching as Chris guided the tow. With quiet assurance, Chris took the sharp turn toward the long line of buoys which run past Fishing Battery, a horseshoe of an island plopped carelessly in the wide expanse of the flats. The breeze was crisp as it blew through the open window, bringing with it scents of salt air and diesel smoke. The low rumble of the engine was coupled with the sound of water rushing by the hulls and lapping at the sterns. Now and then, a duck, disturbed in its sleep, sprang up, protesting.

The darkness and cool air altered the atmosphere of the tug for me. It now had a magic aura, a feeling of specialness, engulfed as it was in its own world of sound and sight and smell. No longer were the grime and rust important. In the dark, Gary stood pressed against my length, side by side. Our pleasure communicated itself without talk.

Four bridges span the Susquehanna like glittering diamond necklaces strung between the rocky cliffs. As we passed beneath the second bridge, Wylie's Manufacturing yard came

6

into sight, looking like a peculiar little city. The buildings were hulking shells, littered with pieces of half-constructed subway tunnels and ship's houses, and here and there burned the sharp burst of a welding torch.

Chris brought the barge into the dock, sending Gary down on deck to catch the lines. In minutes, they had pressed the barge against the bulkhead and moored it. On deck, Gary released the pushing cables, then scampered onto the barge to take the cable loops off the bitts. After dropping the pushing cables back onto the *Progress*'s stemhead, he cleared the deck, winding the excess cable back onto the winch drums. By the time Gary had come up the ladder again, Chris had turned the tug for home. He then relinquished the wheel to Gary and lay down in the captain's cabin, leaving us alone.

I think it was then that I began to feel more at home on *Progress*. Gary stood behind the wheel, his chin lightly resting on its top, and wrapped both my arms around his middle to hug me to him tightly. Laying my head on his shoulder, I drank in the night in deep draughts. He appeared to feel such confidence in his control of this machine. The humming engine and the crested bow wave were constant reminders of the power at his fingertips.

Alone in the wheelhouse for the first time, we hardly spoke, preferring to immerse ourselves in the sensual pleasure of the night. We ran across the flats into the Sassafras, wending our way up the serpentine river past familiar trees and houses which cast spectral shadows in the moonlight. As Gary slowed the engine to approach the harbor, Chris popped his head out of the cabin to inquire where we were.

"About another ten minutes to Sassafras docks," Gary told him.

"Ummph."

Chris came out to put the tug to dock, his control so complete that to watch was a pleasure. Dawn crept over the horizon, more an intimation of a day than a trumpeting. The sky lightened imperceptibly, giving gradually more distinct form to the surrounding scenery.

We stumbled home to bed. Although I was tired, I was exhilarated at the realization that tugboating was indeed romantic, a communion with nature not found anywhere else. I think it was like the first taste of a drug, intoxicating, seemingly harmless, but the beginning of a slowly growing addiction.

The next trip was nearly the antithesis of the first. Gary had been looking for an opportunity to introduce me to the working side of the life when Bob Atwater, a friend who was working aboard as cook/deckhand at the time, wanted the last five days off of the trip in May. As it was a last minute request, Gary presented me as a last minute solution. He phoned on the seventh, and on the eighth, I was coaxing Bob's underpowered Toyota up the inclines of Route 9 which skirts the Hudson River.

The tug and barge were crammed into a slip cut out of the shoreline. The flat barge which belonged to S.C. Loveland Company was being loaded with a steam turbine, and the barge chasers, two of Loveland's men, were busy directing the welding of chain plates, while tightening guy wires to secure the mammoth piece of machinery to the vast deck. The crew of the *Progress* was meanwhile turned out to paint the deckhouse a stunning canary yellow. Bob and two other young men were lined up on the rail, splashing paint onto the pitted bulkhead and telling each other jokes. When Bob saw me pull up on the sandy shore beside the tug, he put down his brush and ducked into the cook's cabin to grab his bag and hoist it over the side onto the bulkheading of the slip. He unloaded my bags and stuffed his duffle into the backseat amid the clutter of beer cans, then flopped into the driver's seat and shut the door.

"Uh, hi, Bob," I stammered, nonplussed at his lack of ceremony.

"Hey, Nance. How's she been running?" he grinned.

"Pretty good. Isn't there anything you should tell me?"

I had hoped to be eased into this job.

"Oh, yeah. I got some pork chops out to thaw over the stove, but they might still be a little hard."

"Thanks. What else is there? How do you usually cook for these guys?" I quizzed, hoping to coax him out of the car and into some sort of guided tour of the culinary side of tug life.

8

"Do whatever you want, Nance. You know how to cook," was his no-nonsense reply.

"Thanks a lot!"

"No problem!" he assured me cheerily as he revved his engine. "Have a good time. And thanks!"

He waved, turned the car around, and was gone.

I knew what was expected of the cook/deckhand, at least approximately. The watch, instead of being broken into two six-hour shifts as it was for the rest of the crew, ran from the time I got up to make breakfast at four-thirty, until I had finished the dinner dishes after six o'clock in the evening. Gary had told me that things could be flexible for the cook, one could choose to work in the morning and catch a nap in the afternoon, or vice versa. In any case one was expected to put in at least a twelve-hour day and when we were making up tows, or pulling hawser, turn out at any hour to help, making the days sometimes fourteen or fifteen hours long. I had known that the cook must also paint and do maintenance with everyone else, and generally fill in where needed, except when meals intervened. I was determined to fit in as part of the crew, ask for no quarter, and do the work, but my apprehensions mounted as I stood before the tug, watching two strangers slosh paint around without a sign of welcome from Gary.

I handed my bag over the side to Chris Schlegel, the deckhand, who introduced himself and the new mate, David Gray. They grinned and shook hands, then returned to their work. I changed into work clothes and climbed over the high sill to introduce myself to the galley. I hoped the relationship would prove a mutually satisfying one, but if first impressions were to be borne out, our association was off to a rather bleak start.

I had never before really studied the galley. I had sat in the sticky grey interior and breathed in the diesel smoke which rose in copious quantities from the center of the big black iron box that was the stove. I had drunk the thick, rancid coffee which brewed continually in a pot at the back of the stove. I had wondered how anything so perfidious could produce nourishment. But I had not, until this moment, actually had to get to know the galley.

9

Wandering over to the port side of the space, I could see the stove surreptitiously taking my measure in a decidedly defiant frame of mind. Ominously it burped a cloud of black smoke. The stove took up one corner of the galley and was bolted to the bulkhead on the starboard side. The oven, a yawning, toothless cavern, opened beside the carburetor which regulated, after a fashion, the flow of fuel into the fire-box. Bob had once mentioned being able to gauge the temperature of the oven by the color of the top, but although I was to spend much time studying the varying hues of the iron slab, ultimately the talent eluded me.

On a shelf over the stove sat the pork chops, dripping a stream of blood which sizzled on the iron top. I dumped them into one of the two deep sinks coupled to the black monster, and scanned the overhead shelves, counting plates and cups, checking on the age of the bread and biscuits stuffed into one of the partitions with the bowls. A rusty counter flanked the sinks and had one edge chewed off like a raw wound. In the gap left by the dismembered counter, sat a small cabinet which was stocked with condiments, packets of gravy mix, and one glass jar of molassas which had opened and was glued to the bottom in a congealed puddle.

The refrigerator, a double-doored affair with a painted grating at the bottom, clicked and whirred. Beneath the table which ran the length of the forward part of the galley, were cabinets stocked with pots and pans, one bent muffin tin, gnawed-open bags of flour and sugar, and jars of Vienna sausages. The table was surrounded on three sides by a bench whose hardness was only partially eased by a cracked vinyl cushion. It was later that I discovered that while sitting with one's back against the forward bulkhead during rough weather, one could feel the wall move at each pounding wave.

Until I had begun my resolute acquaintance with the galley, I had never had reason to descend into the forepeak by the ladder under the trapdoor on the starboard side. There were the freezer and the pantry, as well as shelves filled with spare parts, gasket material, and copper tubing. Though eroded with rust and covered in sweat, evidence of its efforts, the freezer chugged away with admirable determination. It was

10

bolted to the wooden decking, and inside were unmarked white packages of unidentifiable meats, piled on top of frozen bacon and fatback, and a couple of cans of orange juice. Ten gallons of milk took up one corner, and an abused, empty box of ice cream sat on top.

The cabinet at the forward end of the forepeak contained a jumble of cake mixes and bottles of ketchup and mustard, interspersed with huge cans of ground coffee. Several boxes of rice had fallen to the bottom, and one large bag of navy beans spilled out of its plastic to surround a pipe which erupted from the deck. There were boxes of things stacked on bags of things and here and there were oddly shaped corners crammed with jars and cans of things. Without ready access to groceries, the larder needed to be well-stocked. I collected an armload of potatoes and onions from the box on the floor, and climbed the ladder to the galley just as Gary stepped in through the door.

"Hey, Babe," he cried, coming over to help me and give me a swift kiss. "Good to see you."

"Joe," he said, turning to the man who had followed him into the galley, "this is my wife, Nancy. Nance, Joe Weber. He and John, out there, are supervising the loading."

Joe and I shook hands. Then he flopped into the booth by the door and ran his hand through his thinning hair.

"Gary tells me you're going to be cooking," Joe grinned. "Your first time?"

I nodded.

"Well, I think that's great. Thanks, Gary," he said as Gary handed him a cup of coffee.

"I wonder how great everyone else will think it is," I murmured, sipping at the mug Gary had poured for me.

"They'll get used to it," he assured me with a smile. "I know a family in Florida that lives and works on a tug. They run with all three kids and teach them on board. Scared me to death the first time I met them. The two-year-old was climbing the mast and I was ready to go up after him, but his mother just said something like, 'Oh, they've all done that. Don't worry.' She wasn't worried at all. Maybe you and Gary could get your own tug too."

I smiled and took another gulp of bitter coffee.

11

"When're you going to let us out of here?" Gary asked, glancing out of the porthole at the activity on the deck of the barge.

"I don't know. The surveyor hasn't been here yet, but he's due down in the next couple of hours. If he clears you, you can go on the tide tonight."

"I'd better get some sleep then. See you later, Babe."

To my chagrin, he kissed me, patted me as though I were his golden retriever, and disappeared. My disappointment must have been apparent, for Joe ducked his head and took a meditative draught of his coffee, waiting for a few minutes before speaking.

"How long have you two been married?"

"Too long, maybe," I grumbled.

Joe snorted, hiding his mirth, and watched as I began to peel onions and potatoes for supper. I rummaged through the cabinets, looking for pots and pans, taking mental inventory of the meagerly stocked spice rack. Joe finished his mug in silence, staring out of the door at the overhanging trees on the opposite side of the slip.

"Want some more?" I asked, tipping the pot at him.

"Thanks."

To my surprise, he was in no rush to leave and seemed happy to sit there, sipping at a bit of domesticity. It made me feel, if not accepted, that at least there was a friendly face to be found occasionally. Looking at him as I puttered around preparing dinner, I realized his prematurely receding hairline made him at first appear older than he was. His gentle eyes had only the first hint of the cluster of lines a face spent outdoors acquires, and his gestures were vigorous. As he studied the tree leaves outside the door, his eyes took on a wistful expression, and I found myself wondering what he was remembering with such sadness.

"You married, Joe?" I asked after a while.

"Separated," he replied laconically.

"Sorry. Maybe it'll work out."

He shook his head. "I've got a boy. I hate to lose him."

"I can imagine. Is he far away?"

12

"Not really, but I don't get home much. And my wife and I aren't exactly on friendly terms."

"That's rough. I'm really sorry."

"Yeah. This kind of life's hard on a marriage, you know? I think I've been home maybe thirty days in the past six months. She got lonely and I guess maybe she decided she could do better somewhere else," he continued pensively.

"I think that's one of the reasons Gary wants me here," I said, surprised at his candor.

"You don't often meet men out here who are married to the wives they started out with, that's for sure. Being apart so much is really rough on a relationship. You know, we came up here on a day and a half job. If the surveyor doesn't clear the tow this evening, it'll turn out to be three days. It's like that all the time. There's no way to plan anything. You're on call all the time. Sometimes when I get home, I'm so tired all I can do is sleep," he said, shaking his head.

It was not until three years later that Joe told me he and his wife had separated only that week. It had been obvious the wound was a painful one, but at the time I had no idea it had been so newly inflicted.

"What're you making now?" he asked finally.

"Cherry pie. I was hoping to win a few hearts with a heavy-duty spread," I smiled ruefully. "Do you want anything to eat?"

"No, thanks," he smiled in return.

"Do you think we'll leave tonight?" I asked, wondering if I would have an opportunity to get accustomed to cooking on the cantankerous beast in the corner before having to deal with it in motion.

"Hard to say. You can't get out of here without the tide, so if you don't leave here tonight, you'll have to wait for the next high tide tomorrow."

"Where are we taking that?" I inquired, glancing up through one of the galley portholes at the turbine components being wired and shackled to the deck of the barge.

"Cousins Island."

"Where's that?"

"Maine. That thing's insured for fifteen million," he added.

"Good God! Dollars? Fifteen million dollars?" I gasped.

Joe chuckled, enjoying the response. "Yeah."

I rolled out pie crust in stunned silence, musing over Gary's responsibility for fifteen million dollars' worth of machinery. Pie crust is about my speed, I thought.

We stayed in Hudson, New York, that night, still tied inside the narrow slip in front of the barge. David and Chris had eaten dinner and then strolled up the road to see a movie, the main entertainment in that sleepy town, while Clarky Collins, the engineer, Gary, and I sat on the fantail, chatting over coffee in the cool night air. Clarky had hung a fishing line overboard all day, periodically pulling up eels and flinging them into an increasingly crowded bucket. The three of us listened to the night sounds, a bird splashing into the river after its prey, the soft lapping of the water at the steel hull, an occasional car passing down the rough road. Clarky enjoyed an audience and told us hair-raising stories of rides down the coast on injured and dying tugs, and of some of the characters he had known in his thirty-odd years on the water.

"I remember one time coming up to the wheelhouse," he said, munching on a wet stogie. "We were going down from New York. I'd been in the hole workin' on a pump, the main bilge pump, since we were takin' on water, and things didn't feel right. I don't know what it was, but somethin' just didn't feel right. Anyhow, I got up to the wheelhouse, and the captain was passed out drunk, just layin' on the deck behind the wheel. I ended up havin' to take her around the bottom of Cape May myself. I figured if she didn't go down, I'd pile her up on the bar and the barge would run us down. I'd never been at the helm goin' around there. I'd seen it a lot, but never done it myself. Well, we made it. Captain came to. God damn! I mean, Boy! That guy could drink!"

Gary sprawled out on his back on the rough plywood boards which covered the steering quadrant on the fantail, listening to Clarky's stories with a hint of a smile playing at the corners of his mouth. Absolutely at home, he looked serene and contented.

14

"What are you going to do with the eels?" I asked finally.

"Eat 'em," Clarky grinned.

My stomach rolled over, but, hoping to win my way slowly into his good graces, I offered to cook them for him. He raised an eyebrow.

"You ever cook eel before?"

"No, but I'll do them any way you say."

He looked skeptical. "I always roll 'em in flour and salt and pepper and fry in grease."

"Fine. I'll do 'em for you if you clean 'em," I persisted, not having the temerity to reach into that writhing bucket to catch one by the tail, beat it into submission, and chop off its head.

"Okay. I'll leave 'em in the refrigerator for you."

"Fine," I gulped.

Gary had eyed me during this exchange, fully aware of my motive and watched with amusement as I struggled with my culinary inhibitions. A sudden splash arrested Clarky's attention and he hauled the thin line up, hand over hand, swinging a long, glistening eel out of the dark waters to pitch him onto the warm metal deck. The fish squirmed, still conscious, and tried to make good his escape under the boards covering the fantail. Clarky jerked on the line again, and swung the eel over his head to bring him down hard on the deck with a wet slap. He then bent down to disentangle the hook from the slack mouth and chuck him into the bucket on top of the others.

We stayed until evening the next day, painting the deck with the warm May sun on our backs. Finally, just after supper, we hooked up the hawser, dropping the spliced wire eyes of the bridles onto the two forward bitts of the deck barge, and easing it out of the slip into the channel. After clearing up the supper dishes, I poured a couple of cups of coffee and climbed the forward ladder to the wheelhouse. Clarky and Gary had let the hawser out so that the barge trailed several hundred feet behind us. That done, Gary had retired to the wheelhouse to perch on the pedestal that contains the throttle controls, and pilot the tug and tow down the darkening water of the Hudson.

The impression of the Hudson is one of color. The sun, which had descended behind the trees, illuminated the river with a golden haze, edging the blue-black rocks that jut out along the shore in gilt. Emerald lawns sweep down to the water, decorated with a profusion of blossoming trees and shrubs, and an occasional mansion majestically surveying its domain. The river itself is myriad shades of blue, from slate to a shimmering azure, to indigo under the overhanging cliffs. As they funneled down the banks, the winds brought with them the land scents of earth, flower, and sun-warmed rock.

Steering with his right hand on the wheel, Gary leaned out of the window, his chin cupped in his left hand, absorbing the beauty. I set the mugs on the compass pedestal and snuggled under his arm to nudge against the warm, compact body and share the heady joy of the evening. The barge followed obediently as we steamed past the outcroppings of rock, curving around the channel bound for Manhattan.

I served breakfast at five-thirty, passing plates of sausage and eggs in between glances out of the door to watch the dawn outline the blocks of granite and cement with a subtle rosy hue. After shortening hawser, we rounded the Battery and chugged through the East River as the sun burst over Brooklyn, cascading down the sides of the UN building. Joggers trotted along the pavement, sandwiched between the river and the roaring traffic. Strangely removed, we watched the scene as though from a seat in a theater. We sat in the wheelhouse, Gary and I, sipping coffee and studying the frenetic movements of millions of people on the shore, as untouched by their plights or their joys as they ours. It was as though they were part of a vast play of which they themselves were unaware and we the solitary spectators. The world seemed to be in perpetual motion. As we passed under the Queensboro Bridge, we could hear the thunderous clamor of taxis, cars, and trucks pelting from one borough to another.

Gary had been gradually reducing speed since the Queensboro Bridge, trying to compensate for the fair current. As we approached Hell Gate, he slid off the throttle stand and braced himself behind the wheel. His broad shoulders tightened and his movements, until now, facile, became tense. Darting back and forth between the wheel and the windows, he checked the chart, then snatched the radio microphone from its holder on the overhead and made a security call, informing all

16

interested traffic that we were headed for Hell Gate with a tow on a short hawser. He might have added that we had a following current which pushed us through the channel, slewing us this way and that as the passage narrowed. Until we had rounded the last curve into Hell Gate, the barge had been strung out neatly behind us, but when the rocky fingers of the shores closed in on us, we were suddenly in a roiling kettle, careening uncontrollably toward one rocky bank. Gary's bearded face was puckered in concentration.

"Watch out the back window and tell me when the barge comes up against the hawser," he ordered as he gave the throttle a short burst of power.

The tug was headed straight for the cement and rock riprap on the western side of the strait, but the barge had taken on a life of its own. I looked out of the back window of the wheelhouse as the barge swung across the stern, headed for the other shore, slowly taking up the slack hawser. When the barge had run the length of the line, she continued to strain, hauling persistently until the tug had heeled over to starboard, putting her shoulder into the churning water.

"Okay, she's come taut," I said, trying to make my voice sound as calm as Gary's.

Gary stuck his fist into the spokes of the wheel and spun it, cranking it around like the starter on an old Model T. *Progress* shivered and heeled over even farther, trying to pull her stern away from the insistent barge. We were being carried through Hell Gate on the roaring current, sliding farther and farther into the narrowing channel. The barge stopped her clambering for the east shore, hesitated, then took off in the opposite direction, headed for the rocks at the base of the Triborough Bridge abutment. Gary stood at the wheel, feet splayed out to brace himself, and glanced over his shoulder at the lump of metal slicing by our tail, goosing the throttle again to take up the hawser slack.

"God! Is she going to miss us?" he cried. "Nance, take a look and tell me quick."

I stepped outside the door and watched as the barge swung past the battered fantail.

"Well?"

17

"I think so. Yes, it looks like it. Okay. She's by," I stammered breathlessly.

I came in and closed the door again, only to be confronted with the bridge abutment looming up before us. Gary swung the wheel again, swearing under his breath as the tug hesitated before answering the helm.

"Come on, you bitch, turn!"

Barge forgotten, I stared in horror as the currents carried us toward the jagged rocks, and the tug, helm hard over to port, moved inexorably forward. Suddenly, the boat shuddered, and leaned into her turn, missing the riprap by what seemed to me like a few feet. The barge had nearly gained the rocks of the opposite shore, so narrow is the gap. Instead of repeating this ever more nerve-wracking dance, however, *Progress* righted herself and held a forward course, regaining her equilibrium and stepping out into the channel in sure-footed determination. The barge stubbornly continued its zigzag course in diminishing arcs, but the tug had her, pulling with confidence for the passage between the Brother islands.

"Phew!" I let out a long breath.

Gary grabbed me in an exuberant bear hug, his contained tension exploding into a victorious grin. He had obviously loved every minute of it, I thought incredulously. The man is a crazy person.

Is this what tugging is all about? Is this why he loves it?

"Well, Kiddo, we made it!" he chuckled, seeing the astonishment on my face.

"Yeah. You weren't scared at all, were you?" I demanded.

"Hell, yes. What are you? Nuts?" he grinned.

"But you love it, don't you? You love that excitement," I shook my head, understanding the exhilaration of the triumph but not understanding his obvious willingness to do it all over again.

"Sure. Don't you? We made it!" he hugged me again, trying to include me in his joy. "I'm glad you're here."

"Well, me too, Gare. That is pretty exciting, I've got to admit. I don't know, though. I don't think I could learn how to do it myself. You were so calm! You knew we weren't going to end up on the rocks, didn't you?"

18

"Yeah. I wondered for a minute if the barge were going to run us down. That would have been a problem, but I knew we were going to be okay."

A problem? Being run down by a barge in a whirlpool is only a problem? That's what made it possible for him to keep going out and enjoying his work, I decided. People do it all the time and make it through. Why shouldn't he?

"Those currents in that East River are voracious," Gary reflected as we turned out into Long Island Sound. "I saw a helicopter once crash right behind a ship near the Battery. They got a rescue team out there in minutes but they couldn't find the guys or the helicopter. It just got swept out by the undercurrents, they guess. Scarey." he said, shaking his head.

"At least!" I muttered sobered by thoughts of our fate had things not gone our way.

But it had gone our way. That was what mattered. Miss by an inch is as good as a mile, my dad claims. Though he had never put his life philosophy into those words, perhaps that was what Gary believed too. Perhaps it is what I believe. After all, most of us get into a car every day, despite the statistics. And statistics do not include the keen sense of being alive that running along the East River in the May sunrise infuses in those fortunate enough to drink of that cup.

Because of the weather reports, we had taken the inside passage toward Maine, snuggled in behind the barrier of Long Island. We chugged eastward through the Sound, plowing into the corrugated grey water as the wind increased. Gary had warned me that things might get a bit rough toward evening when we would be running into the teeth of a northeast gale. Although the May morning had dawned clear and warm, the day had gradually disintegrated into a bleak, windy replica of March.

The cook has a cabin on the main deck, the first door on the port side aft of the galley door, but I had stowed my gear in the captain's cabin which was nestled behind the wheelhouse on the boat deck. I had not even bothered to make up the cook's bunk. The captain's cabin is about nine feet square with a bunk the size of a small twin bed attached to the port bulkhead, and a desk bolted to the floor on the opposite side. It also has the luxury of a sink that runs hot and cold water, and a pair of metal lockers wedged into the slot at the foot of the bunk.

While it wasn't elegant, I had on occasion thought of it as cozy. Despite the narrowness of the bunk, Gary and I shared it, one smashed against the chilly bulkhead and the other clinging to the radiator by the edge of the mattress in order to keep from being pitched onto the bare deck. Though cramped, it had not bothered us and we slept contentedly.

By two A.M. the tug, which had been pitching with increasing ferocity, was taking fat chunks of green sea over the top of the house. I had been dozing, unable to sleep deeply since part of my concentration was devoted to staying in the bunk. Finally, able to deny the call of nature no longer, I rose. Leaving an essentially warm bunk and cabin to be hit by a blast of cold air, make a long, arduous passage to the glaring light of the head on the lower deck and back again in rough weather deserved consideration. The cabin was dimly lit by the reflected masthead lights, giving me enough glimmer to locate my clothes. Sitting on the floor, braced against the bunk, I struggled into my pants and shirt, then crawled over the bouncing deck to the door.

David and Chris stood in the wheelhouse chatting above the din of the waves pounding on the windows. They turned with mild interest when they heard the door creak open.

"My God! It's sleeting!" I cried.

Chris only chuckled.

"But it's May!"

"Where're you going?" he asked.

"I've got to get to the head."

"You can't go below like that. You'd better get your foul weather gear," David advised.

I nodded and returned to the stuffy enclosure of the cabin to search out some rain gear and boots. By the time I stood at the top of the cabin steps, peering at the vague outlines of the wheelhouse visible in the fluorescent glow of the radar, I felt queasy. Steadying myself for a moment, I grasped the starboard door handle to prepare mentally for the attack on the head.

"I think you'd better go down the port side and around the fantail," David told me. "I'll slow the boat down for five minutes, okay?"

"Yeah, okay," I gasped, hoping the shock of the cold air would settle my stomach. "I'll just stay below, I think. Chris, wake me up in the cook's cabin for breakfast, okay?"

Chris nodded agreement, and David eased the throttle up, leaning into the wheel to brace himself against the center button as the motion of the tug changed. The pitching took on an almost languorous quality as the tug slid down into one trough, then up and over the crest of the following wave to come crashing down again in a slow motion fall. The time between the waves had lengthened, making it possible to dash between the thundering mountains of water as they slammed onto the deck.

"Watch for your opening," David suggested, seeing me frozen uncertainly at the door, unable to make the commitment. "You just go. I'll close the door."

"Thanks."

Keeping my eyes on the waves, I tried to discern a pattern in their assault—two fairly swift crashes and then a pause, and a deep trough before one giant one followed, reaching out a thick fist to pound the flooded deck. One, two, *now!* I took a deep breath and jumped out onto the landing outside the wheelhouse door. Feeling the door pulled from my hand, I kept my eyes on the railing which surrounded the decking at the top of the wheelhouse ladder. Crouching, I ran around and slid down the ladder, landing with a wet thunk of my sea boots on the deck. Not daring to look behind me, I scrambled around the covered vent, and behind the protection of the galley bulkhead as the grasping fingers of another wave reached for my retreating back. I clung to the handrail and half-slid, half-ran down the deck, stopping by Clarky's door just before the fantail. The water coursed over the wide deck like a racing mountain stream as it rushed freely through the large scuppers. Every few waves, *Progress* would lift her stern enough to drain the deck. I waited, feeling the tug squat down into the next wave before rising again. As the deck lifted, the water slowly flushed away through the scuppers, and I made a dash, encumbered by the

21

suit of foul weather gear and the boots. I took too long to swing both legs over the hurdle of the taut hawser, and the next wave came sloshing over the deck, mounting my high boots and filling them with icy water. Trudging to the rail on the bulkhead behind the capstan, I slogged up the deck to the head.

The head door was cracked open, held by the eight-inch-long bronze latch to allow the fresh air access to the tiny cubicle of toilet, sink, and shower. Reaching up to unlatch the door, I discovered that the force of the waves beating against the door had crushed the hook and fairly welded it to the door. In frustration, I yanked at the door with no result. The waves came sluicing along the deck, slurping up my rubber-clad legs and diving into my full boots. Hoping I could squeeze through the narrow crack, I began to force my body through the opening, pushing frantically until my chest wedged into the slot. I felt the tug increasing speed, the engine ringing as it revved to its full power. The cadence of the seas changed again, becoming sharper, more ferocious. Stuck as I was in the door, I could not escape the waves that smashed down the side of the deckhouse and sent cold rivulets down my neck. I pulled myself out of the door and realized I would need reinforcements.

As I struggled up the starboard deck into the full fury of the seas, I suddenly remembered seeing an old documentary film of a trip around the Horn through the Roaring Forties. The man in the film, Irving Johnson, said that when the seas hit the vessel, you had to run quick to put your head flat against the wooden bulkhead. If there were any gap at all, the power of the waters would crack the skull like a nut. At each wave, I laid my head against the throbbing cold metal, waited until it had passed, then continued my trek up the deck.

By the time I had reached the foredeck, my hands felt frozen. As I tried to round the corner, wading in between the tall vent and the pushing cable winch that was welded to the foredeck, the tug dove, throwing me off balance. I reached out for the sharp-edged winch but could find no hold. Before I could drag myself back toward the railing along the deckhouse, a great dark sea poured over the side, knocking me to my knees, spluttering. Another wave followed on its heels, flattening me against the deck and washing me partway back to the head,

22

clawing and flailing for a handhold. Another wave poured over me, sluicing me farther toward the scuppers like so much flotsam. Angry, both at myself and at the indifference of nature, I grabbed one of the dogs, the latching handles, on the engine room door, and pulled myself to my feet.

"You are not going overboard on your first trip out," I told myself sternly, "and certainly not on a trip to the head!"

Having decided that, I clung with determination to the rail, bracing myself against the seas as though it were now a contest of wills. When I stepped into the wheelhouse, I was thoroughly soaked. Standing with my back to the closed door, I dripped loudly onto the cement decking as Chris and David stared at me.

"I can't get into the head," I panted. "The damned latch is jammed."

Chris sighed and pulled on his foul weather gear, then led me back to the head. Apparently thinking that I had simply not been able to dislodge the latch, he reached up to push at it with the heel of his hand.

"No wonder you couldn't get in," he laughed. "The latch is wrapped around the hook."

"I know," I sighed. "That's why I needed help."

The two of us fought with the door, wrestling until the bronze snapped and the door swung free.

"Thanks," I cried, jumping into the brightly lit interior.

Chris dogged the door behind me.

Sodden and cold, I made my way back up the port side and climbed into the dark hole of the cook's cabin. In the blackness, I stumbled to the bunk and fell in, still clad in soaked rain gear. After kicking off my boots, I pulled the army blanket to my chin, ignoring the squelching and squeaking of oilcloth. As I lay there, stiff and shivering, I suddenly thought how frail is the human lifeline, and how easily and abruptly snapped. Had I gone overboard, no one would have realized I was missing until more than two hours later when Chris came to call me out of bed to make breakfast. Rolling myself in the thin blanket, I wedged my body against the bulkhead and coaxed myself to sleep. So much for idyllic.

At breakfast, the galley felt as though it had a motion all its own, jolting wildly and setting up a cacophony of rattling plates and cutlery. I had tethered the frying pan to a metal rail on the stove, but was unable to keep it from skating in wide arcs on the flat surface. The grease from the bacon splattered over the edge of the skillet, starting little grease fires which I put out with the salt. Finally, I dredged out a pound of limply fried bacon and laid it in a bowl on the shelf above the stove. Pouring out the excess grease was a physical impossiblity, so I simply dumped the leftover potatoes into the shimmering pool of fat. Having found several rolls of refrigerator biscuits, I gave fervent thanks to Pillsbury and stuck them in the oven.

Clarky appeared at five-thirty and eased himself into his place by the port door. Silently, I poured him a cup of coffee, and traversed the seemingly expanding distance between us, weaving uncertainly with the scalding coffee. He casually lit a cigarette and puffed as he watched me pour cream and sugar into his cup as he held it with one hand.

"How do you want your eggs?" I asked, trying to sound nonchalant.

"I'm not hungry, Gal. Just a couple of pieces of bread and butter, maybe. Stomach a mite upset?" he wanted to know, eyes twinkling with satisfaction.

"I'm okay," I insisted between clenched teeth. "I've got biscuits instead of bread if you want. I'd be happy to fry you a couple of eggs."

"No, thanks. Biscuits'll be fine."

I fixed his plate and placed it before him, glad when the Buffalo china became his responsibility. Chris stepped into the galley, smiling cheerily. He slid into the booth beside Clarky and began the routine of passing along the watch information, describing work accomplished, position of the gauges, how much fuel had been pumped up and when.

"What would you like for breakfast?"

"Nothing, thanks, Nance. I had a jar of those little Vienna sausages and a peanut butter sandwich before I called you."

My stomach lurched. Two down, two to go. I knew Gary would want only a smile on a morning like this. I hoped perhaps David would pass on breakfast, and I would have little washing up to keep me in the galley. David came down grey-faced and

24

tired. He won't want anything to eat, I thought. He slid into the booth and leaned heavily on the table.

"Stomach upset?" Clarky asked cheerfully.

Chris grinned but said nothing. I found their satisfaction distinctly annoying.

"Got any juice?" David began, looking around the galley for some evidence of breakfast.

"Yeah." Surprised, I fumbled in the refrigerator and poured out a tall plastic glass of juice.

"You want some eggs?" I asked, praying that he would be content to drink his breakfast.

"Yeah. Could you make it three over easy?"

Over easy? I'd be lucky to get them in the pan.

To my astonishment, he ate a huge breakfast with gusto, dipping a biscuit in the gluey yellow yolks, chasing the last piece of potato with his fork. Clarky sat in his corner, meditatively sipping coffee and puffing on a cigarette. Chris had disappeared, leaving after he had completed the ritual of watch change. As David finished the last of his meal, I took the plate and put it in the sink, poked in the stopper, and began running hot water over the sticky egg. I felt the engine slow, the persistent rumbling whine dropping in pitch and intensity until we were riding up and down the waves in a leisurely undulation. Without a word, Clarky stubbed out his cigarette and rose to put on his jacket, then slipped out the galley door.

While crossing the open waters of the sounds in our approach to the Cape Cod Canal, the hawser had been strung out nearly its length, all twelve hundred feet snapping and groaning in the tug-of-war between the two vessels. As the load on the barge was too large to see over with it strapped to the bow in pushing gear, Gary had decided to tow it through the canal on a short hawser, fifty feet off the stern being the required length.

Leaving the dishes in the sink, I pulled on foul weather gear jacket and gloves and followed David down the deck to the stern. Clarky stood by the capstan on the starboard side, another cigarette stuck in his mouth as he squinted through rain-washed glasses at the unseen barge. Gary leaned over the rail of the upper deck, one hand on the after controls as he watched Chris stow the chafing gear. When Chris had stowed

25

the piece of slit fire hose which had been wrapped around the hawser to keep it from rubbing on the metal stern, he took up a position beside the port horn of the bitt. With the reduced strain, the hawser, which moments before had been stuck out over the fantail rigidly, had begun to contract, gaining a new mobility. It began to sway in answer to the dance of the two vessels. Gary took the throttle out of gear, and a loud spurt of air issued from the engine room, a sigh from the pneumatic controls. The tug ceased its forward momentum, retarded as it was by the pummeling winds and waves, and bobbed unpredictably. The hawser had draped itself over the stern like a limp boa constrictor, its barge invisible behind a hoary wall of sleet.

"Okay. Take it off!" Gary shouted above the noise of the wind and gear that rattled and crashed against the steel hull.

Chris began uncoiling line from the port horn of the towing bitts, hauling at the stubborn nylon, stiff with salt water. Clarky had flipped his cigarette overboard and stood leaning toward Chris, waiting to grab the end of the hawser.

"Sit on that hawser! Hold it down!" Gary shouted to me and David.

We rushed to squat on the hawser, pinning it to the deck as though it were a brawling drunk. Clarky had started the capstan with a twist of a valvelike control by his shoulder. The drum rumbled around on uneven bearings, spinning freely without the load of the hawser. When he had freed the line, Chris hurriedly handed it across the deck to Clarky who struggled to put three wraps on the capstan before the line could get away. A second wrap took hold. The capstan groaned, dropping its carefree grumbling to a panting bass. Clarky had braced both feet and leaned back against the strain, pulling the hawser in hand over hand, and letting it fall in a convoluted pile at his feet. As soon as Clarky had control of the line, David grabbed me by the sleeve and pulled me off the hawser rack out of the way. I watched the heavy, dripping line snake over the stern to lead through the H of the towing bitts and around the capstan, bringing with it pieces of seaweed and an occasional jellyfish.

"Okay, Dave. You can go to bed. Thanks," Gary called to him.

26

Chris had climbed over the moving hawser to stand beside Clarky and begin the slow process of coiling, faking it onto the wooden hawser rack which kept the coil from freezing to the deck. Chris laid down the first loop of the coil, carefully twisting the laid line into place so that it would lie flat. Once I saw his intention, I stationed myself at the opposite end of the rack, laying down layer upon layer in tandem with Chris while Clarky tailed. Foot by foot, we piled up a two-and-a-half-foot-high mound as the barge slowly emerged from the bleak, grey dawn about a hundred feet away. It inched its way toward us, a hulking slug rising from the deep.

"Okay, hold her there!" Gary finally shouted.

We had watched the bridles creep up to the fantail, hearing the shackle which fastens the wire bridles to the spliced eye of the hawser, clatter and thump against the stern. Clarky held the line in place, easing back enough so that the capstan spun freely without drawing in more slack. Then he shut off the machine with one hand and swiftly threw off the three wraps with the other, passing the end to Chris who made it fast on the horn of the towing bitts. As soon as the hawser was secured, Gary sprinted back into the wheelhouse to get on the radio. I trudged up the deck to get on with the dishes.

Although the stench of diesel hangs like a shroud over the galley, in cold, miserable weather, it can be the most welcoming place aboard. Toasting one's rump against the furnace of the stove is a sensual delight not to be missed in this lifetime, particularly if it is accompanied by the aroma of freshly brewed coffee and fried bacon and potatoes. While contentedly roasting myself, I stretched white, puckered fingers over the stove to rub some blood back into them, and enjoyed the calming of the motion as we snuggled up under the lee of the land.

The northeast gale had brought with it a blizzard which had downed many of the electricity lines in Massachusetts and forced the schools to close. Gary radioed for permission to traverse the canal, then, receiving it, made several calls to find out what weather conditions were on the eastern side. He began to get reports of seas ranging from eight to fifteen feet, kicked up by the fifty-knot winds. Deciding against going through, he cast around for a place to wait out the weather. The dolphins, clusters of pilings on the south side of the western end of the canal, were clogged with two tugs and their barges. As I opened the door to the wheelhouse, I heard Gary ask one of the captains for permission to tie up next to his oil barge.

"Only if you drop over some fenders, Cap," came the reply. "I got a fifty-thousand-barrel gasoline barge here. We don't need no sparks."

"Roger, I got ya. Okay, then we'll be bringing our barge alongside in about twenty minutes. Thanks."

He turned to me and Chris, who was draped casually over the throttle stand.

"We don't have any fenders. You guys go down and coil up any spare line you can find. Leave out three to tie up to the barge but coil everything else into fenders so we can drop them between the barges. He probably has mooring lines on his barge. We'll pick her up on the hip when you finish."

I followed Chris to help him with the long, thick polypropylene lines, stowing them behind the forward ladder as we made them up. Unable to anticipate the routine of any job once I'd left the confines of the galley, I followed Chris like a puppy, eagerly watching and hoping to be able to learn to pull my weight. Gary made efforts to explain how things would work, how the rituals of the job operated, but often he did not have the luxury of time, and I had to trot after Chris or Clarky, asking questions when I dared, hoping to discern what needed to be done.

When we finished, I trailed after Chris to the stern where Clarky waited, one foot up on the rail, glaring into the mist. Gary wanted to pull the hawser completely, loosing the barge with Chris aboard in order to pick it up again alongside, on the hip. Having some idea of the procedure, I followed the same routine as when we had shortened hawser, sitting on the line while Chris released it from the towing bitt and passed it to Clarky. As the bridle shackle approached the bitts, Clarky shut off the capstan. Gary, who had been at the after controls overhead, eased the tug down to bump the bow of the barge with our stern. Clarky and Chris climbed over the debris on the fantail and stood close together on the uneven boards of the

28

stern. Clarky locked his fingers together and braced his hands against his knees as Chris put a foot in the cupped palms to vault over Clarky's shoulders, landing on his belly on the slick deck of the barge. As I watched in awe, I wondered how many had been killed or maimed doing this feat of acrobatics. A drift away from the barge at the wrong moment would have dropped Chris between the two jouncing vessels.

Unperturbed by my speculations, Chris had mounted the barge with determined grace and trotted to one of the bitts on either side of the bow, ready to drop the wire loop of the bridle back onto the fantail. Clarky had wordlessly rushed to grasp the wire where it draped over the side and yanked it slowly aboard. Realizing he was struggling to get it aboard before it could become entangled in the propeller, I stumbled over the mess of line and wire to help him walk it up the deck and flip the eye onto the top of the pile of hawser. After repeating this procedure for the second bridle, Clarky left me to unravel the fantail while he went forward to catch lines to the barge.

Once we had cast off, Gary had gone back to the wheelhouse and spun the tug in a wide arc, keeping a careful eye on the barge's grey form in the sleet. By the time I had laid the bridles, doubled, back along the deck, we were approaching the barge again, nosing up along its after end on the port side. Between them, Chris and Clarky secured a double quarter line, bow line, then stern line, pulling us against the barge so tightly the lines creaked. I began handing the makeshift fenders up onto the barge's deck, then climbed up after them, standing out of the storm behind the cover of the huge turbine. The barges moored to the dolphins became visible as apparitions, and I could just make out the shadowy outlines of houses perched on the rockbound shore.

We hung our coiled-line fenders overboard at each cleat, then scanned the deck of the gasoline barge as we approached it, hoping to see some mooring lines in plain view. Gary gingerly sidled up to the huge bomb with our unwieldly equipment, relying on Chris and Clarky's hand signals to guide him. The gap between the two barges narrowed. There was a sharp rasping of metal against metal, then silence, as the flat barge came parallel. Chris leapt the gap to scout out some lines. As

29

soon as the two barges came together, the three of us struggled to secure them with the deck lines Chris had found, trying to keep the maneuvering between the two barges to a minimum.

While school children all over Massachusetts were just listening to the happy news that school had been cancelled, we were all in the galley, swigging our fifth cup of coffee for the day. It was on this trip that I began to learn something of the tedium of life on the water. We spent two days waiting out the storm, drinking gallons of coffee, eating, trying to fill the time constructively. Clarky always had some project going in the engine room, always some pump or bucket of oily parts to be reassembled into a useful machine. The rest of us read, played cards, talked with one another, listened to the radio. The weather closed in around us, obscuring even a glimpse of the dock only several hundred yards away, and appeared to shut us off from the world entirely. I had begun to ache for a lemon meringue pie and decided to cross the two barges to the other tug in hopes of doing some trading.

Not having seen any of the other crew since our arrival, I descended the ladder to their deck with a slight twinge of apprehension, suddenly aware of being a woman alone. Twinges notwithstanding, I pounded on the galley door with my fist, but when no one answered, turned the dogs that held it and swung it open. I was confronted by a ring of faces, all sitting in stunned silence at my appearance.

"I was hoping I could trade some onions for a couple of lemons," I stammered, abashed at the obvious shock on the faces of the men. "I want to make a pie," I explained when the statement failed to elicit a response from the open-mouthed cook.

I had stepped just inside the door and stood with the handle still in my hand, ready for an escape if necessary. After what seemed like minutes, the cook, swathed in a white apron, woke from his trance and spoke.

"Lemons?"

"Yes, lemons, if you have any to spare," I said, grateful for a break in the silence. "I'd like to make a lemon meringue pie. You know, it can be pretty boring and I thought I'd try to perk things up a bit," I babbled.

30

In taciturn silence, the man handed me a small bag of fresh lemons, then backed away a couple steps.

"Oh thanks so much. That's too many," I blurted, peering into the bag. "Aren't you going to need some of these?"

"Nope. Take 'em."

"Here. Here's some onions in exchange," I said, proffering my barter.

"Nope. Don't need 'em. You take the lemons."

"You're sure? Well, thanks. I appreciate it. If you need anything, don't hesitate to come over and ask. We're just over there," I gestured stupidly, feeling hopelessly awkward and out of place.

I turned and fell over the door sill in an effort to get away. No one rose to help dog the door down as I left, and I found myself standing in the chill rain, cranking the six dogs around the door back into position. Climbing back onto the barges, I traipsed back across to the *Progress* which suddenly looked like the cozy hearth of home, and scrambled down into the galley to pour myself a steadying cup of coffee. Never again, I promised myself. Never again.

Crew change came at the change in the weather, and we left the tug on a gloriously bright morning, ferrying ourselves to the dock at Massachusetts Maritime Academy to trade places with the others. I wondered what the rest of the trip to Maine would be like, and what sort of place Cousins Island would be. When I learned that we were flying home out of Boston, I almost pleaded to stay. I hate to fly.

T W O

THE NEXT TIME I was aboard, I was a passenger again, a less comfortable feeling now that I knew what it was to be a contributing member of the crew—not that the others accepted me with unqualified enthusiasm. Clarky, being of the old school, found it hard to swallow the idea of a woman aboard a tug, though he was friendly and never deliberately made me feel burdensome. Chris and David, of another generation, seemed to have fewer reservations about my presence. Regardless of their personal feelings one way or the other, they always treated me with respect and courtesy, a fact I very much appreciated. While I was working, however, their acceptance was of less importance: I had a legitimate reason to be there. While a passenger, I was a fifth wheel, dependent upon their approval. However, Gary was resolved that we would take every opportunity to be together on the water, partly in order to familiarize me with the workings of the tug. It was this resolution that made me a passenger for three days in June.

The *Progress* had a tow from Port Deposit to the Potomac River Basin in Washington, D.C. Gary phoned and asked me to come. Even had I not been delighted for the chance to see the river, I would have come to be with him. So, on a scorching June day, kit bag in hand, I negotiated the railroad tracks, the debris, and potholes of Wylie's on the Susquehanna.

Tied to the bulkheaded dock lay a just-completed section of subway tunnel, looking like a giant caterpillar. Wylie's had sealed both ends of the tunnel, making it one long, air-filled compartment. It had been ballasted in order to partially submerge the free-floating structure enough to make it a stable tow. Watertight doors were fixed to the center of the sealing plates. Welded across each end were single I-beams which would serve as handles by which *Progress* and *Miss Elizabeth*, the other tug hired for the job, could hold the tow.

As if in deliberate contrast to the last trip, the weather had turned sultry. Little breeze made its way into the trough between the cliffs of the Susquehanna, and the sun beat steadily against the shining steel of the deckhouse, baking the occupants. The open glass ports hung disconsolately on their hooks, and an occasional fan stirred the heavy air. The galley, formerly a haven in that northeast storm, had become purgatory, its black iron box roaring with a constant flame, and filling the galley with sticky soot. Two wall fans whirred at either end of the compartment, one oscillating dilatorily, the other glumly spinning in place.

Gary met me at the dock, grabbed my bag and led me up the ladder to deposit me and my few clothes in the wheelhouse. I settled into the port corner by the open window at the throttle stand, trying to lean into the little pool of shade the overhead offered from the slanting sun, and enjoy an elusive breath of air. Gary trotted below to pour a glass of iced tea for me before leaving to check on the tow.

David and Chris were wandering over the top of the tunnel, picking up scraps of re-bar, the reinforcing rod used in construction, and pitching ashore odd pieces of metal and bent nails. Clarky slept as best he could in the hotbox of his cabin. I sat alone feeling awkward and tried to look inconspicuous to the prying eyes of the workers onshore. The back of my neck prickled as much from the sense that I did not belong there as from the heat. All about me were men. I was the only woman in sight, and one whose sole function, it appeared, was decorative, a position I fill less than comfortably. Still, Gary had wanted me there; I had wanted to come. We had obtained permission from one of the owners. That should have been enough.

The river was tawny by the time Chris and the new cook hung over the narrow edge of the I-beam, shackling the heavy wire towing bridles in place. *Miss Elizabeth* pushed her bow against the center of the I-beam at the opposite end of the section while her crew hooked up her pushing cables.

Imperceptibly, as the sun began to set, the day shook her hazy cloak and a breeze sprung up, bringing with it the fresh, sweet fragrance of the flowers on shore. The ride out of the Susquehanna is fairly straightforward, complicated only by the railroad bridge, the blockade to the upper reaches of the river that is the needle through which all tows must be threaded. It is at times a test of eyesight and nerve. Although the chart claimed the gap between the wooden abutments was one hundred feet, Gary had tried to turn the eighty-six-foot tug end for end inside the fender system, out of curiosity over the actual space. He discovered that, rather than one hundred feet, the gap was closer to eighty which meant that the tow would have five feet of clearance on either side. After a lengthy discussion by radio with the captain of the *Miss Elizabeth*, the two of them decided that *Progress* would tow the tunnel section straight ahead, quarter speed, while *Miss Elizabeth* backed gently to maintain the alignment. Muscles tensed, Gary headed for the center of the narrow opening.

"How're ya lookin' up there, Gary?" came the voice of *Miss Elizabeth*'s captain.

Gary snapped the microphone off its holder.

"So far so good. It looks like it's in pretty good position from here. What's it look like there?"

"Man, all I see is a *beeg* wall," the other answered, chuckling.

"Yeah, okay. So far so good. Back a hair to port, will ya?"

"Backin' to port."

"Okay. That's good. Back a bit straight rudder."

"Backin' straight rudder," came the reply.

"Lookin' good," Gary told him after a pause.

His blue eyes twinkled as testament to the enjoyment he took in the challenge. Together we watched as the tunnel section crept toward the tiny bridge slot, looking like a five-pound sausage trying to squeeze into a four-pound casing. It

34

was not until the forward end of the tow was actually inside the wooden fender system which jutted out into the opening that they knew for certain that she would fit.

"OOOOOhhkay! Looks like we're in there. Back her down a bit, Cap, port rudder."

"Backin' port rudder."

"Can you see the fender system yet?" Gary wanted to know.

"Not yet. Wait a minute, here she comes! Yeah, man, we got her now!" the other man crowed.

"Great. I'm going to put a little more juice to her to get her around this buoy," Gary replied breezily.

"Okey dokey."

A few moments passed while Gary pushed the throttle down slowly, listening to the engine rumble in a more commanding baritone.

"Okay, Gary, we're through. We got her. How're ya doin' on the buoy?"

"Well, I'm around it, but it looks like the tow's going to run over the can. Yep. There she goes. Keep an eye out so it doesn't pop up on your deck," he said casually.

As the tug made the sharp turn by a triangle of buoys at the mouth of the river, the long, cumbersome tow had swept overtop the black can, submerging it temporarily. Gary listened for confirmation of its return.

"Yep, got it right here," the other man chortled. "She just missed jumpin' up in between the cables and the boat by a hair, but she came up outside our cables."

"Sorta bump alongside, did it?" Gary teased.

"Yeah. Woke up the deckhand," the other laughed.

The glassy expanse of the Susquehanna Flats sprawled out before us like a vast mirror whose uniform surface was broken only by the silhouette of Fishing Battery Island and the marshy shore in the distance. As the light dimmed, we swung around the marks, past the island, bending slowly around the final turn to head for the flasher off Turkey Point and then chug down the languid bay.

I sat in the wheelhouse sipping at a tall glass of iced tea and pondering the peace of the summer stillness. Gary pored over

35

Gary at the wheel, checking the compass. Photograph by Charlton A. Gunter.

the chart, then checked the compass deviation, squinting over the wheel to line up the buoys as best he could. He flipped open the red log book to record the time, followed our present location, weather conditions, and direction of the current.

"Turn on the weather channel, will you, Nance?" he asked as he filled the line in the book. "Channel two or three."

I turned the knob until the penlight shone through the numeral on the dial and sat back in the tall wheelhouse chair to listen to the continuously droning voice on the radio. Gary stared out of the back window of the wheelhouse at the dark form of the tow close on our stern. As we angled round into the channel at the mouth of the Elk River, he radioed the captain on the *Miss Elizabeth.*

"Cap, I'm going to start slowing her down to let out some hawser. How about knocking it out of gear for me?"

"You got it, Gary."

Although we had left Port Deposit with the tow about fifty feet off our stern, Gary had planned to let out the hawser to full length once we reached the open waters. With the barge towed up close, the tug had more control over the tow, but the tug's prop wash fought the forward motion of the section, slowing our speed by about a knot.

I followed Gary out on deck to stand beside him at the after controls. Clarky was below, waiting by the turns of hawser wrapped around the port horn of the towing bitts. When the tow had stopped moving, Clarky threw off the wraps and let the line run free, watching it leap off the coiled pile on the deck to whiz through the bitt. Gary had put some power to her, speeding up enough to feed the line out evenly, then took it out of gear, allowing the tug to coast forward until only one flat layer of hawser remained on the wooden rack. Then he reversed the engine long enough to stop the tug, and Clarky quickly snatched two turns around the horn again, throwing on two more when they had tightened down. After securing the hawser, he carefully positioned the split section of fire hose that served as chafing gear, and tied it in place so that as the line stretched, it would cover the spot where the hawser rubbed on the taffrail. His work finished, he glanced up at Gary for confirmation of his dismissal.

"Thanks."

Clarky waved a hand in acknowledgment and meandered back to the engine room. I followed Gary back to the wheelhouse, grateful to be out of the enveloping diesel smoke which wafted down from the single stack to hover over the afterdecks. Diesel smoke permeates everything aboard, sticking to hair, clothes, and skin. By the end of a two-week stint aboard, the dense oiliness clings to the cloth lining of foul weather gear, and floats up from the pages of books hidden in the lockers. No amount of scrubbing of bodies or airing of clothes completely dissipates the smell. It penetrates the material possessions of the crew much as the addiction for the life infiltrates the psyche.

We ran down the channel toward Pooles Island, following the winking lines of channel markers. In the distance, the Chesapeake Bay Bridge spanned the gap between the two shores, surmounting what appeared to be a black wall to the south which was decorated with streams of moving lights passing over it in two uninterrupted chains. As we passed Tolchester, a ship steamed out of Baltimore, bound for the Chesapeake and Delaware Canal and headed toward us in the long finger of

37

Brewerton Channel Extension which reaches from Baltimore Harbor to the Eastern Shore near Swan Point. Gary radioed him, apprising the pilot of our tow and the fact that there was an unseen tug behind in the vulnerable pushing position. I watched, marveling at how Gary had distinguished the distant lights of the ship from the series of red and white lights blinking in a sketchy outline of the channel, all partially obscured by the bright glow of the city. Looking down the black bay, I wondered how many unidentified vessels lurked, all differentiated by their lights. The vessels melded with the backdrop of the scenery, and I thought with chagrin that I would never develop the capability to discern a threat. Gnawing at my mind, too, was how difficult a time I would have in this fraternity, being one of the few women with the audacity to try to join the ranks.

It was an all male world. While I was aboard, the girlie magazines which littered all corners of the tug were discreetly turned face down on the seats or stuffed, folded, behind the radiator in the head. For Clarky, who swore as a vivid punctuation to his stories, my presence was a hindrance, every few sentences stumbled over in an effort to delete the expletives. I often felt as though I had walked into the boys' locker room inadvertently, my entrance followed by a loud silence.

Although I was determined to fit in as best I could, I still could not change the fact of being female. Despite their fears, I had no intention of rearranging the atmosphere aboard, my main interest being the job itself and sharing the experience with Gary. Swearing was something I had expected in that rough working atmosphere. While I made no bones about the fact that I appreciated their deference to my femininity, I could take the worst of it unblushing.

Perhaps the worst of it for them was the exposure of frailties that this living situation entails. The work is physically demanding, and it requires a certain amount of pure bravado to endure. Exhaustion and heat stretch nerves, and facades grow thin, allowing glimpses into the soul in unguarded moments. I had begun to feel as though it was this exposure that the men feared most. They live two wholly separate existences and find incorporating one into the other a constantly fraying experience. They leave family, friends, and comfort ashore to step

38

into another dimension, an existence whose boundaries are the confines of the tug and whose isolation is complete from all but the reality of day-to-day running.

While working, I was part of the drudgery and the pleasure, but as a passenger, I was merely a spectator. The new cook, particularly, resented my being there and made every effort to make the time unpleasant. He was a man with a disturbingly broad, insincere smile whose handshake had immediately sent a foreboding chill up my spine. He served the men supper before he would allow me to eat, trying even to prevent my sitting at table with them while I waited for everyone ("the ones who are really working") to finish. Over the very short period of our trip down the bay, I had come to fear him, feeling a sharp prickling at the back of the neck that instinct tells you means danger. For whatever reason, he had taken an instant dislike to me, and intuition warned me he could be violent. Finally, thinking I was losing my perspective, I asked Clarky about my apprehensions.

"If you've got that feeling, Nance, believe it," he told me seriously when I confessed to him that I thought the cook would willingly do me harm. "I've known of guys who for one reason or another made enemies, and they went overboard without a trace. It's pretty easy out here."

I shuddered but was at least confirmed in my own sanity. My fear of this man made what would otherwise have been a time of leisurely enjoyment, instead, a study in endurance. I resolved never to be alone with him.

The ice of the previous winter had shifted and removed many of the navigational aids in the Potomac. Even this late in the season, the Coast Guard, burdened by an abundance of work and a dearth of manpower, had not replaced the river's full complement. We lumbered up the dark Potomac, guided by an occasional temporary ice mark, and enjoyed the cool evening air. I had brought yet another pair of mugs filled with coffee to the wheelhouse to sit with Gary, touring the river from a vantage point few are fortunate enough to encounter.

"I feel like a cookie," Gary said out of the blue.

"What?"

"Doesn't that sound good? A nice, warm, chewy cookie!"

39

he said slowly, lovingly drawling out the words, a puckish grin spread over his face.

"Gary, I don't want to make cookies now," I told him, thinking of the cook's reaction should he catch me in his galley.

"You steer and I'll do it!" he said, undaunted.

"No! I can't!"

"Sure you can. Come here. Look, we're right here on the chart," he said, putting a finger on a buoy which was absent in actual fact.

"Gary, I can't!"

"You can! You've been reading charts all your life," he insisted, exasperated at my reluctance.

"But I always knew where I was. And I wasn't hauling that monstrosity," I moaned, waving an arm in the general direction of the tow. "And what if someone calls over the radio?"

"Answer. Look, Nance. You can do it. Look here at the chart. See that buoy? It's that one right up there," he said, pointing toward a flashing white light standing off a point on the shore. "I won't be long. I saw a cookie mix in the cabinet."

With that he was gone. I stood behind the wheel, flashlight and chart clutched in one sweaty hand, binoculars hung around my neck. Thankful that we were running against a current that had slowed our progress to little more than four knots, I hoped at least I would have some warning of impending disaster. Minutes dragged by. I peered through the binoculars, then studied the chart, easing the tug around toward the next pair of buoys upriver, praying I had not mistaken the lights of a house or car for the buoys I hoped were in place. The longer Gary was gone, the more fantastic were the calamities in my mind. Glancing back to be sure the tow was still following, I wondered how soon it would run us down and kill everyone aboard if I were to ground the tug on a bend. Finally, able to stand the self-inflicted pressure no longer, I set the helm on a straight course, and bolted down the ladder to call in the open galley porthole.

"I can't stand it. I'm not sure where we are and I'll come down and take your place. You get up here!"

Without waiting for a response, I took the ladder two steps at a time, jumped back into the wheelhouse, and grabbed the wheel again. *Progress* chugged toward the lights, unchanged in her heading. Gary came up the ladder, an amused expression in his bright eyes.

"What's the matter?" he asked, putting a reassuring hand on my shoulder.

"I'm not sure where I am. Are those two, these two marks?" I asked, pointing first to the lights ahead, and then to the chart.

"One is, the other is on shore, I think. The next one, that one," he said as he laid his finger on the chart, "should be a little farther away."

"Look, I'll go down and do your damned cookies. Just don't tell anyone I did them. As far as anyone is concerned you baked cookies," I instructed.

"Okay."

I went below but did not step into the galley before glancing down both decks to see if anyone else was about. Periodically throughout the watch, Clarky stopped in the wheelhouse, taking a break from the noise and heat of the engine room while puffing on a stogie or downing a cup of coffee. He was nowhere in sight. Probably crouched on the oily grating inside the engine room while fiddling with a piece of machinery, I decided. I stepped into the galley and found the cookie dough in a bowl beside a tin sheet half-filled with blobs. I finished dropping dough onto the two tin sheets and tried to open the oven door as quietly as possible in order to slide them inside. The heavy iron latch slid reluctantly, squeaking shrilly. As I was pushing in the second cookie sheet, I felt a hand on my shoulder. Jumping up, I nearly cracked Clarky under the chin.

"My God! You scared me!"

I shut the door.

"Who'd you think I was, the devil?" he teased.

I studied him for a moment before admitting, "He won't let me in the galley much less cook anything. They'll be done in ten minutes."

"Mmm good. Don't think he'd approve, huh?"

I shook my head.

"As far as you're concerned, Gary baked these, okay?"

He nodded. We sat down to talk until the cookies were

41

done, his presence taking the edge off my anxiety about discovery by the cook. The deed was done undetected, and with a sigh of relief, I climbed the ladder to the wheelhouse with a warm plate in hand. Clarky followed with two glasses of milk and the three of us chewed warm peanut butter cookies and swigged cold milk as we threaded our way toward Washington, D.C.

I arrived for breakfast the same time as Clarky and slid into the booth beside him to watch the cook flip eggs with spasmodic jerks of the spatula. He poured out a mug of coffee for Clarky, ignoring me with studied care. By the time David stumbled into the galley, cook was in a full-blown swivet. Finally, after huffing and puffing like a wet hen, he stopped and fixed me with an icy stare.

"I see someone was making a mess in my galley last night. *Someone* baked cookies. They're not very good!"

I felt Clarky's knee press mine under the table.

"You mean you don't like my cookin'?" he asked sweetly, a bland smile turned on the agitated cook.

"*You* baked them, Clarky?" the cook asked suspiciously.

"Sure. I can cook. What's the matter? Don't you like my cookin'?" he repeated, warming to his part.

"Oh, I didn't say I didn't *like* them," the cook stammered, trying to retrace his steps. "They're not bad at all as a matter of fact. You're welcome to use the galley anytime."

"Well, good. I just got hungry for some cookies last night. You don't mind, do you?" Clarky smirked into his mug.

"Mind? Of course not. You know, they're pretty good," he burbled, glancing at me, then at Clarky and back.

I sat poker-faced as the exchange took place and pressed Clarky's knee surreptitiously to acknowledge my appreciation. It was a moment I will never forget and for which I have always been grateful to that proud, complex man.

In the Potomac Basin the water was hardly visible for the countless pieces of construction equipment perched on barges and pontoons that clogged the muddy stretch between the two shores. There seemed to be men and metal everywhere, and the shore teemed with activity. Before reaching the conges-

42

tion, the crew of *Progress* had pulled hawser and retrieved the bridles, releasing the tunnel section to the tug *Miss Elizabeth*, while we steamed around to the side, readying the tug to push the subway section into position. That done, I stood by with my satchel, waiting to be put ashore on a barge accessible to terra firma in order to journey home via bus connections and sundry rides.

While my family was occasionally disconcerted at the casual way Gary left me on various bulkheads and piers, expecting me to find my own way home, I found his confidence in my resourcefulness a compliment. Rather than seeing it as negligence or lack of concern, I viewed it as a firm belief in my ability to cope. That summer was an alphabet soup of gardening, home maintenance, canvas and sail repair, candle-lit dinners with my visiting husband, and my forays into tug life.

THREE

THE TUG *Progress* was owned and managed by two men, Chris Berg and Jerry McCammon. They were in many ways a marriage of opposites, but each had something that the other needed and in the original partnership, the relationship was completely symbiotic.

Chris, F. Christian Berg, Jr., the son of a man who had owned and run a tug company for years, had grown up working on tugs. A graduate of the United States Merchant Marine Academy, at Kings Point, New York, he was also a southern gentleman of the old school. More important, he was a boat handler of the first order. A Norwegian by descent, he could coax a tug into doing virtually anything he wished. Because of his years of association with the tugboat industry, his contacts and savvy made him the point man for the operation, managing the day-to-day details of the tug crew, provisioning, maintenance, and contracts.

It was Chris who found the 1943 vintage tug and recruited Gary, in his efforts to crew the tug quickly. The *Progress* had been built by the Defense Plant Corporation, a government agency which constructed a series of tugs of the same design that were known simply as DPCs. The battered vessel was a bargain that required a complete engine overhaul as well as some welding and cutting of body parts, but she was a member of a group whose reputation was one of dedicated service. Originally, she had six cabins, one of which was then converted to a storage locker for lines, running lights, batteries, and after several years of washing clothes in buckets, a wringer-washer. Since she was designed for eleven- and twelve-man crews, a tremendous crowd on the eighty-six-foot tug, she was luxurious in having one cabin per crew member for a five-man crew. In that respect, she offered far more privacy than most tugs whose sleeping arrangements included something closer to a barracks, or at least double bunking.

Jerry McCammon, a former stockbroker turned farmer, was also an energetic entrepreneur. His background in no way prepared him for a partnership in a tug company; nonetheless, he was hardworking and willing to learn, not only keeping the books, issuing paychecks, and arranging financing, but occasionally crawling down into the engine room to help change an engine blower or rebuild pumps. Consequently, a natural flair for the mechanical gradually ripened into a detailed knowledge of the engine and its idiosyncracies.

Chris and Jerrry were also partners in an enterprise in the Gulf of Mexico for which Chris provided the same service as he did for the *Progress*. Often, things in the Gulf would get chaotic, and Chris would be called on to fly down with parts or to sort out crew problems. It was on these occasions that Jerry was in complete charge, and that Gary saw his chance to get me on the tug. While Chris disapproved of my being there, let alone working, Jerry had none of an old salt's inhibitions about a woman aboard. I was convenient and would come at a moment's notice, making his problems with last minute crew shifts manageable.

In 1976, crew problems appeared to be almost constant. It was a time when it seemed as though everyone associated with the water had bought or chartered a tug in hopes of benefiting from the many jobs abounding. Crews were at a premium, particularly reliable wheelhouse crew. Chris shuttled back and forth between Wilmington and the Gulf, delivering parts, overseeing mechanical repairs, crew negotiations, and contract difficulties.

In June of that year, Gary had been on for three weeks instead of the usual two in order to give his opposite number an extra week at home. Gary and I had driven to Rehoboth to visit his mother the day after he had gotten off, and it was there that

45

Chris chased Gary down by phone. The other captain had fallen ill and had to get off the tug in Norfolk. Chris needed Gary immediately to stand in for a short time. Although the nebulous "short time" sounded like a year to us, Gary, reliable as always, was on a bus that afternoon bound south.

Finally, in July, with no end of the trip in sight, Gary phoned to ask if I would meet him at Wilmington, ride to Baltimore, then get off again in Wilmington. Craving his company, I agreed, and drove to the fenced-in yard in Wilmington that the company used as a headquarters. Leaving the car safely locked behind the tall chain link fence, I caught a ride to Wilmington Marine Terminal and climbed aboard with my little blue satchel in tow.

At about midnight the next evening, we left Baltimore with a collection of barges that looked more like a pudding stone than a tow. There were a couple of war-ravaged flat barges which had seen hand-to-hand combat with longshoremen's cranes and docks all over the Atlantic coast. These were tied to the port side of five LASH barges, grey steel boxes thirty by sixty by ten feet which were made up end to end, comprising three hundred feet of tow. The *Progress* had been made up in pushing gear behind this conglomeration. The barges were lit with a port bow light on the outboard end of the forward flat barge, and a starboard light on the forwardmost corner of the LASH tow beside them so that from head-on at dawn, the arrangement must have looked like a walleyed whale. The tug itself was, as always, lit to the nines, dressed in her spangle of lights as though ready for a night on the town. A ring of yellow deck lights circled the brim of her lower deckhouse, and the running lights sat atop the wheelhouse like bangles on a hat. To crown this were the white masthead lights which identified the nature of the tow—two (according to the old inland rules) for pushing—one for the boat and one for the barge. In the old inland rules, three lights strung one over the other indicated a tow on a hawser—one light for the barge, one for the towing line, and one for the tug—although this has changed because of recent legislation, and some of the lighting is dependent on length of tow as well as disposition.

I had collapsed just before midnight and fallen dead asleep before Gary could even get off watch so that he was relegated to the outside of the narrow bunk. Despite the assortment of barges, it had seemed like a run-of-the-mill tow, and we steamed out of Baltimore Harbor to make the turn past North Point Light and run across Pooles Island Flats. In my sleep, I vaguely heard the long, deep blast of the horn, repeating its warning over and over. The cabin door creaked, and Ed Watson, the mate, who was on watch, leaned into the darkness.

"Gary, I think you'd better come up here."

Gary rolled out of the bunk and pulled on a pair of shorts, padding up into the wheelhouse barefoot. I lay there for a few moments half-asleep, and then realized the tug had stopped. I had felt no sudden nudge to indicate we were aground, and rose to my knees to peer out of the porthole over the bunk. The searchlight swept back and forth over the cloudy water. The engine kicked into reverse and we backed hard, rattling the lockers and clattering the plates in the galley. Back to neutral, and then forward, full, sending a struggling shudder through the tug as she strained to push the massive weight in front of her, then back to reverse. We were crabbing sideways, hampered by the resistance of the tow, but for what reason I could not discern. Fully awake now, and curious, I rose and dressed as Gary sprang back into the room and snapped on the light to tie his shoes.

"What's happening?"

"Somebody's hit the tow," Gary informed me in clipped tones.

The urgency in his voice communicated itself, and I came out to see if they would need help. Ed stood behind the throttle pedestal, steering with the small electric tiller on the port side by the window. He swept the large search beam over the surface of the water, and then, focusing on a small, motionless speedboat, continued his efforts to back and fill the tug and tow. One man was slumped behind the controls of the little boat, his head drooping onto his chest. As the white beam of the searchlight hit him, glaring off the console in front of him, his arm came up, and without lifting his head, he waved us over toward him. Visibly shaken, Ed leaned out of the window.

"We're comin', Buddy! Hang on, we're gettin' there as fast as we can!" Ed cried.

Gary was on the radio, calling the Coast Guard. he described our location and the size of the boat. As we neared, we could see an inert form in the bottom of the speedboat.

"She's still floatin'," Ed commented nervously. "Thank God she didn't go right down. I wonder if she's leakin'."

I leaned out of the door, trying to see the damage. From where I stood, the main damage was a crushed bow, clearly showing the boat had hit squarely, but there did not seem to be any water in the bottom.

"God, Gary. I blew the horn, but by the time I saw them, they were just headed straight for the side of the barge. They were flying. Never even slowed down that I could see. I flashed the searchlight over the barges, but they never even slowed down," he explained unhappily.

Gary nodded without comment. The radio barked, and he snatched it off the overhead to confirm our location to the Coast Guard. We were drawing up to the boat which bobbed alongside the barge. Gary went below to help Bob Atwater, who was decking on this crew, get the boat secured to the side of the tug.

My heart pounding, I went out on the top deck to stand by. Together, Bob and Gary snagged the boat with the long boat-hook and dragged it sideways to secure it to the after quarter bitts. Inside the speedboat were two men, one slumped over the steering and the other semi-conscious on the carpeting.

"Gary!" Ed shouted from the platform outside the wheel-house door, "Coast Guard wants to talk to you."

"Okay!" he called. "Nance, get a couple of blankets and come down here to hold this guy's hand," he said to me as he stepped out of the boat.

Numbly, I did as I was told, climbing into the boat and draping a blanket over each man. Bob had disappeared on another errand, leaving me temporarily alone with the two injured men. The seated man moaned and rolled his head, eyes closed. He was pinned behind the steering and appeared to be only stunned, but from every terrifying thing I had ever heard about accidents and internal injuries, I feared to touch him except to clutch his hand in support.

"My knee, stretch my knee," he groaned.

He was in shorts, and as I studied his knee in the light from the tug, I could see that it was extremely swollen.

"My knee," he said again, "move it."

"Okay, I'll make it better," I assured him in a shaking voice.

Rather than move anything, I worked my hands up and down his calf in a massaging motion, hoping to make him believe that I had changed the position. I could only guess that his knee was dislocated or broken.

"Oh, move it!" he groaned.

"What's your name?"

"Jim. How's my buddy?"

"He's going to be fine, Jim. So are you. They're getting help now."

"How's my buddy?" he slurred, turning slightly to locate his fallen friend.

I realized then that he was drunk as well as stunned. Harry Truitt, the engineer on this crew, had come into the speedboat and sat by the other man's head, patting him and offering soft words of reassurance.

"He says he feels sick, Nance," Harry told me quietly.

"Oh, God, Harry. Both these guys look like they're pickled. What do you think we ought to do? We don't dare move them, at least not much. Do you think he's really going to be sick?"

"I don't know."

"Maybe we can just turn him on his side enough so he doesn't choke if he does."

Harry and I tried to find a place to hold the man and ease him onto his side, but as soon as we touched him, he began to moan loudly, and we gave it up.

"Maybe you could just watch him and if he starts being sick, turn his head," I suggested.

"Oooohhhh," the man groaned. "I swear to God, if we ever get outta this I ain't never gonna drink another beer in my life. I swear!"

Harry and I chuckled in spite of ourselves, and I went back

to massaging Jim's leg. It seemed like hours before we saw the lights of the small Coast Guard boat speeding toward us. They wasted no time in tying to our starboard side and setting to work. One man brought a stokes litter and Harry and I vacated the speedboat to give the Coast Guard men room to work. They laid the prostrate man in the litter and parked him on the fantail while they pried the mutilated wood and fiberglass from the driver, freeing him from the console.

Finally, the two injured men lay on the deck of the Coast Guard patrol boat, skimming toward a hospital, their ordeal just begun. We were ordered to wait for a Coast Guard inspector to arrive who would take down a report and retrieve the smashed boat. Unable to sleep, Gary and I lay down side by side on the bunk, our skin sticking where it touched in the muggy stillness. Ed stood watch by the radio, gulping hot coffee by the pot and lighting one cigarette from the last.

The dawn oozed up, lighting a steamy, flat morning that felt like the grim prelude to a day spent in sweat-soaked misery. Gary rolled off the bunk at five-thirty, peeling the damp bedclothes from his back.

"What's going to happen now?"

"I don't know," he said, frowning as he tied his shoes. "We've got to wait for the guy from the Coast Guard to get here, and then see from there. I've got to call Chris and let him know," he muttered.

There was little reason for talk. We sat around the tug, drinking coffee, and pondering the ramifications of the accident. I wandered up the ladder to sit on the landing by the wheelhouse while Ed hung out of the open window, puffing thoughtfully on a cigarette. The tow sat in front of us, surrounded by the slick grey of the water, as though we were in a murky reflecting pool.

"Seems like everybody's suing everybody these days," Ed mused, his eyes on the hazy outline of Pooles Island in the distance.

I glanced up at his worn face, his usually twinkling eyes dull and tired.

"I hope those guys are okay. They looked like they mighta been hurt bad."

50

"I think the guy behind the controls dislocated his knee," I murmured.

"I hope they're okay," he repeated.

When the Coast Guard arrived, they wanted to hear the entire story from Ed, but were as interested in Gary's sea experience, license, and record as Ed's, studying his papers and checking through the log. When they left, Ed sat up for a while, staring out of the window while Gary continued the tow on its way over the monochromatic grey of the flats.

"You think Ed will be sued?" I asked after he had gone to bed.

"It wouldn't be Ed. It would be me," Gary told me woodenly.

"What?"

"The master is responsible. If anyone is going to get sued, it'll be you and me."

"Geez, do you think we will?"

It is the captain's license that is at risk as every decision aboard is, technically, his. In actual fact, the mate makes many of the decisions which would affect the outcome of a job. If the tow is made up during the mate's watch, he decides how it will be made up, oversees the lighting of it, and chooses the route unless otherwise stipulated. The captain has it within his authority to override any decisions and may take over at any time from the mate. However, in practice, when two people are trading wheelhouse duties every six hours for fourteen days at a stretch, many decisions rest with the mate. Regardless, the captain is ultimately responsible.

The ride through the C&D Canal was one of the most miserable trips I can remember on the water. What little breeze there was followed us so that we felt as though we were caught in a vacuum. The current fought the tow, slowing our passage to three knots over the bottom, a crawl punctuated by the bridges and docks. The sun poured down over the house and decks, leaving nowhere to hide from the heat. Bob and Ed and I sat in the wheelhouse drinking endless glasses of iced tea while the perspiration soaked what few clothes we wore. My head throbbed with a headache born of heat and worry.

When we finally turned the jetties at Reedy Point and

headed north up the Delaware, the breeze picked up a fraction, breathing a hint of freshness through the open windows and doors. Gary had come on watch and we sat in the shade of the wheelhouse after supper, watching the sun sliding down toward the marshes. After the claustrophobic heat of the day, the sun dripped buttery pools over the water. Gulls and herons glided by, lethargic in their flight.

Waiting for the Coast Guard had pressed the job for time; the tug was due in Philadelphia posthaste, leaving no time to put into the Wilmington Marine Terminal to let me off. We approached the Delaware Memorial Bridge, fighting the current, and Gary began casting about for a way to get me back to my car. Seeing a young couple in a speedboat skimming upriver, he tooted the whistle and stood on the landing outside the wheelhouse door, waving his arms. Uncertainly at first, they slowed and consulted each other. Gary continued to shout at them, waving them toward us. As they closed the distance between the vessels, Gary descended to the lower deck to meet them. If they were surprised to be stopped by a tug captain, they were even more nonplussed at his request.

"Can you drop my wife off on that barge over there?" he said, pointing to the oil barge tied at the outermost bulkhead of the marine terminal.

Gaping, the man said something to his wife who, though wide-eyed, nodded affirmatively.

"Yeah, okay."

"Great! Get your bag, Nance! Quick!" Gary shouted to me.

Thoroughly embarrassed at the audacity, I ran along the deck, jumped into the boat, and huddled in a corner trying to look unobtrusive.

"Listen, thanks a lot," Gary said, sticking out his hand. "Nance, I'll call you when we get up there to make sure you get home all right."

I waved and then, as we careered away from the tug, apologetically introduced myself. The two refused payment, even for the gasoline their taxi service cost them. They deposited me on the barge, waving with incredulous smiles as they backed away.

52

After scrambling to my feet, dragging my bag with me, I walked across the barge, climbing over the maze of pipes and lines toward the small cabin at the stern. The men who sat in the deckhouse wore the same astonished expression as had my ferry tenders, when they saw me threading my way over the barge toward the catwalk which led to shore.

"Where did you come from?" one asked as he lumbered toward me.

"From that tug," I said, pointing out into the river where *Progress* slowly moved upriver. "A speedboat just dropped me off."

"What's she say?" his friend called from the door of the cabin.

"She says she just got off a tug," the large man shouted back at him.

"Tug?"

"*Progress*," I offered. "Out there."

"What?"

"Never mind!" the big man told him in exasperation. "He's a little deaf. Where're you headed?" he asked kindly.

"I've got to get to my car. It's locked up in a yard upriver here," I answered, smiling in appreciation of his obvious goodwill.

"Come on. I'll call a cab for you. There's a phone in that booth at the end. I've got a key."

I followed the burly figure down the narrow walkway, looking down through the slats at the water and rocks beneath. The man waited with me for the cab, chatting about mutual acquaintances and tugs. The sun had dropped behind the warehouses at the far end of the vast terminal, and the mosquitoes had begun to bite my bare, sticky limbs.

"Listen, you tell that cab driver to wait for you to get into the yard for your car," the man instructed. "That's no place for a woman to be wandering around alone."

"I will, and thanks a lot," I said, shaking his hand.

I had begun to feel like Blanche Du Bois, always dependent on the kindness of strangers. The cabbie was gruff and little interested in the fare, particularly not one which took him down a road whose only pavement had crumbled away years

53

before into deep holes. It was moonless and completely dark when we pulled up at the chain link fence. After paying the fare, I got out and turned the dials of the combination lock while the cab driver focused his lights on the gate. Nothing happened. I pulled out the slip of paper on which Gary had written the combination. According to the scratches on the slip, it was the right set of numbers. I tried again. Still nothing happened.

"Come on, lady. Are you gonna open that lock or not? I got another fare to go to," the driver called.

"I can't get it undone," I explained.

"Listen, do you want me to take you anywhere?"

"No, I've just got to get this lock undone," I repeated.

"Look, lady. I gotta go."

So saying, he backed the car around and took off down the rutted road, leaving me standing tantalizingly close to the car, yet unable to reach it. A streetlight cast an uncertain glow toward the lock, just enough to distinguish one digit from another, and I tried the combination again, this time yanking it ferociously once the proper squence was set. No result. The lock dangled from its hole, taunting me. Looking at the fence, I debated scaling it and trying to find something with which to cut the lock off but then realized I could not in good conscience leave having broken the only piece of equipment between the cars of the rest of the crew and the local enterprising car renovators.

Docks are rarely in anything but the seedier parts of town, or at least in parts where it is unwise for a woman to walk alone unless her intentions are other than mine. However, I had little choice but to find a telephone and try to persuade a friend to drive the hour to Wilmington to collect me. I'd worry about the car later.

The mosquitoes had made a pincushion of me, and my skin was covered with red welts and perspiration. Limp strands of hair were glued to my sweaty neck and face. Gathering my bag and pocketbook, I began the half-mile walk to the nearest gas station. The road is lonely and dark, lit only by a streetlight at either end of a long corridor which is grown up on one side with brush and unwanted piles of debris and fenced along the other by a series of industrial yards. Lumps of broken cars take on new character in the dark, aided by the humming chorus of a thousand attacking insects. The walk felt like a silent gauntlet where lurked unseen predators, both animal and human. Taking long, determined strides, I kept my eyes fixed on the distant lights of the gas station, and hummed, "Whenever I Feel Afraid," over and over to myself.

Once inside the telephone booth, I could not decide whether I preferred the bright lights which made apparent my solitude, or the anonymous darkness of the lane. Wasting no time, I began to dial, hoping to reach one of three friends from home who could have driven up to Wilmington, however reluctantly, at ten P.M.

All phone calls went unanswered. No one was home on a Friday evening, and I was stuck in the heart of the docks of Wilmington, alone. Finally, I phoned Jerry to confirm the combination of the lock. Although he lives almost an hour's drive away, he offered to come down and open it for me. Shamed that I should put him to such trouble, I demurred, resolving to either get the lock open or spend the night sleeping in the car after climbing the fence.

I trudged back to the yard and attacked the lock one more time. The combination Gary had given me had been correct, Jerry had said, had I tried yanking it? I turned the numbers slowly, aligning them with meticulous care. Holding my breath, I pulled hard. The lock would not budge. Furious, frustrated, tired, I stepped back and kicked it with a roar. The lock fell open.

It was past eleven o'clock before I fumbled the key into the front door lock of our house. I could hear the telephone ringing as I tried to jam the key in the slot but it stopped as I turned the knob. Without even turning on the lights, I climbed the steps to the bathroom, washed my face, and brushed my teeth. Too exhausted to shower, I stripped off damp clothes and climbed into bed. The phone rang again. It was Gary.

"Thank God! I've been calling ever since we got to the dock. What happened? I was worried about you!" he poured out in a rush.

"Well, the lock wouldn't open on the gate so I had to walk

55

and call—oh, Gare, it's late and it's too long a story. Are you okay? You sound worried."

"Well, I was! I expected you home an hour ago."

"What happened at the dock?"

"The lawyer came to talk with us and look over our copy of the Coast Guard report. He wants us all to give depositions as soon as we get off."

"Did he say what it looked like?"

"He didn't sound too encouraging. He said something about an ambulance chaser being at the hospital talking with those two guys."

"How are they?"

"Not too good."

"Look, keep a good thought, Love. You know it helps. And he's a good lawyer. You know you did everything right?"

"Yeah."

"Then don't worry. It'll be okay."

"You're all right?" he asked, somewhat bolstered.

"I'm fine. I just miss you already."

F O U R

FIVE DAYS LATER I was changing crews with Clarky Collins, Chris Schlegel, and David Gray to go aboard for two weeks as cook. As a result of more crew problems, the cook who had so unnerved me was needed to fill in on the other boat in the Gulf. While Chris Berg was still not enamored of the idea of a woman working aboard an oceangoing tug, he had come to regard my availability as a last minute crew replacement with a certain sangfroid and in fact had been the one to ask if I could get on with the rest of the crew that July. I had agreed immediately. Gary had been aboard for six unrelieved weeks, and we yearned for a little time together.

Although it was wiltingly hot, I anticipated a pleasant trip without the threatening presence of the cook, and scurried around for two days, trying to set our home and garden in order while looking forward to the radical change of pace a hiatus on the tug offered. After taking our cat off to my parents, and leaving instructions with neighbors about picking the garden and watering the plants, I packed my suitcase. Cramming in paint-splotched clothes, the survivors of various careers as house painter and yacht maintenance person, several pairs of rubber gloves, several more of work gloves, foul weather gear, sea boots, and a lone dress, the expression of a hope which had so far gone unfulfilled, I prepared to leave modern conveniences behind for life at sea. As there was no washer aboard at the time, the choices were to pack enough changes for the entire two weeks, wear the same thing until the rest of the crew

57

began making comments about compost, or hand-wash underwear in a bucket and hang it on the clothesline strung tenement fashion through the engine room to dry stiff and smelling of diesel smoke. I packed changes.

While everyone traveled to and from the tug dressed like the rest of the world, once aboard, the uniform looked more like rejected Goodwill donations. More often than not Gary spent his time aboard wearing hopelessly mismatched socks, ripped pants, and shrunken shirts with the insignia of his former employer peeling away from the pocket. The others were little better. Cutoff shorts were the norm with tattered T-shirts as a bow to propriety at meals.

Wednesday morning I sat in the shade on the brick stoop beside my suitcase, my skin already itching with the heat although the sun had barely skimmed over the east-facing kitchen. The company van thumped into the driveway and stopped. At the wheel was Chris Berg and beside him, Clarky laconically puffed on a cigarette. David Gray sat in the second seat, smiling in welcome as I approached with my case in tow. Chris jumped out of the van, took my case, and heaved it into the back while I climbed in beside David. There was little conversation. Chris Schlegel was added in Annapolis, and we roared over the highway toward the Potomac.

Progress was tied to a bulkheaded stretch of river which skirted a park that was more a wish than an actuality. The trees which lined the shore did not quite shelter *Progress*'s yellow deckhouse, and she sat naked in the blinding sun. When we skidded to a halt on the gravel and sand quay, the other crew poured over the gunwale, their bags in hand, eager to escape. Although showered and dressed in respectable clothes, everyone looked disheveled, the sweat soaking round blotches in their shirts and beading their faces. Curl's bald head glistened in the sun.

"I got yer dinner in the oven," he growled, giving me a gap-toothed smile. "You got some taters down thar and some onions. And they's some meat in the freezer. Ought to have enough for a few days."

"Thanks," I said as I yanked my suitcase out of the back and dropped it in the dirt. "Got much salad stuff?"

58

"Naw, we done run out," he scoffed.

I always had the feeling that he thought salad was for sissies. Curl's cooking style was unadulteratedly Southern Tugboat. Beans and fatback were staples as well as cornbread, biscuits and gravy, bread pudding, and pork in all shapes and incarnations. The men on Curl's crew were, for the most part, older and had been accustomed to the heavy meals traditionally served on the water. A breakfast of pancakes, eggs, and scrapple would be followed six hours later by a dinner of roast pork, potatoes, succotash, biscuits, and gravy, followed by supper six hours after that of fried ham, applesauce, mashed potatoes, peas, and dessert. It was easy to see why, in a job of predominantly heavy labor but little exercise, so many men carried with them a considerable paunch.

Although the thermometer read ninety-four degrees, Curl had the iron stove top glowing cherry red, the flame in its belly roaring at full capacity. I reached into the oven and pulled out the dinner he had made. The bones on the roast stuck out like the twiggy arms of a windblown scarecrow. The succotash was grey-green and the potatoes, carrots, and onions swam in an inch of rendered grease. As I laid the pan on the green-painted tabletop, Gary jumped into the galley and snatched me up in a sticky hug.

"God, it's good to see you, Babe!"

We stood glued together for a moment, drinking in each other's embrace. When I stood back, I could see how haggard he looked. Dark circles ringed his blue eyes, and his hair and beard, untrimmed for two months, looked wild, curling in all directions. He wore shorts and socks and work boots.

"How're you doing?" I asked, taking in the exhausted slump of his shoulders.

"I'm bushwacked!"

"I guess you are! Are you going to be able to come home after this two weeks?"

"I sure hope so!"

"Have you heard anything about those guys who hit the barge?"

He shook his head.

"The lawyer talked to Chris, and he says they're still in the

59

hospital. Apparently, they both had a lot of internal damage."

"Oh God. Anything permanent?"

"I don't know. Everybody who was there that night has given depositions but me. I'm supposed to go to the lawyer's office whenever I can get off. Then we've just got to wait to see if they're going to file suit against us."

"I don't see how they could file suit," I murmured, knowing full well how they could. "How long do we wait?"

"Three years from the date of the accident."

"You're kidding!"

"Nope. It's a bitch, huh?"

"Three years!"

"Have you had anything to eat?" I asked finally. "You want me to serve you some lunch?"

"God, no! I had a sandwich a little while ago. I'd better go talk to Chris," he said, giving me a kiss before disappearing out the companionway.

The others had trooped aboard and dispersed to their cabins. Gradually, they stepped into the galley, scanning the table and its contents. After setting out the china and cutlery, I left them to make what they could of the meal while I changed into shorts and shirt and wrapped a bandanna around my head to keep the smoke from coating my scalp. Rummaging through the linen locker in my cabin, I laid out four sets of clean sheets and pillowcases, worn to gossamer, then stacked up four small towels. After parceling them out into each cabin, I joined the others in the galley to eat a sandwich and gulp down a glass of iced water.

Clarky sat in his accustomed place by the port door, munching quietly through the pile of food on his plate. Senior to the rest of us by at least twenty years, he had spent the better part of his life working on tugs. He had been with the old Berg Boat Company when Chris's father had owned it and run a fleet of tugs. When that company had dissolved, Clarky had hired on with Jerry and Chris. He and Curl had known each other for years both as neighbors and shipmates. They had worked on tugs before the protection of a union was common to seafarers, and Clarky particularly was a convinced union man. He often told stories of tug life before union contracts. Without a set

60

Harry Clark "Clarky" Collins. Photograph by Charlton A. Gunter.

schedule, he and many others worked almost constantly, afraid to walk off a tug to go home for fear of losing their jobs altogether. Clarky's first wife packed up their daughter and most of their belongings and left him while he was away working. The first year of his second marriage, he saw his wife a grand total of thirty days. He talked of the fight for decent grub, of demanding more than a diet of beans and fat-back meal after meal. He told of running tugs so shorthanded that he had been forced to stand an occasional wheelhouse watch in addition to tending the engine room. Clarky therefore had little patience with the complaints of our generation.

Our contention, that the men who ran unions were money-grubbing con men, was met with a set jaw and a sharp lecture. Clarky, convinced that people had not changed, was certain that without the unions, however corrupt, the old days would return with a vengeance.

Clarky is a complex man, intelligent and hardworking with a stubborn streak and his own ideas about how things ought to be. Born to a farming family on the Eastern Shore of Maryland, he had wanted to be a doctor but dropped out in the final semester of college. Eventually, he had worked his way onto tugs and had been there ever since. Although not happy at the idea of a woman aboard, he treated me with respect and affection, often chatting with me in the evenings as a father to a daughter.

After the other crew had left, we cast off and cruised downriver behind the barge, sliding over the glassy water toward Norfolk. I cleared up the dishes, climbed the ladder to the wheelhouse to let myself into the darkened captain's cabin to lie down beside Gary in the close heat.

By afternoon of the following day, we were meandering through the first few miles of the Inland Waterway. Since the hopper barge on our nose was empty, Gary climbed on top of the wheelhouse, bringing the remote controls of the steering with him. Chris Schlegel and I joined him, admiring the view. The sun on this hot, bright day glinted off wet carpets of marsh grass that covered the shore to the water's edge, and the shimmering blue of the canal wandered carelessly between low-lying shores.

At every opportunity, Gary had me practice my aim with the deck lines by standing on the fantail and firing loops at the towing bitts. Despite my height (five feet, eight inches) which gave me an advantage over Gary, who is shorter, my strength could not match his, and I had to develop a sidearm pitch coupled with a thrust of my whole body in order to get the distance that a man of Gary's size had. However, my aim was improving marginally, and when we nosed into the murky slip on the southern end of a small shipyard, which threatened to slide off the banks into the canal, Gary sent me out on the hopper barge with Chris. Chris went forward and shouted directions back to Gary, stabbing stiff fingers in the air to indicate the number of feet the barge stood from the pilings and dolphins.

Having spent most of his life in and around the waters of the Chesapeake, Chris seemed to be completely at home on boats. I envied him his easy surefootedness on the rolling decks of the tug in rough seas. An avid reader, he devoured books by the dozen and often sat in the galley curled up in a corner while I cooked. Additionally, and more important to the job, his commonsense knack for decking and his ability to anticipate the next move made both his job and the work in the wheelhouse appear easy. Seeing firsthand how interdependent everyone aboard is, it becomes apparent that a good deckhand can make even an incompetent boat handler appear to be better than he is, while a poor deckhand, or worse, one who deliberately obstructs, can make even the best boat handler look as though he is less than what he is. It is soon evident how this mutual reliance can also translate into mutual vulnerability.

The hopper barge, a large box thirty-five feet wide by one hundred and ninety-five feet long, has a coaming around its top the height of a man's chest which supports the sliding hatches. It leaves just enough room on deck to accommodate cleats and inspection ports welded to the steel deck at approximately forty-foot intervals. As often as they act as aids, they are obstacles to the unwary deckhand dragging a hundred feet of two-inch-thick line. I followed Chris, hauling a line with one hand and running my other hand along the thin rail attached to the coaming. Twice the line snagged on a cleat, stopping me abruptly in midstride as though I had slammed my coattails in a door. Unlike Chris and Clarky who were usually able to give the line a cavalier flip to free it, I was forced to stop each time and trudge back to extract it from the jaws of a cleat or piece of angle iron welded to the inspection ports.

"Looks good here, Gary!" Chris called over his shoulder while taking a bead on an upcoming dolphin.

"Okay! Nance, catch that piling coming up on you, that one just forward," Gary called to me as he leaned out of the window.

I stopped just aft of a cleat and, hauling up some extra line around my feet, readied myself to throw. I grabbed the handrail in my left hand to keep from going overboard off the narrow walkway while I threw the rest of my body into the toss. Keeping my eyes on the fast-approaching piling, I leaned back as far as I could, adding a roar for oomph. Instead of the line's eye dropping neatly over the tar-covered pole, it fell down the side of the barge, splashing into the brown water. Frantically, I pulled it back aboard, grunting with the added weight of the water. Knowing that I had only one or two more wholehearted pitches left in me, I geared myself mentally for the second shot.

Keep your eye on the target, Woman! Easy now, it's not a calf, it's moving steadily, just calculate, watch it. Lean back now, give yourself enough slack, you can do it. Don't take your eye off that piling. Okay, now *heave!*

Joy! The loop opened casually as it soared over the top of the pole, dropped down, and hung there. Did it! Now, make it fast before she takes off with you. Quickly, I bent down to flip several figure eights around the cleat at my feet, then backed off as the strain pulled the wraps taut, creaking. That done, I wandered toward Chris who was coming down the deck toward a line draped over the hatch. The yard foreman, who had watched us tie up with mild interest, took two steps over the rubble on the shore to stand on the edge of the bulkheading.

"It needs to come in two more dolphins," he finally informed Chris.

"What?"

"I said it needs to come in two more dolphins," he repeated.

"Oh. Okay, Cap. It's your ball game," Chris responded, his annoyance barely concealed.

Although it was the first time I had witnessed someone who had stood by while we worked to put a barge in the wrong place, waiting until we had completed the ordeal before mentioning the mistake, it was not to be the last. By the time the push cables were draped back over the stemhead, and we turned toward Norfolk again, I was bushed. I stepped into the galley to get a cold drink and apply it to my dripping forehead. The bread dough which I had so lovingly kneaded that morning, and laid to rise in a pair of pans on the shelf above the stove, had climbed well past its peak and collapsed in the center, but not before fat tentacles had cascaded onto the greasy shelf, the whole mess looking like a miniature of the Blob that ate Milwaukee. Back to refrigerator rolls.

At Norfolk, home of the navy as well as many tugs and shipyards, the supermarket stays open twenty-four hours a day. Ah! That air-conditioned market! It made what was usually a chore a happily anticipated two-hour respite from the heat. Although the food budget on many tugs is virtually unlimited, ours was strictly delineated in a union contract. For a crew of five, we were allotted three hundred and fifty dollars for two weeks of consumables which besides food included soap, paper towels, used at the rate of about one roll a day, cleaning products, mops, toilet paper, and sundries like aspirin and Band-aids. This translated into five dollars per man per day, not extravagant, but in 1976 adequate.

Each cook stocked not only for the two weeks aboard, but tried to help maintain a store of staples and condiments below in case the tug were out of grocery range for a long period. Since meals can either bolster or quash morale aboard a tug such as this, I made every effort to please with variety and imagination. At every opportunity, I read cookbooks, studying Fanny Farmer as though she were the key to warmth, comfort, and the American way. For the most part, any experiment was welcomed by the rest of the crew. Clarky, the only one who was distrustful of anything he could not recognize on sight, would taste in meditative silence, then would either eat or excuse himself to come back for the reliable virtues of a baloney sandwich a tactful time later. Gary, Chris, and David, on the other hand, dove into each new dish with the enthusiasm of a panel of professional taste testers. Their interest engendered in me a determination to live up to their expectations and, bit by bit, they helped to shape my repertoire.

David Gray, the mate, was another King's Point graduate who, as it happened, not only resembled my brother but who nearly shared a birthday with him. His culinary tastes were developed in his mother's loving care, and he appreciated anything that smacked of the carefully prepared dishes he had loved at home. Often, after everyone else had packed up and gone about their business for the next six hours, he would sit in the galley while I cleared up, pushing remnants of a meal around his plate with the last biscuit and offering praise or suggestions for the latest entrée. His mom had added a bit more oregano, or simmered a little more or less. While this sort of conversation had more than once landed Gary in a simmering kettle, David's suggestions merely appeared to be an exhibition

65

of interest, and were received with due consideration.

Kitchens, of whatever persuasion, are relaxing places, places in which to feel secure and surrounded by love. Feelings and convictions mingle easily with the steaming soup. Confidences mosey out into the conversation, meandering into the thread of talk, sidling up to a coffee cup, leaning casually over the bread pan. Gradually, the essences of a person flow out in small dribs and drabs.

I had come to realize that there are no typical tugboaters. They may be disgruntled insurance salesmen, retired navy, or uneducated men who have gone to sea as boys to feed themselves and their families. They may be farmers, car mechanics attracted by the possibility of higher pay, maritime academy graduates, romantic sailboaters, drifters, drunks, or men running from the law. There are Tarheels, Tennessee hillsmen, and lunatics. There are several who had hopes of something better in their lives and with hard work and sheer love of the water bought tugs in all states of disrepair in order to carve out a different life for themselves and their families.

That July was one of the hottest on record. The thermometer at the fuel dock near the navy yards read one hundred and five degrees. A broiling sun glinted off metal pipes and soaked into the oozing tar which coated the dock. I had turned the stove back, adjusting the carburetor until the top was a rusty brick color. There was no place to hide from the heat.

As we were on charter to S.C. Loveland, Company, we took our daily orders from their office. Unless we were running in the ocean, Gary and David had to call in at least twice a day, often several times, confirming orders which would then be changed, cancelled, shuffled, and reissued. From our end, it appeared the office was in constant flux.

Gary strode across the dock, having phoned in again while Clarky and I listened to the water gush down the tube on deck to the fresh water tank. Our next job was to go back down the Waterway and take a barge from another of Loveland's boats which was coming up from Florida. He came down into the shade on the port side where Clarky and I sat on the rail.

66

"They said something about Fall River," Gary said casually.

Fall River! Massachusetts! Ocean breezes, no mosquitoes.

"What are our chances?" I asked, my spirits rising despite the logic that told me not to anticipate a miracle.

"Who knows?" Gary smiled ruefully, his blond curls stuck to his forehead in wet ringlets. "We leave this afternoon to meet *Evelyn Doris* and that's all I know for sort of sure."

Once again we headed down the Inland Waterway, the hazy mugginess producing a Dismal Swamp atmosphere. The waterways teemed with bugs of all kinds. In the Pungo River Canal, we saw a small deer, grazing on the green-carpeted floor of the woods. We met the other tug in the wee hours and turned around so that by the time I rose, we were trying to drag ourselves over the shoal waters of Currituck Sound, sanding off bottom paint. The fuzzy bills had arrived during the night, coating everything. Instead of responding to shooing away, like mosquitoes or even gnats, they stuck. Table, plates, and counter all needed scraping before I could serve breakfast. The rising sun lit the steamy marshes with an eery haze.

After docking the barge we refueled and watered, ballasting in hopes of a coastal trip. While we refilled, Gary went to the telephone, taking his time to make his phone calls in the air-conditioned office. Clarky and I saw him as he walked back across the dock, a peculiar smile playing at the corners of his mouth. He jumped down on deck, able to contain himself no longer.

"We're going to Fall River!"

"Hot damn!" Clarky crowed.

"We've got to take a bunch of turbine engine components. I'm going up to listen to the weather."

I followed him up the ladder, both relieved at the reprieve from the sweltering heat of the harbor and bay, and dreading cooking meals while seasick. I prayed for calm weather. Later that evening, we were headed out Thimble Shoal with the barge strung out on the hawser. At night, the Chesapeake Bay Bridge-Tunnel is a magnificent string of pearls looped across the seventeen miles of water at the mouth of the Chesapeake

Bay, with only two small black gaps through which the shipping passes. Thimble Shoal Channel is a narrow slice through rock and concrete riprap, passing near the feeding grounds of the hammerhead sharks that throng the shallows. There was a breath of southerly breeze as we rounded Cape Charles and rolled north, dragging the bulky turbine components lashed to the deck of the flat barge.

Many commercial seamen pick up some knowledge of ornithology and sea lore, if not by design, then by accident as they watch the terns cut through the air then plunge kamikaze fashion into the water after their prey, or notice how the little warblers light and stay on the tugs in grim weather. Large gannets float placidly on the waves, reminiscent of the Ancient Mariner's albatross. The evenings are often a pause between the long day and a longer night, a time for a contemplative mug of coffee enjoyed in the wheelhouse as the gulls swoop and cry.

The breeze, though still warm, felt fresher, wafting in the unadulterated scents of salt spray and seaweed. A gentle swell rocked the tug, lulling us as we slid past the flatland of the lower Eastern Shore. Until we reached the tall buildings of Ocean City, the shore was undistinguished, our forward motion marked only by the buoys which bobbed past, one by one. Away from the cloying heat and mosquitoes of the Inland Waterway, the days rolled by in an even progression from dawn to dusk, followed by indigo nights laid out under a bright canopy of stars.

There was just enough spray coming over the rail to prohibit painting on deck, so my days consisted primarily of cooking meals interspersed with odd jobs like clearing out the dank compartments in the forepeak. In between chores, I could legitimately spend time with Gary in the wheelhouse.

On the second day out, annoyed at my lack of enterprise, Gary sent me below to grease the turning buttons and pushing cables. The buttons are a fixed sheave, turned sideways and welded into slots cut in the rail on either side of the tug slightly aft amidships. They are the corner on which the pushing cables bend. The cables feed from the winches fixed to the foredeck, then snake down to the buttons, turn and lead through the slots to hang outside the rails, draped along the tire fenders to the

68

stemhead. I searched out the grease, a gelatinous bronze glop kept in a five-gallon bucket which was wedged behind the engine room ladder between the fuel pump and the buckets of spare parts. I dragged the bucket up the steps, gritting my teeth each time it bashed my legs. After reaching the landing, I hoisted the bucket over the twenty-four-inch sill to the deck. With a stick and gloved hands, I smeared generous quantities of the grease into the deeply grooved metal of the turning button, then slathered handfuls into the cable. Once finished, I kicked the bucket back into its hiding place, cleaned myself, and crouched down on the foredeck, in the shade, out of Gary's sight to savor my last half-hour before starting lunch. The only sounds were the distant humming of the engine, echoed by the throbbing deck, and a soft whoosh as we plowed through the glittering waves.

We shot straight up the coast toward the outcropping of Montauk Island. Gradually, the wind clocked around to the north and the motion changed to a pound and a heavy splash, sending the ketchup sailing off the table to smash in a bloody pool in the corner. I tried to look at cooking in an enclosed, diesel smoke-filled galley as a challenge, but more often saw it as an exercise in masochism. Determined that I would not fail at this job, and clinging to a vague notion of upholding the good name of American womanhood, I dragged myself around the galley, willing the meal together. Lasagna seemed a reasonable compromise between nothing and a five-course dinner. Even so, the preparation was interrupted now and again for a salutary gulp of fresh air. The starboard door was the only ventilation. The rest of the galley was shut tight against the spray, airless and hot. I straddled the open companionway, drinking in fresh air, and making forays into the galley's interior to check on the progress of the contents of the oven.

Clarky, who appeared to take perverse pleasure in the disruptions in my gastrointestinal tract, stepped into the galley and poured himself a cup of coffee before sitting down to light a cigarette.

"Mite rolly," he observed.

I nodded and stretched a smile over gritted teeth.

"You ready for supper, Clarky?"

"Yeah, I guess. What is it?" he asked, eyes sparkling with mischief.

"Lasagna, salad, bread, tea," I told him from my perch in the companionway.

"Umm, lasagna. Nice and juicy, I hope."

"Yeah, good and gooey. You'll be able to slop it all over your plate and down your chin," I said, trying to keep from being sick.

"Nothin' goes down my chin like mushrat gravy," he said pensively, glancing at the reaction this piece of news would have on the color of my face.

"I can imagine."

"Yeah, mushrat gravy is the best, I think, nice and greasy with plenty of buttery biscuits to soak up the fat," he continued maliciously.

"No doubt."

"But possum stew runs a close second," he continued, still intent on his fishing expedition.

"I'm sure. Look, do you want dinner?"

"Sure, yeah, serve it up!" he cried heartily.

Wrapping himself around his plate, he spooned in lasagna and salad, pushing slippery pieces of pasta and sauce around his plate with a relish that was positively disgusting. Chris and David were not much better. Fortified by youthful appetites, sharpened by a day in the fresh air, they ate with gusto. David, while not unsympathetic, gulped down seconds before rising to drop his plate in the sink. Clarky finished his meal and put his dishes on top of David's, then came to pour himself a cup of coffee. Patting my shoulder, he looked down at me.

"Stomach giving you trouble?"

"Some."

Finally, they were all finished—finished slurping up the meal, finished making dirty dishes, finished talking. After they left, I sat in the companionway, mustering the strength to scrape crusted cheese off the lasagna pan. In a debate with my conscience over whether to wash the pan or simply cast it over the side, virtue won, and I set to with the Brillo, bracing my hips against the sink. After what seemed hours, I jammed the

70

last pot into the cupboards and escaped to the clear air of the wheelhouse.

"You know, I'm starting to feel hungry," I murmured, watching the lights along the bluffs of Block Island.

"Hold her and I'll get you a sandwich," Gary told me.

He showed me the chart, told me the compass course, and disappeared, leaving me alone with the night air and the ghosts of all the seamen who had plied these waters over the centuries, cargo creaking in wooden holds, sails snapping overhead. When Gary's face popped up above the window, I thought how lucky I was to be there with him on a night that breathed all the beauties of nature.

"Boy, it's rough down there, isn't it?" Gary said as he handed me a ham and cheese sandwich.

"I'm sure glad you think so. Clarky gave me a hell of a time."

Gary chuckled. "I can imagine."

In rough weather, I invariably slept below in the cook's cabin, while in calm seas Gary and I shared the bunk in the captain's cabin. Nights like this were a judgment call. Gary would stuff life jackets and rolled-up blankets under the bunk, rolling himself into the mattress like a hot dog in a roll, a strategy that was designed more for one than two.

"Where should I sleep tonight?" I asked finally.

"It should calm down after we turn the corner. Why don't you stay with me?" he said, cuddling up beside me where I sat in the chair, steering occasionally with my feet.

I grinned. It was hard to imagine the magic going out of a marriage that was so constantly off balance. Never knowing whether or not you will enjoy the privilege of sharing your mate's bed adds a certain spark.

At dawn we approached the slip, rounding the corner into Mt. Hope Bay just before sunup. The plan was to ground the tug lightly at absolute high tide, shoving the barge as far ashore as possible. From there, two bulldozers would haul it ashore by lines secured to each of the two forward bitts on the barge.

The basin was rimmed by a dock and a cement bulkhead that formed an L on the east and south sides. On our far right, the bulkhead connected to a concrete ramp where the men and

71

equipment waited in the twilight before dawn. Gary stopped at the dock, and we cast a line in order to wait out the tide. Sipping a mug of coffee, Gary sat on the quarter bitts and peered over the side at the current eddying around the pilings. Joe Weber, the barge-chaser I had met on my first trip, sprinted along the bulkhead and finally jumped down onto the deck beside him.

"Hey, Gary, Nance. How're ya doing?" he grinned.

I handed Joe a cup of coffee.

"Gary, I've been talking to the guys at the plant and they say there's a pile of rocks partway in, right about in the middle."

Gary opened his eyes wider. Grounding the barge and tug was going to be a tricky enough maneuver without the added threat of an obstacle whose location was nebulous and which was capable of damaging the vessel in such a way that we would not discover it until halfway down the coast.

"They say you have to shove it right along the face of the dock until you get it past the rocks, then turn in the corner," Joe said.

"Sounds like fun," Gary observed. "I wanted to wait until the current stopped completely before trying this. I don't need anything shoving me around any more than necessary."

"Yeah," Joe agreed.

Gary and Joe went to study the chart together, meanwhile glancing out of the wheelhouse window at the slackening current. Clarky sat in the galley, hunched over a mug of coffee and puffing on a cigarette when Gary called out of the window.

"Okay, Nance. Tell Clarky to crank her up."

Silently, Clarky rose and went down the deck to the engine room. In a few moments, the tug shook and rumbled as the engine revved up.

"Cast her off, Nance."

I fumbled with the line, bringing it back aboard and coiling it on deck while Gary put the tug in gear. Behind me, Clarky leaned on the vent cover, taking the last few drags on his cigarette before pitching it overboard and climbing up onto the barge. I followed, trotting after him like a puppy.

The air was dewy as the dawn broke over the eastern horizon, lighting the huge storage tanks on shore with a gentle

72

aura. Joe stayed in the wheelhouse with Gary to help guessti-
mate the location of the rock pile. Out on the barge, the sound
of the engine dimmed to a distant churning allowing us to speak
in conversational tones.

As we eased forward along the dock and then overlapped
the cement bulkheading, I could hear the water rushing along
the hull like the sound of a breeze through wild grasses. Clarky
stood on the port bow, holding up fingers to indicate the
distance the barge held from the bulkhead as we edged toward
the flat turn. When Clarky held up ten fingers twice in quick
succession, Gary began his turn, a close backing and filling to
ratchet the barge around the corner between the bulkhead and
the phantom rock pile. Each time Gary changed gears, we
could hear the loud hiss of the pneumatic controls. Standing
just behind the two port bitts which were welded one in front of
the other like lead soldiers, Clarky kept Gary apprised of the
distance between the corner of the barge and the bulkhead.
Two fingers, three, two, one. Metal scraped concrete with a
shriek, chipping away little chunks from the bulkhead. One
finger, two. As the light came we could make out figures
onshore, John, the other barge-chaser, and the men who stood
by the bulldozers, where they crowned the ramp that led to the
water. One finger, another screech. One finger, back and
forward again. Two, three, four. We were around the turn and
heading slowly for shore as Gary brought the barge parallel
with the bulkhead, lining up with the bulky machinery on the
ramp.

"Nance, come get the monkey's fist," Gary called out the
window.

As I trotted over the deck, I could feel the tug ground.
John was cautiously edging his way down the slime-covered
ramp when I returned carrying the long yellow polypropylene
line that had a heavy ball woven into one end. Knowing
Clarky's pride would not allow him to stand idle while I threw
the heaving line, I gave it to him. He dropped the bitter end
onto the deck and put his foot on it before holding the rest of the
coils loosely in his hand and swinging the ball over his head.
When the line sang, he let it fly to land in the water two feet shy
of John's grasp. Clarky reeled it in, coiling it again, this time

73

standing on the edge of the bow while making his toss. It fell short. John came farther down the ramp, wading partway into the water, skidding on the slippery moss. On the third toss, John clawed after the ball, snatching the line as it slithered back down the ramp.

I had dragged one of the bow lines over to Clarky to let him tie the end of the heaving line into its loop to send it ashore. By the time we had the second line attached to the bitts, strung across the water, and latched to one of the two bulldozers, Joe had come out of the wheelhouse and begun to check the guy wires which had held the component parts in place.

"Thanks, guys," Joe said as he passed us, shaking our hands briefly.

"See you later."

"I'm sure."

Clarky and I went back to the tug to break her out of pushing gear. Gary hung out of the window waiting, studying the spectacle of the men onshore. While Clarky stood by the starboard cable which was looped over the bitt, I climbed over the tug's thick bow fender to loose the cables. The dog which held the starboard winch was stuck, locked in place by the pressure of the drum, so that I had to stand in the spokes of the winch wheel in order to let it go. Careful to jump back and pull my foot out of the spoke simultaneously, I let the wheel spin, whirling around until it had spun off several feet of slack. Then, bending down, I pulled out enough extra wire to allow Clarky to work the loop up off the stern bitt and sidestep to drop it onto the bow fender while I yanked the excess out of the water alongside the tug. In short order we were free, finished with our job and headed out of Fall River in gloriously bright, clear weather. The sun climbed into a cloudless sky and sparkled off the rooftops of the houses perched along a jagged shore. A breeze, the remembrance of spring days, whistled through the open ports and companionways, blowing out the dank smells of mildew and diesel smoke and leaving behind a hint of salty, mussel-strewn beaches.

Gary was in the wheelhouse, nose in the air like a retriever, searching for lobster boats. Spotting a small wooden fishing vessel picking up a run of pots along the southern side of the river he throttled back and eased over to him. David and Chris were up, and we all stood on deck rummaging through wallets and pockets to pool our money for a lobster feast. By the time Gary had closed the distance between us and the little scoop-prowed dory, I held a fistful of bills. The man, seeing us approach, had continued to pull his traps, and as we watched, yanked a wire cage into his boat, emptied its contents, and baited it again.

"I don't know, Nance. They don't look like lobsters to me," Chris said, squinting.

"I know. What the devil's he putting in them?"

"Got me."

"Whatcha got there, Cap?" Chris called over the fifteen feet of water between us.

"Whelk."

He held up one of the pots, showing us the conchs intermingled with the cracked horseshoe crabs he was using for bait.

"What do you suppose they use whelk for?" I asked Chris under my breath.

"Why don't you ask him?"

The fisherman had stopped pulling his run and brought his boat over to our side, bobbing in the gentle waves. We all leaned over the rail to peer into the bottom of the boat, staring at the piles of mollusks around his feet.

Scooping up a five-gallon bucket full of them, he handed it over the side.

"What do you do with them?" Gary called from the wheelhouse landing.

The fisherman looked up at him and grinned.

"I sell 'em to a company in Fall Rivah makes chowdah out of 'em."

David had retrieved the battered galvanized bucket from the head and emptied the conchs into it, then handed the fisherman's bucket back over the gunwales.

"In the Caribbean they make cracked conch and conch fritters," Chris said, smacking his lips as he eyed the buckets.

"It's some ol' good."

"Thanks a lot. How much do you want for them?" I asked, leafing through the dollar bills I held.

He shook his head and dismissed my question with a wave of his hand.

"Just try 'em and see how you like 'em" he said.

"No, please, let me pay you for them," I persisted.

He shook his head again and pushed the wooden stick he used for a throttle forward, easing away from us, a smile still playing around his weathered eyes.

"Many thanks!"

Once the transaction had been completed, Chris had gone into the galley for a pot and began sorting through the bucket of spiral shells. With authority, he carted the load to the afterdeck and set to working the unsuspecting whelks out of their homes, his eyes glittering in anticipation. I followed him.

"Down there they work a long, thin-bladed knife into the tail of the shell, right here," he said, producing one of the galley knives and applying it to the small hole in the pointed end of the shell. "Then you work it until you sever the muscle."

He screwed up his face and dug with the knife. Whelk juice ran down his arm and dripped off his elbow.

"They do it without any trouble at all. It always looked like to me anyway." he said, trapping the shell under his left hand and continuing to grind with the knife. "Just drops right out."

Dubiously, I watched him. After five minutes of work, he had managed to produce the creamy lump of muscle and lay it on the chipped blue paint of the plywood boards.

"Now you need to pound them," he told me.

I looked into the bucket at the pile he had yet to detach from their shells and decided to try to steam a few out. With a small bowlful of half-cooked shell-less whelks and a washed ballpeen hammer filched from the engine room, I returned to the afterdeck to pound the muscles to tenderness like a cutlet. Well, almost like a cutlet.

Beginning with two sheets of waxed paper from which the conchs slid like wet soap, I resorted to applying hammer to muscle first on the washed cutting board, and then anywhere the thing happened to dodge. It was like pounding a lacrosse ball to tenderness. Finally, with a bucket of whelk juice and partially flattened whelk, I went back to the galley, followed by admonitions from Chris as to how they should be cooked.

"I thought I'd try conch *chowdah*," I said just before he stepped into his cabin.

"Well, you *could* do that," he said with obvious disappointment.

As a compromise, I laid out a whelk smorgasbord—cracked conch, raw conch marinated in lime juice and herbs, conch fritters with jalapeño peppers dipped in batter and deep fried, conch chowder, both New England and Manhattan style. The reception was enthusiastic, the men reaching for the various bowls on the table and passing the relishes back and forth, chatting as though we were all on holiday, the weather perfect, the company good. It was good to be alive. It seemed a long way from the sweltering docks of Norfolk.

We ran down the coast light tug, that is, without a tow, heading back for Philadelphia and a LASH tow. Since we rarely traveled light, the company being naturally anxious to make both ways of a trip profitable, we took the opportunity to run through the little Cape May Canal, cutting off the longer journey around Overfalls Shoal at the bottom of the Delaware Bay. Gary still had hopes of a lobster dinner before we entered irrevocably the Land of Pleasant Living.

We turned at the sea buoy off the harbor just before dawn and nosed into the tiny harbor through a luminescent mist that rose off the waters, surrounding scores of small fishing boats at anchor. No one stirred. Disappointed, we tooled through the narrow canal which is like a tunnel cut between overhanging, grass-fringed shores that broaden and flatten gradually as they move west.

The suffocating heat of the week before had receded, leaving behind the clear brilliance of a July morning. As I kneaded bread and thawed steaks for Sunday dinner, I watched the blue-green marshland of the Delaware scoot by the companionways, interrupted now and then by the passage of a buoy or a ship bound for sea. As we chugged upriver, however, the fresh sea scents gave way to the heavier smell of damp earth and then to diesel smoke and industry. By the time we were tied to a crumbling pier where the LASH barges were tethered like so many ducks, the acrid odor of melting tar was palpable.

Putting together a LASH tow in July has all the charm of being popped into a convection oven for hours on end. The water reflects a blistering sun, doubling its intensity.

The barges, thirty by sixty feet long by ten feet deep, are grey steel boxes into which goes cargo as varied as mink coats, army jeeps, and television sets. We once approached a group of LASH barges which were still in the process of being loaded, and discovered a pair of beautifully painted bright green and yellow railroad cars bound for Iran. Once loaded (and sometimes sealed to prevent pilfering by enterprising longshoremen and tug crews alike), LASH barges are shuttled up and down the waterways either strung out on the hawser looking like a parade of circus elephants, one holding the next by the tail, or made up in a semirigid block for pushing.

Making up a LASH tow is sheer drudgery which harks back to the chain gangs of the Old South, sledge hammers, sweat, chains, and all. Although we rarely left a dock in anything other than pushing gear, it was necessary to prepare to tow them as well in case the weather kicked up. That meant that the initial step in the process was unloading enough LASH straps, each weighing about eighty-five pounds, to link the barges together. As a rule, *Progress* kept about twenty of the straps on the upper deck in a jumble of hawser ropes, wire eyes, and galvanized thimbles the size of the Gutenberg Bible. Flinging them one by one over the upper rail, across the five-foot space between rail and barge to land with a resounding *bang!* on the hatch of the barge required coordination as well as strength. Generally, two of the men held the strap between them, swung it, one, two, and then let it fly on three. I was the dragger, being more suited to hauling around my ball and chain than lofting it. Once there were sufficient straps unloaded, enough to hook two between each pair of barges, then the barges were lined up and we all swarmed over the hatches to begin making them up into a movable tow.

As we wandered around in the baking sun, dragging straps, iron pipes, and sledge hammers, I wondered whose brainchild these models of efficiency were. I could see their creator in his air-conditioned office, dapper and clean-shaven, making unerased drawings of the barges, the winches intact instead of frozen with rust, three-quarter-inch cables wrapped neatly around the drums instead of sprung, kinked, and snapped in pieces on deck, and bitts welded firmly to the deck instead of now and again raised off their moorings as evidence of a narrow escape from a broken tow.

In theory, putting together the barges has all the simplicity of a child's game. First, the straps are hooked over a pair of bitts, one on the end of each barge. Second, the cables are wrapped around and around these same sister bitts, bringing the two barges smack against one another, like winding a string around two pencils, until they lie as close to each other as possible. Then the tow is cast off.

In practice, the equipment is often recalcitrant, the weather a fight, and the job is back-breaking drudgery. Sledge hammers are used to beat obstinate winches and handles into submission, as well as to pound slack into the cat's cradle lacing

Coming into Hampton Roads at dawn. Photograph by author.

of wires that secure the barges one to the next in order to tighten the wires on the winches. Iron pipes are slid overtop the stubby winch handles in order to add leverage in the tightening process. Patience as well as brute strength are required when one after another of the winches is without cable, when the gears are broken, when a bitt is pulled out of the deck altogether. It is a knuckle-scraping, frustrating job that takes an average of an hour per barge to complete.

By the time we had finished putting the tow together, my head throbbed with the heat, and I began to feel the beginnings of heat prostration. The others, red-faced and sweating, sat along the rail in the shade munching on supper without enthusiasm. We looked like piles of dirty laundry. Once supper was finished, we made the tug up in pushing gear. After tightening the pushing cables, Gary backed the tow out of the slip, and settled down for the tedious days of creeping to Norfolk. By the time I sat in the wheelhouse chair with a glass of iced tea, grateful for the breath of air coming in the windows, every muscle throbbed. Fall River seemed a long way away.

F I V E

In NOVEMBER of that year, I returned to fill in for the absent cook. Five of us—Gary, Clarky, David, Chris Schlegel, and I—drove up the New Jersey Turnpike and across the Brooklyn Bridge to pick our way amidst the fenced-in warehouse lots and derelict buildings along the East River. Finally, we arrived at the scrap metal yard affectionately known as the Pit which encompasses approximately two patchwork acres of mud and gravel and lays claim to one bulkheaded finger of cement that juts into the river. An old brownstone warehouse sits adjacent to the sugar refinery next door, soaking in the pungent odors of sour mash and half-rotted cabbage leaves that are the residue of the refining process.

The scrap yard was covered with little mountains of fenders and torch-cut sheets of old deckhouse or railing that spilled down from the tops of the piles into the maze of muddy roads. Twelve-ton trucks wended their ways through the labyrinth, ferrying between one crane that dumped load after load of scrap onto the truck beds, and another that unloaded the cargo into Loveland's barges at the dock. A week-long downpour had made the last hundred yards of road impassable for the company truck. Forced to stop, we pulled on sea boots, then lifted our luggage onto our heads to slog through the knee-deep mud to the tug.

Joe Weber stood on the outboard side of one of the two hopper barges moored at the bulkhead, conducting the loading with understated hand signals. As we trooped between truck and crane, Joe waved, then returned to watch the crane operator drop the bucket jaws into another bite of debris. The other crew sat in the galley gulping coffee in contemplative silence, waiting.

A colorless, drizzling day served as a foil for an already disheartening place. Everywhere were mud and noise. The crane screeched back and forth, picking up lumps of scrap from the conveyor belt of the trucks, slinging them over the water to drop them into the barge with a hollow *thud!* Trucks ground their gears and roared through the morass, splattering mud over everything. The galley floor was coated, with little trace of the white and black tile underneath. The sides of the crane, the trucks, and our boots were all the same murky brown. The other crew looked as bleak as the day, speaking in monosyllables, all anxious to escape to hearth and home.

We relieved them, exchanging the minimum information, then helped them with their gear. It was hardly the changing of the guard at Buckingham Palace. Curl had left a paperwrapped parcel of porkchops on the counter to thaw. It was, I discovered, the dregs of the freezer. After stowing my gear and changing into coveralls and workboots, I climbed back into the galley and, in an attempt to lift our sagging spirits, began leafing through Fannie Farmer. The rest of the crew felt the leadenness as keenly as I and busied themselves with unpacking and reacquainting themselves with their other home. After sautéeing the chops in a little butter and splashing in some sherry and herbs, I took a mug of hot coffee to Joe, inviting him to lunch as I handed the cup over the corner of the hatch coaming. With his usual smile and thanks, he accepted both. By the time I swung onto the foredeck, Gary was coming down the ladder.

"How many days' worth of food is there?" he asked.

"I don't know. Maybe three. Curl said there wasn't much. When he says that you know we're running low."

"Jerry gave me two hundred dollars for groceries. Maybe Joe'll lend you his car after lunch."

"Great. I wonder where to go?"

I thought of the empty buildings and warehouses we had passed trying to find this scrap heap.

"Maybe Joe knows some place."

By the time the car was crammed with packages which filled its interior with the pungent odors of salami, cheese, fruits, and vegetables, I had forgotten the grim weather and cruised back to the tug with my spirits lifted. When I returned, the guys descended on the bags and, while helping to carry them, poked inquisitive noses into their enticing contents.

The barges were to carry two separate loads, one a heap of miscellaneous scrap, the other a load of one-ton cubes of pressed metal which looked like a child's building blocks. Although we had expected to leave the day after crew change, the crane pulled a sprocket, and sat waiting for a part for two days. Jerry grabbed this opportunity to race up the highway with a main engine blower loaded in the back of the pick-up in hopes of getting the blower manhandled into place before the crane was fixed.

The blower, which looked like a giant vitamin capsule, barely fit through the engine room door, and it took all six of us and a series of handy-billies and come-alongs to work it into place, suspended over the engine before being lowered and bolted into place. Once we had fought it in the companionway, I was dismissed, but the men worked with little break for the rest of the day to remove the old blower and attach the new one. While they wrenched and swore, I sat in the galley, cooking and trying to make myself useful. Cleaning was a waste of time in that migrating filth. Hoping to produce a bright spot for them in an otherwise dreary day, I roasted a leg of lamb, complete with mashed potatoes and gravy, and a smorgasbord of vegetables and salad, ending the meal with a lush bowl of English trifle which quivered with its mounds of whipped cream every time I opened the refrigerator.

Out of orneriness, the stove revolted and refused to raise its temperature above a lukewarm approximation of cooking temperature. The lamb oozed its juices into the pan, and the potatoes sat in bathwater. The men were unconcerned, however, as suppertime came and went without an appearance from anyone. By nine-thirty, the meal had reached a reasonable stage of readiness and Chris, Gary, and David scraped their hands clean and trooped into the booth. Clarky and Jerry remained below, fiddling. Too tired to care about a meal, they all pushed down several mouthfuls of food, then retired, leaving me with a mountain of greasy dishes and a fervent wish to be home.

The next morning, Joe arrived with an agent from the company in South Carolina which had ordered the scrap metal. The agent had been sent to inspect the load and the entire operation which had by now been delayed by two days. The dapper little southerner in beige was an incongruous sight amidst all the mud and grease. Looking more like an opera star in his camel's hair coat and white scarf than an employee of a steel company, he had managed somehow to get through the mire without a spot as though he had been dropped by parachute on the wrong target. Joe had brought him to the tug, promising a hot drink and a meal.

They stepped into the galley which I had scrubbed with qualified success, Joe leading the way. Glancing around the interior with obvious disdain, the agent furtively sought a clean place to sit. Finally, spotting a newspaper, he inspected it, then laid it on the seat and eased himself down, carefully tucking his coattails under him so as not to come in contact with the stained vinyl. He stared at me, dressed in olive drab coveralls and men's work boots with the paint-splotched bandanna around my head, and his face furrowed.

"Would you like something to eat?" I asked. "A couple of eggs or a sandwich?"

His gaze touched my hands which were seamed with dirt that defied scrubbing.

"No, thank you," he replied.

"How about a cuppa?" Joe grinned, enjoying the sight of the agent trying to avoid the grime, like a cat who attempts to lift all four paws simultaneously.

"Sure."

I poured out a mug and handed it to Joe, then turned to the agent.

"One for you?"

"Do y'all have tea?"

"Yes."

He sipped his tea while Joe and I talked, then put his cup

84

in the center of the paper towel I had given him for a napkin, and touched the corners of his mouth with his handkerchief.

"I guess we'd better go," Joe said, as he dropped his empty mug in the sink.

As they stepped out of the companionway, I couldn't help hoping that the fellow would be marked with at least a little mud, proof of his actually having been there. Finally, the barges reached their Plimsoll lines, the markings on the sides of the hulls that determine a safe load, and we were off, headed south. The trip down the coast was a rolling one, awkward, as the condiments bowl slid around the galley table during meals, but not uncomfortable. *Progress* swaggered along cavalierly, taking spray over her deck as we passed the mouth of the Delaware the following day and continued down the Eastern Shore beaches to round Cape Charles. Once we plowed through the Chesapeake Bay Bridge-Tunnel, the rolling diminished, and we dragged the two barges, strung out on the main hawser with an intermediate hawser between them, into Norfolk. Instead of making the entire trip to South Carolina with the two barges, we handed them off to another tug then ran down the Ditch to Morehead City, North Carolina.

I looked forward to churning down the swampy canals in cool weather. The mosquitoes would not have been able to withstand the November frosts and the ride would be bugfree. The dense growth that hovers at the edge of the narrow channels between the sounds would have thinned with autumn, providing an occasional glance at the interior of the thickly grown woods. Generally, Gary put off ballasting with fuel and water if he knew we had a trip down the Inland Waterway and since we were lightened by the run down the coast, the shallow, silted channels gave us little problem.

Although many barges are identifiable only by what sounds like an all-points bulletin, for example, "three hundred feet long, forty wide, crunched coaming, used to be red," others are numbered, displaying their markings prominantly. Fortunately, the one we were to fetch had numbers as more than one tug has waltzed off from a dock with the wrong barge, only to have to sheepishly return it.

Guessing accurately that I had an abiding fear of snakes,

Clarky had spent a good deal of time on the way from Norfolk regaling me with stories of how the poisonous snakes dropped on hapless deckhands to slither down their clothes, biting all the way to get out. Cool weather was the worst, he told me gleefully, " 'cause they go sorta limp and cranky." By the time we found the barge, shoved into the marshy bank just north of Morehead City, he had me thoroughly spooked. Gary eased *Progess* up to the barge, and Clarky and I made up in pushing gear, tightening down cables together while I shot nervous glances at the trees.

"You go ahead," he told me when we had finished. "I'll be right out. I want to check something first."

I stalked out onto the barge, turning up my collar against possible intruders, and wondered how fast I could peel off my clothes if a snake dropped down my shirt. Suddenly, I felt something clammy slap at my neck.

"Look out! There's one now!" Clarky cried.

"Aaagggh!"

I whipped around, arm in the air to fend off the monster, nearly punching Clarky in the nose as he jumped backward with his length of hose. On the tug, Chris and Gary cackled delightedly. Annoyed I had not inadvertently connected with Clarky's jaw, I tried to salvage what little composure I had left and squared my shoulders.

"Okay, you got me. Congratulations."

Clarky chuckled, eyes twinkling at the success of his joke, and patted my arm solicitously.

"Did it scare ya, Nance?"

I glowered as we walked out on the barge together and listened to the sniggers behind me. The bow of the barge was tied with a ratty mooring line full of loose ends with loops pulled out of the laid strands. It had been cleated, flung around the trunk of a dead tree on the embankment and wrapped overtop the first set of figure eights. Clarky deftly unwound the top wraps then threw the line ashore and began to haul it around the tree from where he stood on the barge. He had pulled in about six feet before it hung up on a broken branch. Together we yanked with no result. The line was jammed onto the limb in the manner of a Chinese finger link. The more we pulled, the

86

tighter it stuck. Chris had sauntered out on the barge and the three of us studied the situation.

"Damn!" Clarky muttered as he took off his cap and scratched his head.

I smiled quietly, seeing my revenge around the corner.

"Looks like someone will have to climb on down there to get it off," Chris observed.

Clarky shot him a glance but said nothing. My delicacy having been so recently established, I was able to stand back and wait, hands in pockets.

"Looks kind of snakey," I murmured.

If Clarky heard, he gave no sign. Backed into a corner of machismo, he sent Chris and me for the ladder and prepared to descend into the marsh. We tied the ladder to the barge to keep its rails from sinking into the spongy peat and held it steady while Clarky lowered himself to the knoll. Cautiously, he thrashed through the brush, pushing suspect bushes aside until he could reach the tangled line. Despite his furious wrenchings, it refused to budge. Swearing, he tugged at the branch in an effort to break it.

"See any snakes?" Chris wanted to know.

Clarky glared at him momentarily then returned to his battle. I stood on deck, bathed in satisfaction.

"She's not comin'," he said finally, panting.

"Gary," Chris shouted over his shoulder, "We can't get her loose. You'll have to back her off."

Gary waved in acknowledgment and waited until Clarky had appeared on deck and we had dragged the ladder back onto the barge before putting the tug in reverse. The line pulled freely for a couple of feet, then stuck again and we could hear Gary push down the throttle. Suddenly, a *pop! crack!* and we scattered as the tree crashed onto the deck, splintering. The line was intact. Having had enough diversion, Chris returned to his cabin while Clarky and I cleared up.

My first real taste of winter tugboating came in February when the cook on Gary's crew wanted the first five days of a two-week stint off. The weather had been uniformly cold, laying sheets of ice over the rivers and bays which had been crushed, scattered, and refrozen a hundred times with the passage of water traffic. The cold penetrated everything, shackles, pushing cables, the bulkheading inside the cabins. Everything felt frigid. The wind whistled in the cracks of the warped doors, slicing through Swiss cheese blankets to chill the marrow.

Going to the head in the middle of the night, leaving the relative warmth of a bunk to tramp down and back in the frost was like having a tooth drilled without Novocain. Taking a shower sometimes required days of consideration. Although the rest of the compartments had been fitted with watertight doors, the head had retained its old warped door, gaps and all. Going from being wrapped in layers of clothing to blue-skinned, goose-bumped nakedness sometimes took sheer determination. If a bitter cold blast of wind did not come through the broad slot in the door, then the elements would have their revenge in the shower stall. Since water was almost always at a premium, navy showers were the rule. Water on. Needles of exquisite pain until the temperature can be adjusted. Sluice down. Water off. Lather. Avoid the ice-encased outer bulkhead. Yeeouch! Water on! Wow! Is that cold! Water off. Done. Rub down and dress. Oh Lord, not again for a while!

Decking in the cold means bundling to ward off frostbite. Gloves are pulled over chapped hands, hats, sweaters, coats, never scarves (never anything to get caught in machinery or on projections on the equipment), boots, sometimes foul weather gear—all act as insulators, but as impediments as well; getting around on narrow decks in thick layers of clothing is awkward and dangerous. Hypothermia is a constant worry in weather that increases the chances of going overboard. Chipping deck lines out of a prison of frozen spray, wrestling them into place, pulling hawser with watersoaked gloves, all are part of a job so closely tied to the elements.

Once, while jumping in between the top deck of the tug and a LASH barge, I landed on a patch of slippery deck and crumpled against a hatch, grabbing at the small piece of pipe that sticks up on the side. After checking to be sure that I was essentially all right, Gary remarked, "It doesn't matter if you end up in a heap, just be sure you end up on the barge." It was advice I remembered.

While the snow can bring land traffic to its knees, an accumulation after a blizzard has virtually no effect on the movement of water traffic. It is the bitter cold, clear days, strung out in an unbroken chain of bright jewels that slowly clog the waterways with thickening ice. I had gotten aboard with the rest of the crew at Wilmington Marine Terminal, armed only with my standard cold weather gear and enough underwear for five days. Our first job, a trip to Artificial Island in Delaware Bay, gave us a taste of things to come as the thermometer hovered around the teens.

The currents and the turbulence of the water traffic had stirred the masses of slab ice, and they had grown into jagged, rangy icebergs, slamming into hulls with deafening *thunks!* Running through the clogged river required constant attention in the wheelhouse, and Gary and David spent their watches creeping through the obstacle course, trying to avoid collision with the larger chunks. We picked our way down to Artificial Island bound for a slip on the west side of the Salem Nuclear Power Plant where one of Loveland's flat barges sat. The barge was corked into the slip with a mass of slab ice that had been washed into the mouth of the slip with the tides. She looked as though she were barricaded by a bed of crenelated glass. Gary sidled up to the slip, driving the wedge of the tug between the ice plug and the barge until he had nudged our bow against her stern. Clarky climbed over the stemhead with a bow line in hand and dropped it over the stern cleat of the barge, then held his hand out, waiting for the loop of the port pushing cable. As he sidestepped it over to the bitt, I worked my way quickly down the deck, taking the cable off the quarter bitts in order to let it run free up the side of the tug. The slack cable dangled in the water. Gary tried to work the tug to starboard to hook up the other cable.

The packed ice which had been crushed even closer together as we worked our way toward the barge now began to mount the sides of the tug, pushing white blades up between the tires and the naked metal hull. On the barge, Clarky hunched down further into his jacket and turned his back to the wind. Working the tug back and forth, Gary managed to get the starboard side close enough to wind the cable out and drop the

89

loop over the starboard bitt, but it left us hooked up at a skewed angle to the barge. The brittle layers of ice that covered the river rustled and crackled with life as they undulated in the swells.

Clarky climbed down onto the foredeck to tighten the cables with me. Then we crawled over the stemhead and skated toward the mooring lines which were looped from the tall pilings like the graceful cables of a suspension bridge. Clarky eyed the lines sullenly and rubbed his shoulder.

"Arthritis bothering you?" I asked.

"Some."

Times like this presented a dilemma for me. Knowing I was neither as strong nor yet as skilled as the men, I was nonetheless the deckhand and owed any help I could give to the job. But I was still a woman, dealing with the fragile egos of men in a man's world. The question usually came down to when and how to step in rather than whether to or not. If it was quietly offered, help was usually accepted. I waited through two abortive attempts, then stepped up behind Clarky and laid my hands directly behind his to shadow his movements. Once we had conquered the first line, the rest fell like defeated soldiers and finally we were coiling the lines in the center of the barge, away from the bow spray.

We cast off, and Gary backed the barge out of the slip, chewing up the ice with the propeller as he swung her around and headed for the clearer waters of the shipping channel. After Clarky and I squared up the tug to the stern of the barge, letting off slack on the port side and laboriously cranking it in on the starboard, we were finished and trudged down the deck to get some coffee and take a break in the wheelhouse.

As I sat in the chair sipping at a steaming mug and watching the sea of white before us, I gave thanks that my responsibility did not extend to fording this morass. The sound of ice hitting the hull was reminiscent of the crashing and thumping of railroad cars being coupled at the end of a line.

At times, tugboating is simply running errands twenty-four hours a day. We left the flat barge at a pier in Philadelphia, then ran light tug up to Northern Metals several miles away to wait for the tide in order to collect another barge and deliver it to Paulsboro in New Jersey. It had begun to snow on the way downriver and by the time we passed Chester on our way to tie up in Greenwood for the night, the visibility was reduced to a minimum. The radar, which was notoriously antipathetic to precipitation of any kind, particularly disliked snow and expressed its pique with a blurring of the outlines on the scope. The radio crackled with calls back and forth among pilots and captains, confirming locations, checking speed, in constant efforts to avoid collision with one another. Gary was familiar with the river by now and could devote his attention to the radio and the traffic without having to consult the chart. I sat in the wheelhouse after supper, silently listening to the voices on the radio.

"Is that you, *Intrepid*? I see a set of running lights just off my port bow headed south on Bulkhead Bar."

"Roger, *Intrepid* heading south on Bulkhead Bar. We're pushing the Ocean two-fifty and I'm hanging way over to the black side, Cap. So I shouldn't bother you. I got you on my radar."

"Good, *Intrepid*. Roger that."

"Security, security, security. This is the *Emma Maersk* clearing Reedy Point in ten minutes to head upriver checking for all interested traffic."

"Yeah, *Emma Maersk*, this is *Intrepid* coming down Bulkhead Bar. I've got a fair current and I'll be at Pea Patch in five minutes. Keep an eye out for me."

"Roger, *Intrepid*."

"*Diplomat* calling the *Maersk*. We're headed up to Delaware City pushing but I'll cut her back some more so we stay clear of you."

"Roger that, *Diplomat*. Thanks."

"This is *Sea Tiger* passing under Commodore Barry Bridge. I see a set of running lights ahead coming north. Is that you, *Brandywine*?"

"Tug *Big Mama* to *Sea Tiger*. I think it's me you see, Cap."

"*Brandywine* behind you, *Big Mama*. We'll hang over to the red side. You got us on radar?"

"No, you're in my shadow, I guess."

"I got you both on radar, *Brandywine*."

"Okay, *Sea Tiger*. We'll stay over to the red side for ya."

"Roger on that, *Brandywine*. Thanks."

"No problem."

"Gary," I ventured when a break came in the chatter, "how can you keep all that straight?"

He smiled. "None of them are going to hit us."

"But how do you know?"

"I know none of *them* are in range. If we get hit, it'll be someone else. We'll be turning into the river in ten minutes," he replied matter-of-factly.

It was no comfort to think that we could be hit by an unidentified rather than an identified vessel. I looked at Gary, leaning into the wheel, his eyes on the curtain of snow that obscured the usual river lights and softened the harsh metal edges on the tug. He was utterly self-possessed. His concentration was complete, but not intense. Admiring his ability, I also gave thanks I was having the chance to understand so completely his work and his love of it, the thrill he got from being in control of a potentially dangerous situation.

We turned into the Christina River, safely out of the main river traffic and coasted through the bridges to the half-sunken barge that was the office at Greenwood yard. As Gary snuggled *Progress* up to the western end of the crazily tilted barge, Clarky came out of the galley to throw lines at the mounds of white which covered the bollards. The blizzard was dropping inches by the hour on us, coating everything with a fuzzy-edged blanket. Once we were secured, Clarky trudged below to shut down the engine, leaving only the muted hum of the generators and the soft hiss of the falling snow.

By the following morning, the deck was buried beneath two feet of powdery snow. Half of the Atlantic Seaboard states had closed their highways to all but emergency traffic, and power lines were down the length of the coast. After breakfast, Gary slogged over the barge to the little office to call Loveland for orders. Stay put. Feeling like children let out of school for the day, we swept the decks and ladders, throwing snowballs occasionally and stepping into the galley for a mug of hot cocoa.

I had thawed a turkey and served up a country kitchen meal, stuffing, cranberry sauce, gravy, endeavoring to conjure up hearth and home with the fare if not the atmosphere. Only two thin sheets of pitted metal with the remnants of aging insulation in between sheltered us from the bitter cold. Because the blizzard had ground the wheels of commerce to a halt ashore I was now stuck aboard for the duration. With only a few days' worth of clothes, I began to burrow through Gary's reserves under the bunk and to hang damp underwear in the engine room among the long johns and jockey shorts. The following morning, we were on our way up the Delaware en route to another job.

Our orders were to break the tug *Shelley Keen* out of the ice of her home port, then deliver a barge to Artificial Island where ground crews were in the midst of a strike. Ostensibly, we needed the *Shelley*, a wooden tug whose lines brought to mind visions of another era, to help get the barge into a slip which was subject to crosscurrents. In fact, the owner of *Shelley*, Donald Keen, was a card-carrying member of the shore worker's union, and it was hoped that his presence would soften any hard feelings.

Clarky, who had been standing in the wheelhouse while Gary was explaining the job to me, muttered, "I don't want to be a scab."

"We're not scabs," Gary growled.

"I remember the old company sending us into Baltimore one time. They said that there was a job needed doin'. Didn't say anything about there bein' a strike still on. Said it was all settled. Well, it wasn't. They chased us out of there with guns," he grumbled.

"We're not scabs," Gary said again, firmly. "Their strike doesn't have anything to do with our putting a barge in there or not. It's just that sometimes things get out of hand."

"Yeah."

Clarky chewed on his stogie and glared out of the window.

The narrow mouth of Raccoon Creek looked impassable, the ice stretching in overlapping swirls far into the tree-lined inlet. The creek seemed to be the defiant last stand of nature, contrasted as it was with the industrial Pennsylvania shore opposite. The dawn came up in a magnificent blur of color, bleeding orange and pink into the silvery ice. We sat outside the blockaded creek for a few minutes while Gary sized up the situation and planned his attack. Picking up the radio, he called Donald Keen.

"*Shelley* back to the *Progress*. Hey, Gary! Where are ya?" came over the radio.

"We're right outside the creek, Don. It looks pretty thick. When did you go through here last?"

"I came in here night before last, Gary. There should be a path where we came through. I can see one from this end."

"Yeah."

Gary stuck his hand in his pants pocket and laid the microphone under his chin thoughtfully.

"Look, Don," he said finally. "We'll give it a try but I can't promise anything."

"Yeah, okay, Gary. I think if you can make it past the first stretch it'll be okay. The current runs through here pretty swift."

"Okay. Well, I'm going to go ahead and try to break in to you. Can you see me at all?"

"No, not yet. I'm sittin' in the wheelhouse, but she can't see over the trees."

"Yeah, I got ya."

"Gary, can you see where I came through?"

Gary had been eyeing the darker stream of ice which had been broken and then refrozen in an irregular path toward the *Shelley* but from where we sat in the wheelhouse, it looked solid.

"Yeah, Donald. I see your trail, but it's really frozen over."

"Yeah."

Gary pushed the throttle forward and *Progress* surged up over the shelf to come crashing through into the water, leaving chunks floating around her bow. He backed and rammed, chiseling in bit by bit.

"*Progress*, I see your mast."

"We're almost to the first bend. How much farther to you?"

"That's good, Gary. You're halfway there. You're gonna make it okay," he replied enthusiastically.

Gary backed the tug again, sending little hunks sliding over the sheen of water we had churned up. He stopped to write in the log, noting that the ice was eight inches thick, then put the tug in forward again. Warming a mug of coffee between cold hands, I enjoyed the spectacle of the sunrise and the battering as we inched our way in, glad I was not at the helm. Slowly a dapper little tug came into view, tied to a small dock in front of a brick house.

"You're lookin' good, Gary. Not much farther now."

"You got enough water for me to turn around by you, Donald?"

"No problem, Gary. You can stick your nose up by me and swing your stern around."

Finally we had turned and were crunching past the white planked sides of *Shelley* to retrace our broken path which was already beginning to refreeze. After firing up the engine, Don had waved to his wife who stood on shore, and called to his slim son who was casting off the lines. As Gary watched Don ease away from the pier he shook his head.

"I wouldn't want a wooden hull in a mess like this."

"I've got another place to keep her until all this ice clears," Donald said over the radio as though he had read Gary's mind. "I'll wait until the thaw to bring her back in here."

"Good idea."

"Listen, thanks for comin' in after me," Don added.

"No problem."

When we had cleared the mouth of the creek, Gary turned the tug north, keeping the engine at three-quarter speed until *Shelley* pulled even with us. Finally, he suggested that Don tie her to our quarter bitts and we carry her upriver on the hip.

"That'd be fine, Gary," Don responded, sliding the tug over until we had made contact and lashed her to our side.

Once secured, Donald left the helm to his son, Scotty, and climbed over the gunwales to visit. He stepped into the wheelhouse, both shy and outgoing and stuck out a hand to Gary.

"How're ya doin', Buddy?" Gary cried, shaking Don's hand. "This is my wife, Nancy. She's on as cook this time."

"Nice to meet ya," Don grinned, sticking out a hand.

About my height and broad chested, Donald had a face that defied a guess at age. He had obviously spent a good deal of his life outdoors and carried with him a testament in the form of a netting of fine lines around sparkling eyes. I had an immediate feeling of warmth, a genuineness that at once set me at ease. In the years since we first met, I have only added to that first impression an admiration for his industry and generosity of spirit.

The *Shelley* was, he told me, his first tug. He had wanted a tug for years, ever since he had driven a truck when his first two children were small. He would be gone, making pit stops at home while Sandy, his wife, waited with the children, stretching every penny that came in. Finally, they had found the *Shelley* and named her for their only daughter, then set about picking up any job he could to pay for her. She was built without plumbing and with a primitive electrical system but what she lacked in comfort, she made up for in heart, determined to give her best to any challenge.

Despite Clarky's grumbling, the docking at Artificial Island was uneventful and we parted from the Keens at the island. They charged home while we turned south for Lewes Breakwater, deployed to meet a barge coming from New England. It was to go to Baltimore, but since the ice had closed the Chesapeake and Delaware Canal, the run had to be made by sailing the length of the Eastern Shore coast then running up the Bay, a trip of some two hundred and fifty miles rather than the usual hundred and ten.

After the barge had been delivered to Baltimore, we headed back down to Norfolk to stop for fuel and groceries before we met another tow. In the waning light of afternoon, Gary left Chris and me off on a railroad barge which was tied to a bulkhead across the highway from the Open Air Market and took off for the fuel docks. I had left a stew simmering for the others along with a cookie sheet of biscuits and a list of instructions which absolved me of any responsibility for supper. I

96

knew a stack of dishes would await my return, but still enjoyed the break from the routine a trip to the market offered.

Chris, who was generally a happy-go-lucky sort, bounded over the snow-encrusted deck of the barge followed closely by my awkward form wrapped in Gary's leaden commission coat. I scrambled over the rails, tripping on one hidden in a drift, and dropped lumpishly to shore. Chris was in buoyant spirits and trotted the length of the shipyard with me struggling to keep pace.

What the market lacked in charm it redeemed in pure volume. Row upon row of shelves held the best that the American economy could offer. In Norfolk, the addition of a row of wine and beer helped to make an otherwise dull trip something of a lark, and Chris disappeared into the stacks as soon as I had snatched a cart from the line.

By the time I had wheeled the fourth cart to the front of the store, Chris had appeared and was flinging food onto the moving conveyor belt. After unloading one basket, he left the rest with me while he scouted out a dolly and some boxes into which he began stowing bags of food. We pushed and sorted and packed while the other customers gaped until I took the yard-long register tape to the charge counter. Finally, we had our shoulders together, straining to push the laden dolly through the half-cleared parking lot and across the highway. Once we had reached the shipyard, the journey became something of an Alpine crossing. The low-slung dolly pushed a bow wave of snow, halting periodically at hidden objects until we sledged it to the bulkhead by the barge. We unloaded the groceries onto a dry piece of plywood, then Chris left me to take the cart back across the road.

Standing there, flapping my arms to keep warm, I watched the darkness swallow Chris. I stood in a meager pool of light cast by the street lamp some distance away, the only spot of light on the otherwise black quay. Before me, the barge loomed quiet. A steady singing of tires, the sound of the traffic, filtered past the warehouses which divided me from the highway. Suddenly, I felt completely alone, vulnerable. No one moved. Home seemed unreachable. Intently, I scanned the corner of the far warehouse where Chris would first appear in the glimmer of the guard hut light. I counted out ten minutes in my head. Still no Chris. Over the sound of the highway and the wind whistling in my ears, I thought I heard the crunch of boots in the snow. Sweat trickled down my back as I listened. Debating whether to abandon the bags and melt into the darkness or stand my ground, I saw a figure coming toward me from the direction of the chain link fence. Whoever it was would have had to vault the fence in order to come from that direction. Then the light fell on him and I recognized Chris's devil-may-care stride. As I breathed a sigh of relief, I realized my heart was pounding. Chris, unaware of my desperate speculations, advanced on me, sizing up the distance between the bags and the barge.

"Okay, Nance. You stand there and hand the bags up to me one or two at a time," he said taking a short run at the piling and springing up to the top.

Once I had given him a bag, he leapt the gap between piling and barge, and walked across the tracks to put the bags against a clear rail under a car. He repeated this maneuver for the twenty-eight bags we had mushed through the snow, finally jumping down beside me.

"Look, I can't get them on the hand radio. I'm going on down the way and see if I can raise them on one of the radios on those tugs," he told me, pointing to three vessels moored at the far end of the yard.

I clambered aboard the barge and sat down next to the bags, rooting through them until I found the cookies. The wind had picked up, whistling around the cables and lines on the derelict vessels tied to a collapsing pier opposite the slip and searing my cheeks. The lights of the bridges danced over the water in a thousand bright shards. With numbed toes and hands, I gloomily munched my way through the cookies and stared out at the water. An hour passed. Finally, I saw the gay lights of old *Progress* blink into view just beyond the railroad bridge, passing under it and chugging toward me. Relief flooded me as though I had trudged miles to see a glimmer of hearth lights. Chris jumped up onto the barge and stumbled toward me to stand ready to catch a line.

"Where the devil have you been?" I demanded.

"I got to jawing with the guys over there," he answered, taken aback at my vehemence.

While the men delivered the bags to the galley table and floor, I slowly began the job of stowing, pouring myself a mug of hot cocoa, and working my way through the groceries. It may not have looked like much, but to me it was home.

Oɴᴇ ᴅɪꜰꜰɪᴄᴜʟᴛ aspect of working on the tug is the time away from home. Holidays blend unnoticed into the regular two-week-on, two-off schedule. Thanks to a union contract, Easter, Fourth of July, Thanksgiving, and Christmas are paid holidays, adding considerably to the pay packet, but the extra pay can only go so far toward solacing those who sit at home without their men. While many employers may sympathize with the yearnings produced by carols heard over the radio while transferring fuel on a freezing cold deck, business depends on the tug's availability and that availability depends in large measure on the crew.

Gary and I had spent one Christmas together since our marriage and that was from midnight of Christmas Eve, when he dragged through the door and headed straight up to bed, until about ten P.M. on Christmas night when he left to return to work. In 1978, *Progress* was tied up at Port Newark, New Jersey, with little prospect of work through the three-day weekend. Meanwhile, I was in bed with the flu, bemoaning my Gary-less state and wishing he had gone into greeting cards or law. Just home from filling in for the cook who had quit unexpectedly (cooks are notoriously temperamental), I had climbed into bed with a large mug of tea and proceeded to nurse fever and self-pity simultaneously. At eight in the evening, Gary phoned.

"Where are you, Darlin'?" I asked.

100

"Port Newark. Jerry's gonna let us off," he began with a peculiar note in his voice.

"That's great!" I croaked. "When do you get home?"

"We haven't got a ride yet."

I could sense the other shoe dangling, and waited.

"He says if you can come pick us up, we can have three days off, and he'll come get us at Wilmington on Monday and take us the rest of the way back up."

Clunk.

I sighed, pulled the blanket around me, and wondered how much gas was in the car.

"Sure. I'll leave in a few minutes," I said, deciding that what waited at the other end of the four-hour drive was worth the effort.

"Uh, we can't get off until four," he said carefully.

"Four A.M.?"

"Yeah. Can you make it? We'll be tied up right beside the highway at Port Newark across from the airport. You'll be able to see us. You remember," he ventured more boldly now. "Not far from where you met us before we were married."

"Yeah. I know where you mean. Right inside the slip by the warehouse and the gantry cranes."

"That's it."

"Is there anything else tied there I'll be able to see from the highway?" I murmured, rubbing my face at the thought of driving alone up the turnpike in the wee hours.

"No, we're the only ones here. There's not much going on. I'll leave the running lights on for you."

"Thanks. Okay, Love. I'll see you guys in about eight hours."

"Great, Kiddo. Lookin' forward to it," he said and hung up.

Pulling on the equivalent of a feather bed, I went out to fill our old Buick with gas before the station in town closed, then returned and set the alarm by the bed and crawled into the covers for a few hours' sleep. When the alarm buzzed at midnight, I awoke with a head packed with cotton wool. Suddenly, the trip seemed so improbable that I began to think I had imagined it. Switching on the light, I looked over the foot of the bed to where I had laid my clothes, piled conspicuously in a heap topped by my pocketbook, my note to myself of the reality of the trip.

An hour later, I was sailing over the Delaware Memorial Bridge, looking down at the winking lights of the river. The highways had been nearly deserted until then, the headlights of an oncoming car an unexpected break in the monotonous black. The radio kept me company, that and the knowledge that in another three hours I would be snugged down next to Gary who would drive home. The radio stations ebbed and returned, one fading into the static only to be replaced by another. The few cars on the New Jersey Turnpike appeared to be occupied by families or groups of people filled with the ebulliently friendly spirit of Christmas. Rather than feeling alone, I began to feel a part of a sea of goodwill which expressed itself in friendly waves and cheerful courtesy as we sped toward our various destinations. A Ray Henderson medley came on the radio, and I hoarsely sang along with the melodies my father had played throughout my childhood, "Bye, Bye, Blackbird," "Button Up Your Overcoat," "Life Is Just a Bowl of Cherries."

When I approached the exits for Newark Airport, I slowed down and slid over to the right lane looking for a way to get to the water. As I pulled even with the airport, I glanced over toward New York and saw the tug nestled into the dock beside a huge, black warehouse, her lights sparkling from head to toe in welcome. Taking the next ramp off the highway, I kept my eyes on the tug, only to discover as I wound through the tarmac maze that I had entered a nonstop route to Bayonne and was helplessly whizzing past the tug and up onto another highway. I crossed the bridge, peering down as the tug receded from view and, for just a few moments, almost panicked.

Calm yourself, Woman. Just ask directions. It will be all right.

Having fruitlessly searched for a friendly median strip to cross surreptitiously, I ended up at the tollgate, and, as I paid my toll, leaned out to ask the keeper how to get back to Port Newark. His answer was a blank look as he reached for my money. Panicked again, I found a way to turn around just past the tollbooths, and, after waiting in line to pay another toll for the return, asked for directions. This gatekeeper was delighted to talk, chattering away about road signs, ramps, and right-hand left-hand crosses that led to the Kills. Dizzy, I cruised back to the river and, like Jonah, searched for a way to get the sytem to disgorge me at Port Newark. It was fruitless. As I slid down the last ramp, my eyes wistfully on the merry lights of *Progress*, I could look ahead to see that the ramp was a loop. As I swooped down the asphalt, frantically looking for some escape, I could see the tug receding once again as I was being swallowed by Bayonne. By the time I pulled even with the fourth gatekeeper, and held out my money, I was in tears. Sympathetic, he patted my arm and gave me simple directions in a soothing tone. Thanks to his help, I finally managed to disentangle myself from the Gordian knot of cloverleafs and screech to a halt before the chain link fence that separated the car from the tug.

In the headlights which washed the broad parking lot by the inlet, I could see the men file out of the galley, kit bags in hand, and troop across the lot to the fence. Gary held back, saying something to Clarky before jumping over the gunwale to trot toward me. Clarky stood hunched over the gunwale, foot on the rail, elbow on knee, and chin in hand as he watched the others scale the fence and drop down by the car.

"Good to see ya, Kiddo," Gary said, kissing me firmly on the mouth after he had climbed the fence.

"Hi, Sweetheart," I murmured, the relief at seeing him allowing me to relinquish what was left of my tenuously mustered energy.

"How was the trip?" he asked.

"Not bad. Good, in fact, except for the last bit. Could you drive? I feel rotten."

"Sure."

We climbed into the car, and I collapsed against him gratefully. David, Chris, and the new cook who apparently began every meal with the statement: "I didn't enjoy cooking this and you probably won't enjoy eating it"; flopped into the back seat, shoulder to shoulder, anxious to get underway.

"What about Clarky?" I asked as we pulled away from the fence.

"He volunteered to stay. One of us had to," Gary replied. "Poor Clarky!"

"Oh, I don't think he minds that much," Chris said. "He was carrying on about Bah! Humbug, Christmas. He gets all our holiday pay for the day so he makes out like a bandit."

"Oh."

I cuddled down into the warmth of Gary's side while he put a protective arm around me, and wondered what Clarky's three-day holiday would be, spent at a deserted dock on a tug, alone. I pictured him in the galley, making himself a baloney sandwich and a cup of coffee and telling himself that he really did not mind. Then perhaps he would take his meal down the deck to his cabin where he would sprawl out on the bunk, turn on the radio, and open a *Playboy* magazine. The next day, after a breakfast in the empty galley, he might go below to reassemble one of the pumps, or do a little washing in the five-gallon bucket which sat under the spigot near the engine. Another sandwich and a pot of beans for his lunch might be accompanied by another *Playboy* or one of the mildewed murder mysteries that were in a dilapidated box under the forepeak ladder. Perhaps he would take a nap after lunch, lying down on his bunk, listening for footsteps. I wondered if he would feel any apprehension at the idea of being alone in that vast terminal, unable to lock the doors and easy prey to any lunatic or thief abroad. I knew Clarky would never admit to such fears, at least not to me, but the isolation was almost complete. A grim Christmas, I thought, munching a solitary meal of beans and franks in a smoke-darkened galley.

Birthdays, anniversaries, and religious holidays are all of a piece when work separates you from loved ones indiscriminantly. Married life takes much understanding in the best of circumstances but these are not the best. The days run together, and even if a phone is available, often the will to use it is absent, it being easier to pretend that it is just another day rather than that you are missing yet another milestone in your life that might have been shared with family or friends. Trust, a most necessary ingredient to any good marriage, becomes of paramount importance to the seaman and his wife. She must

104

fend for herself completely while he is gone, making the decisions about cars, homes, often rushing a child to the emergency room alone, or simply taking over the day-to-day responsibility for their shore lives together. Fidelity is often a casualty during the long separations, and one grim joke on the boats is "Jody," the guy who sneaks out the back door of the seaman's home while he comes in the front.

For me, the more difficult aspect of shouldering the entire responsibility of home, finances, and cars, was relinquishing it when Gary returned. I was unaccustomed to making decisions in conjunction with anyone else, and the problems arose when Gary was home, expecting to be able to overturn, criticize, or nullify my decisions. From his perspective, he had been working diligently and sending home every paycheck and therefore deserved some power in the decisions, as well as some tender loving care. From my point of view, it simply made me a spacer, a zero to fill in the empty place while he was gone. Floating in and out of responsibility is not something I have ever done well. Having seen how that kind of schizophrenic flopping back and forth between two different lives could affect a marriage, I had made a conscious decision to wrap my life around Gary's insofar as I could without completely losing myself in the process.

Therefore, I did not take full-time work, something that would have given me more friendships, pleasure, and satisfaction than just waiting for my man to come home since he looked forward to our uninterrupted time together. Although it was a conscious decision, it was not as easily carried out as made, and many of our fights centered on how to compromise two lives without losing both.

Understandably, seamen have a very high divorce rate surpassing even the fifty percent of the population as a whole. I had gradually discovered that it was a rare thing to meet a seaman over thiry-five who was married to his original spouse. The knowledge of this was one reason Gary was so keen to have me out there working alongside him. We hoped that if we could share our working lives as well as our home, our marriage would have a better-than-even chance.

After taking the new cook and Chris to their cars, we drove

the hour to our home with David who then took the Buick for the weekend. Gary mounted the TV on a table at the foot of the bed, tucked me under my grandmother's down quilt, and brought me brandy and roast goose until the fever broke. It made the eight-hour drive worthwhile.

In January of 1979, the new deckhand, whose favorite indoor sport was brawling in bars, wrenched his knee in yet another fight and was in a cast from hip to ankle. He phoned the night before crew change to ask if I could go on in his place, standing in until he got his cast off so he would not lose his job. I agreed as did Jerry who shifted the cook to deckhand and sent me aboard as cook.

Gary and I packed up, left the faucets to drip to ward off frozen pipes, shunted the cat to my folks, and turned up the furnace to forestall any major catastrophes. Since we had been married, things happened at home only when Gary was away. A tree came down in the yard, missing the house by inches and leaving me a mammoth trunk to saw up, alone. The bats in the attic descended into the house, taking over its interior while I migrated to friends' and battled from a distance. Pipes burst, flooding the house, and leaving me without heat for several days. When Gary was home, everything ran without hitch.

As soon as we were all aboard *Progress*, we set off for Philadelphia. There, the crew of the *Michael Keen*, Donald's new tug, was hard at work making up a LASH tow. Having decided that the *Shelley*'s size restricted his choice of jobs, Don had bought the old *Delilah*, a sixty-nine-foot tug with the narrow look of an old Bay cruiser. Although *Delilah*, renamed *Michael Keen* for Donald's third son, had more horsepower than *Shelley* and was fitted with indoor plumbing, she was as tender as a new calf, digging her shoulder into the water in sharp turns and heeling over disturbingly. However, Donald, who was licensed for inland work only, seemed unperturbed by this drawback, and instead enjoyed the added versatility she gave him.

Working with the Keens was invariably a delight. Cheerful, hardworking, and willing to do virtually anything, they would all turn out for LASH work, unlike many another crew

106

we had run with, and taking as much pleasure in the job as possible. Scotty, who had gotten his tug operator's license on his twenty-first birthday, was now running as his father's mate, and seemed to thrive on the challenges that Loveland's crazy tows afforded them.

From what we could gather, Donald's tug was something of a Boy's Town of the water. He ran the *Michael* with two deckhands in addition to himself and Scotty, taking on the troubled or high-spirited sons of friends and neighbors. One of the most recent additions to the crew was a young man, slender as a willow rod and as tough, who, according to Don, had gotten in with the wrong crowd and ended up in trouble with the law. Unable to handle liquor, he was without sense or conscience after a couple of drinks, stealing cars and running road blocks indiscriminantly. Once aboard, however, he was a pleasant working companion who, despite a vocabulary rich in obscenities, was good company as we trundled along the hatches tightening winches together.

Scotty, shortly to be married, worked enthusiastically along with everyone else, his cheerful disposition helping to alleviate the drudgery. While he always treated me like a lady, he nevertheless seemed to have little difficulty with the idea of my working beside the men and would help me haul on an iron pipe with the same easygoing friendliness he shared with the others. While he worked, he talked about home, about his and his father's plans and hopes, about the workings of Loveland's company, some of whose employees were family friends, or told good-natured stories about his dad.

Once we secured the tug, we spread out over the hatches with pipes and crowbars in hand to help finish the job of stringing together the ten-barge tow, arranging it so that it was doubled into two parallel lengths of barges hooked together by odd wires and ropes laced through the eyes of the lifting pads. When they were finally made up completely, wired together in a semi-solid block of tow, sixty by three hundred feet, we made the tugs up behind in pushing gear, one lashed to each of the two sections, and set off toward the C&D Canal.

The wind had been gathering strength all day and had raised a deckle-edged chop in the Chesapeake, slapping against the hard chines of the tow and jostling the barges. The tugs had begun to ram their noses against the tow with the jolting determination of pile drivers, and wires snapped and popped, pulling tighter on the winch drums. Just below the Bay Bridge, Gary and Donald decided to string out the tow on the straps, and set up the tugs on the hawser in front. Together, Gary and Don mapped out a game plan, deciding that *Michael Keen* would go up ahead and hold the tow on the hawser while four of us would unlace the lashings between the barges with the help of the *Progress* behind.

Undoing a tow en route is a job which requires both brute strength and dexterity. As the weather disintegrates, often so does the tow, snapping cables and jerking what lashings still hold into tangled masses of wire and rope.

While taking apart a LASH tow underway is disagreeable work, it was only later that I discovered the nightmare of trying to retrieve a tow that had come to pieces itself. At midnight on one sticky August night, Gary roused me out of the bunk and told me that the barges which we had strung out on the straps on the hawser only hours before, had broken apart. After pulling hawser, the mate, the deckhand, and I were dispatched to the barges which by this time were leaping in a St. Vitus' dance, smashing frighteningly into one another. One pair of barges had broken one strap completely, snapping the three-inch-thick hawser line of the strap like a piece of wet spaghetti. The bitt on the other side of the barge had pulled out of its mooring and was gone. The three of us had skated over the decks, jumping between the barges when they came close enough together until we reached the pair that were separated completely, grabbing each other occasionally for balance. When the efforts of the *Progress* and the other tug diminished the maw between the two, the deckhand jumped, landing in a bruised heap on the deck, clawing at a handhold. When he got to his feet again, he dragged the partially escaped strap back onto the barge's deck and readied himself to pass it across the gap the next time the two barges surged together. As they came closer, he stood, feet braced, leaning as far out as he dared while the mate and I pawed at the wire loop. The barge lurched

108

and the mate, who was stretched out over the black gap, stumbled toward the meat grinder between the barges while I snatched at his belt. My heart in my throat, I realized how easily any or all of us could lose our limbs in the chaos. The only light was the tug's search beam which followed us unsuccessfully. The apprehension was exacerbated by the noise of equipment crashing ominously and the threat of more pieces of the tow coming apart to injure or kill any one of us.

Gary had snared the barge behind the one on which we stood, and brought it close enough so that we could finally grab the wire loop and drop it on the bitt before the barges leapt apart again and took our fingers off. As they strained apart, the loop rose up over the ear of the bitt, threatening to drop back off into the gap. The mate and I tried to put our feet on top of it, then frantically worked it back into place when the motion gave us some slack. That done, we tied a scrap of line overtop to keep it from jumping off. The other strap had snapped, and by this time we were without a spare so we had to tie the other sides together as best we could with soft line. By the time we returned to the deck of the tug, we were soaked with sweat, greasy and shaken.

However, as I trudged over the hatches in the cold, I was still unaware of the joys that lay ahead. After nearly an hour and a half of breaking the tow apart together with two deckhands from the *Michael Keen,* both tugs were strung out on hawser, one in front of the other, and southbound for Norfolk. We rounded Old Point [Old Point Comfort] and straggled into the crowded harbor, looking for a snug place to begin bunching up the tow in order to put it to dock. The wind howled down the James River, scudding foam over the tops of the waves to collect in lathery patches around the barges. Norfolk harbor teemed with traffic. After finding a place to work in the lee of the shore, we began restringing the barges, working unenthusiastically, knowing that the job would be negated in another hour when we took them apart yet again to take the straps back aboard.

No one was happier than Clarky, who loathed LASH barges, when our orders were to leave Norfolk with a tow bound for New York. Ocean running can run the gamut from

Towing an empty deck barge as seen from the fantail, port side. The hawser board is scraping over the rail, upper extreme left. Photograph by Charlton A. Gunter.

extreme pain to extreme pleasure with many shades in between, all depending on the weather. In the northwest gales of winter, coastal sailing is a steady roll, a bearable careening along the shores, interrupted only by the dismally rough crossings at the mouths of the bays.

We scurried out the Chesapeake, chased by a hearty northwester that blasted us broadside as we turned the buoy at Cape Charles. Once we had lurched around the corner and stood behind the shelter of the low-lying shore, we settled into a careless swing that rocked the plates in their bins noisily and kept the doors thunking back and forth on their latches.

Usually, I took for granted that we would actually survive the passage, but crossing the mouth of the Delaware, pounded broadside by a nasty chop, I had cause to doubt. The wind had screamed down the length of the bay all day and night, and by the time we peeked out from behind Cape Henlopen-Lewes Breakwater, there were five-foot seas slopping up over the side to pound the deckhouse and splash in the closed doors. The timing was perfect for me. I had finished supper and had managed to get the dishes stowed before dashing for my cabin

110

for the night. The surf of Overfalls Shoal crashed against us, picking the tug up and dropping her unexpectedly into the deep troughs like a carelessly thrown ball. Huddled under a thin blanket, I lay in the bunk in several layers of clothing and tried to sleep. As we reached the center of the channel entrance, the motion grew more violent, and I turned over on my stomach, gripping the side of the bunk to keep from being pitched onto the wet deck. My head swimming, my stomach in knots, I willed myself to sleep.

After an hour, I realized that I had lain there awake listening to the deafening crash of the waves followed by the rush of water down the decks, slurping up into the open spaces of the doors and scuppers. In the bottom of the locker, the pair of ownerless shoes that had been in residence since I had first come aboard thumped back and forth rhythmically. Finally, unable to stand the sound any longer, I crawled out of the bunk and, on my knees in the damp, opened the locker. While holding the sheets and towels that tried to escape, and bracing myself against the locker door which crashed back and forth freely, I searched with one hand, intending to throw them over once and for all. I could not feel them. The door hit me in the shoulder. My suitcase, which had worked itself free, came down against my back. The shoes had stopped thumping. As I crouched there, still without the shoes, I could feel my stomach begin to go, and I opened the door just enough to be sick in the torrent which coursed over the deck. My stomach empty, I clawed my way back to the bunk, kicking the locker closed and leaving my suitcase sprawled on the floor, held in place by the other debris. The shoes began to bang again. As I lay there, panting, I kept telling myself that with each minute's passing, we were nearing the end.

Most of the crew had little trouble with seasickness, and although I usually got my sealegs about six hours out in the ocean, a prolonged stint in the smokey, enclosed galley tested my equilibrium. Engulfed in a veil of diesel smoke, pitching around the long aisle which ran athwartships from the port door to the starboard, juggling plates and cutlery and pots of food, chasing the creamed corn from one end of the flat stovetop to the other were all a challenge to my inner ear, and while

111

cooking, I would spend whole minutes together sucking in gulps of fresh air.

The deep sink became a catch-all where I thawed the meats, made a salad in one of the large steel bowls, and braced the condiments while I served. In rough weather the coffee pot had to be lashed to one black iron rail at the back of the stove by a piece of limp nylon. Opening the refrigerator took a certain calculation. Although I carefully wedged and braced the contents before leaving the galley, cramming virtually everything I could into the box of jams and mustard at the bottom, more than once I had opened the door to find cranberry sauce draped rakishly over the egg cartons or leftover soup dripping into the box of salad dressings.

The discomfort notwithstanding, there were sights which made it all worthwhile. Coming into New York harbor on a clear night can be one of unadulterated splendor. The first time I saw it, we had rounded Sandy Hook after supper on a cloudless night and I sat in the wheelhouse with Gary as we churned toward the Verrazano Narrows. This quiet approach through a black velvet evening spangled with stars made New York seem peaceful to me despite the gabble on the radio. As we dodged the chaotic harbor traffic, Gary leaned back on my knees, his hands on the wheel, and chuckled.

"I remember the first time I brought a tow into this harbor at night," he said, staring ahead at the clusters of moving lights.

"I was running mate to Freddie Carter. We had two hopper barges on the hawser loaded with steel from Sparrows Point and we were on our way to General Dynamics in Quincy. They were using the steel to build those liquid natural gas ships. I don't remember what the tide was doing but we were headed in Swash Channel."

"Swash as in swashbuckle?"

"Yes," he chuckled again. "It's the shallow channel in between Sandy Hook and Ambrose channels."

"Oh."

"Anyway, I was headed in on the ranges and there were three tows, each one with a single barge on the hawser outbound and they were all side by side which made it kinda crowded. I could see them coming out, and I kept calling them on the radio trying to get some sort of response, but there was so much garbage on the radio that I had no idea if I was getting through to anybody or not. I couldn't tell who I was talkin' to. So I just said, "Here I am, I'm comin' up on my side of the range and there it is." I just headed straight on up and kept praying. As it turned out, it was just time for watch change and I called Freddie. He came up and got it and headed it on up the middle of them. Two went on the right side of us and one went on the wrong side."

He laughed, remembering.

"Better thee than me," I said, shaking my head.

The lights of the Statue of Liberty and Manhattan shone on the dark water in shimmering splotches of silver and gold. The lights of the ferries and the other traffic danced over the harbor. From a captain's point of view, it was something of a headache. but from my point of view it was breathtaking.

Coming into Boston Harbor with an empty deck barge on a short hawser, picture taken from the boat deck. Photograph by Charlton A. Gunter.

SEVEN

THE DAY we changed crews in Philadelphia was one of those thoroughly bleak days of which February has more than its share. The deckhand who was still in a cast from ankle to hip hoped to return halfway through the two-week stint and as I looked around the drab docks, littered with papers and scraps of wire and wood, I suddenly felt thankful that my time in this grim atmosphere would be limited. Climbing down from the dock into the galley, I felt a pang of homesickness for the comforts of hearth which were to contrast with the strenuous days ahead.

My return to the *Progress* was made more difficult by the fact that, this time, Gary did not accompany me with the rest of the crew. What had originally been a two-day moonlighting job in the middle of the two weeks off had been rescheduled and had stretched to six days due to severe weather conditions. While he pounded his way down the coast, I packed both bags and lugged them to Wilmington to join David, Clarky, and the cook who had, in the original deckhand's absence, been shifted to the deck. The captain on the opposite crew had agreed to stand in until Gary's return. So, added to the grim mood of the day was the prospect of working under a man whose response to me was something I could not predict.

Like many of the long-time commercial tugboaters, this man's prejudices ran the gamut from blacks through the rainbow to white women in a man's world. His natural antipathy notwithstanding, he treated me with an exaggerated courtesy

114

and interest. I was allowed to cook and wait on him but forbidden to deck. Like many of the older men on tugs, he dyed his hair, a fact I found ironic when the conversation turned to the vanities of women. I realized that, like women, these men equate youth with work, and in a physically demanding job, they often take extreme cosmetic measures, hoping to cling to an image of vigor, fearing, perhaps justifiably, that their working life is easily jeopardized by any signs of aging.

Our run to Paulsboro for fuel brought home the result of several weeks of stinging cold. The ice coverage was about eighty percent with chunks floating that were eight to ten inches thick. Although the captain insisted he was happier in a wheelhouse than anywhere else on earth, he nonetheless craved company, demanding I stay with him while he was up. According to the other crew, it was the same with them as well. He hated to be alone. Despite his constant flow of protest against his "old lady" and home, once he caught sight of Gary coming in on the other tug, he was packed and gone.

The tug was tied to a long warehouse pier in Philadelphia, one of the arthritic fingers that line the riverside roads. Rats scurried inside the vast buildings, squeaking and clawing through the hills of grains, their noises echoing the length of the tin warehouse. Since the tug had no work that day, Jerry decided to hoist off another piece of faulty equipment and replace it. Consequently, the men spent the entire day in the "hole" together, slamming around torque wrenches and long screwdrivers and swearing while I made meals.

It was the following day that we got orders to move. We were to run down to Baltimore and call in, confirming orders for the next night. With the continued buildup of ice in the waterways, the possibility of the Coast Guard's levying horsepower restrictions increased. So, after having gotten our orders, Gary had Loveland's office call the Chesapeake and Delaware Canal dispatcher to check on any problems going through the canal, and he himself called the Philadelphia Coast Guard to check on the disposition of the Delaware. When he received an okay from both quarters, we cast off to chew our way downriver through a ninety percent coverage of ice. It sounded as though we had entered a giant thresher. The noise of the chunks

115

smashing against the hull was enough to drown normal conversation.

David had come on watch by the time we reached Pea Patch Island, one of the last way points before entering the Chesapeake and Delaware Canal, and I sat with him in the wheelhouse in between kneading bread, watching this new world coast by the windows, and chatting sporadically. As usual, he radioed for permission to go through, telling the dispatcher our whereabouts and approximate arrival time at the jetties. The gravelly voice of the dispatcher came back.

"Right, Cap. Keep her comin'."

As we crunched by the buoy at the junction of the Delaware City channel, Reedy Point entrance to the canal, and the main river channel, we saw the *Chinook*, a Coast Guard tug, emerge from the canal followed by a convoy of smaller vessels pushing barges. The *Atalanta*, another Coast Guard tug, took up the rear, and churned out of the pass as we rounded into the canal. David radioed the *Atalanta*.

"Do we need to convoy?"

"No, no problem," came the reply.

Rounding the mark, we crabbed on the currents into the slushy waters of the canal and plowed through alone. With the movement of vessels, the ice had been crushed to the consistency of a snow cone. Running through it sounded like a downpour on a tin roof. As we left the final mark of the western end of the canal, turning past the spiderlike beacon on Old Towne Point, we could see down into the maw of the Elk River.

The scene was desolate. The river was frosted shore to shore with only the dark suggestion of a pathway leading up the string of buoys into the canal in a line of frozen channel. Fragments of ice stuck up like the spikey broken glass on a deserted parking lot. We pushed ourselves through, turning out of the main shipping channel only when we reached the jog into Pooles Island Flats. The radio had been almost completely silent since passing Worton Point, and the upper bay looked abandoned in the last light of evening. By six we were off Southwest Beacon [the local name for Pooles Island Light], ramming and fishtailing through the unbroken armor of ice. In the beam of the searchlight, a seam came into view now and

116

again, and Gary would back the tug, then ram the seam with the bow, hoping to open it enough to push on another quarter of a mile.

By law, as well as common sense, the tug's radios had been on channels thirteen and sixteen, monitoring what little traffic there was. After cleaning up the supper dishes, I had gone up to the wheelhouse with a fistful of cookies and two mugs of coffee to sit with Gary and watch our journey over the wasteland of the once-familiar flats.

Gary stood behind the wheel, gripping it in both hands, listening to the threads of conversation on the radio. Clarky came up at seven-thirty to join Gary for a call to Jerry, hoping for some news of the parts he had ordered. Although the usual hour-long journey had been protracted to four, by eleven that evening, we were tying up to the western end of the police dock at Broadway. Blackened lumps of snow, the residue of the snowfall the week before, crusted the railings and bollards. Everything was strangely silent.

The following morning, Gary sent me off to borrow a car from a long-time friend in order to do the grocery shopping while they went out to meet the *Miss Elizabeth* to help in putting the tow to the dock. By the time I returned to Broadway with Anne, laughing and sharing a beer with her in a Volkswagon bug crammed with grocery bags, the Coast Guard had come and gone. Having left lunch, I came back to find that the deckhand had washed the dishes and David had put them away, enabling me to stuff bags into a clear galley. The deckhand had disappeared and Gary was nowhere in sight.

David met me and Anne at the companionway to help with the groceries. He snatched bags from us, depositing them on the table and floor, but he took little interest in their contents.

"David, where's Gary?" I asked, suspicious at his lack of interest over the food.

"He went up to the phone."

"Is something wrong?"

"I'd better let Gary tell you," he replied, shoving the bags around to make room for yet another one that Anne handed over the gunwale.

"You tell me."

David sighed and straightened.

"The Coast Guard met us at the pier when we came back and charged Gary with a violation."

"What violation?"

"Going through the canal without a convoy. Crossing to Baltimore."

"But that's crazy! He checked. My God! You asked the Coast Guard tug, what's its name?"

"*Atalanta*."

"*Atalanta*. You asked the *Atalanta* if we needed to convoy, and they said no. This is crazy. Is it serious?"

David shrugged. "They sounded serious."

"God."

Once we had unloaded the car and Anne had left, I began to cook dinner and sort through the bags with David. I was unprepared for the sudden appearance of two young men in polyester suits who leaned into the companionway.

"Where's the captain?" one asked without introduction.

I darted a glance at David and guessed by his face that they had been the two from the Coast Guard who had charged Gary.

"Can I help you?" David asked politely.

"We want to see the log books," the other replied.

I shook my head in the negative.

"That's up to the captain," David informed them gently.

"I'm the captain's wife," I told the one who had demanded the log. "What exactly do you want with him?"

"We'll talk to the captain," he smiled indulgently.

I looked at David who watched them evenly and realized that the calmer I stayed, the better. They left us and climbed the ladder to the wheelhouse. Protectively, David and I followed on their heels. Gary found the four of us there, eyeing each other like tigers in a small cage. When Gary stepped into the wheelhouse, shutting the door behind him, one of the men reached into his breast pocket and withdrew a piece of paper, then handed it to Gary.

"It's a summons," he told Gary smoothly. "You are to present yourself before the court to answer the charges."

My mouth went dry, and I could feel my heart quicken. I leaned back against the log book.

118

"We came for your log books," the other man said.

"No way," Gary growled, not looking up from the summons as he skimmed over its closely typed lines.

"Captain Robson, we can subpoena your logs, but it would go easier if you gave them to us," he threatened.

Gary glanced at me with a question in his eyes. I shook my head.

"You'll have to subpoena them," he replied. "Wait a minute! This says I have to appear in court in two days! I'll be halfway down the bay in two days."

"I suggest you make arrangements," the first man said with a hint of a smile.

"Christ! You guys want my license and twenty-five thousand dollars! What the hell is this?" Gary cried as he read through the summons.

"What?" I shrieked.

David stood behind Gary, reading over his shoulder while satisfied smiles spread over the faces of the two envoys from the Coast Guard.

"It says they'll fine me twenty-five thousand dollars and take my license," he repeated angrily.

"But how can they?" I cried.

"Oh, it's well within the law," one of the men said confidently.

I wanted to punch him in his supercilious face.

"He violated the port captain's restrictions."

"Christ! I didn't *know* about the restrictions!" Gary shouted.

"Ignorance is no excuse," the other smiled.

"But we listened to the radio. How the hell do you guys broadcast? Did you only broadcast them once? We just came from Philadelphia!"

"It is your duty to keep abreast of the rules, Captain."

"I *do*, God dammit! Move! I've got to make some phone calls," he said, pushing past the crowd and scooping up some change on the desk in his cabin.

"Captain, we want those logs," the first man persisted.

"Nope!" Gary said without looking up.

I put my elbow on the log book and waited. After several

minutes, the two gave up and descended the ladder to their car and drove off.

"Twenty-five thousand dollars!" I murmured, thinking of the scrimping and saving we had done.

"And his license," David reminded me softly.

Snow had begun to fall in a thick curtain of flakes. When Gary returned, he flopped into Clarky's seat and stared at his hands. David had been sipping a mug of tea while I cooked.

"Well?" I demanded after a few moments of silence.

"I called Jerry and Loveland. They're going to get me a lawyer. I've got to call back in a little while," he said. "The first thing is to get the hearing date changed."

"Do you really think they'll try to take away your license and the money?" I whispered.

"How the hell do I know? That's what the summons said!"

"Look, you didn't do anything wrong. What can they do?"

"I must have done something wrong. They say there were restrictions. And they can do plenty. I got the license from them, and they can take it away."

"Does anyone else know about the restrictions or is it a Coast Guard secret? I spent a lot of time in the wheelhouse yesterday. I didn't hear anything. David didn't hear anything. You sat there until we tied up. You didn't hear anything. What kind of a case could they have?"

He shook his head miserably. Rising, he went back to the wheelhouse. Leaving him to his own thoughts, I finished making dinner and laying it out on the table before joining him. He was talking on the radio.

"Does anyone else know about the restrictions?"

"They do now!" he said. "I've got to get back up to the phone."

He slid off the stool, hugged me, then set off through the snow to the pay telephones outside one of the bars. When he returned, after a long conversation with the lawyer, he had calmed somewhat.

According to the lawyer who had begun scouting as much information as possible, a new commandant had been appointed port captain and, according to a memorandum circulated within the ranks of the Coast Guard, was determined to show the world the Coast Guard had "teeth." Gary was now worried that he would become a scapegoat and be pilloried. Having done what he could, he tried to quash his worries in a haze of activity, updating the Notice to Mariners, straightening out the cabin, washing his dirty underwear. The chores were short-lived, however, as the snow continued, blanketing the city in two feet by morning and laying us up in the harbor with little constructive to do to occupy our time. Thankful that I had been able to do a massive food shopping, I busied myself with frenzied cooking and baking, spending a day in the tedious process of rolling and folding dough for Danish pastries. David hung over the table, enjoying the sight of me in flour to my elbows and anticipating the jam-filled delights that awaited him for breakfast the next morning.

Fells Point had ground to a halt. Shops were shut up, their owners unable to wade through the blocked streets. The brick piazza was deserted, even of the homeless who usually occupied the few benches, and the pushers and prostitutes who roamed back and forth plying their trades. The police had been forcd onto horseback to stop the looting, and a stillness had fallen over the city, broken only by the occasional shriek of a child at play.

After two abortive forays into the harbor, we stayed tied to the dock for five days longer. We had finally sailed the LASH tow with the *Miss Elizabeth*, pulling away from Canton Pier II behind the tug *Drum Point* which Loveland had hired to appease the restrictions, and break ice for us to the Bay Bridge. Once we reached the waters of Sandy Point, the ice had begun to clear, and as we passed under the bridge, *Drum Point* turned for home, leaving us to continue to Newport News on our own.

Rumors had been flying on the radio since Gary's summons had been delivered. The news of it was all over the wires, coupled now with the scuttlebutt of another arrest, this time of a captain who had known about the restrictions in the Nanticoke, but who had lied when contacted by the Coast Guard. After Gary's having been dealt with so peremptorily, the mood on the water was skittish. The Coast Guard had become the enemy. Radio chatter was guarded.

The rapid change in air temperature had produced a fog

which in the twilight obscured the outlines of the piers at Newport News. The sound of the foghorn which sat on the end of the rock-encrusted coal pier was our only guide. As we approached the docks, Gary sent me out on the barges beside Clarky, armed with the hand radio. Two deckhands from the *Miss Elizabeth* already stood on the bow of the tow, chatting quietly to one another. When Clarky and I joined them, they sidled away to perch on the opposite corner of the barge.

"Woman shy," Clarky remarked amusedly.

I pulled the radio out of my jacket pocket to tell Gary we could see no more than he, and was treated to a steamy conversation on the radio betwen two men who were gleefully recounting their sexual exploits along the waterfronts of the Atlantic.

"Can you see the light on the coal pier yet?" Gary wanted to know, interrupting their transmission.

"No, not yet," I said into the radio. "Can you see anything, Clarky?"

"Nope."

"I'll back her down to get it around when we get enough of an overlap on the pier, okay?" Gary asked the captain of the *Miss Elizabeth*.

"Yeah, okay, Gary."

"I just see the outline of the pier," I said over the radio when the red light of the foghorn came into view.

We were much closer than I had anticipated.

"Better back it down a bit. We're about seventy-five feet off it.

"What do you think, Clarky?" I asked, shutting off the transmission until he confirmed my guess.

"Yeah, that's about right," he agreed, spitting a stream of tobacco juice over the side.

"What the hell's this broad doin'?" a coarse voice demanded on the radio.

"Yak, yak, yak," came the reply.

"Okay, Kiddo. We're backin' it around some. Let us know how far off we are," Gary broke in.

"You're comin' up pretty fast," I said to him.

I could see the structure of the foghorn now and the rocks which surrounded the cement base.

"Jack, some damn broad is yakkin' over our frequency. I couldn't hear your last."

"Maybe *Miss Elizabeth* could back down and swing the bow past the rocks," I ventured.

Clarky nodded agreement while straining to see the approaching riprap.

"Get off the radio, you stupid bitch!"

"Okay, guys, it's about a hundred feet now," I said, gritting my teeth.

"Okay, I'll bring her around now."

"Tell 'em she's swingin' pretty good now," Clarky told me after a few minutes.

"It's swinging pretty good now," I repeated into the microphone.

"It's gettin' so these damn broads is everywhere!"

"Okay, I'll drop my line, *Miss Elizabeth,* and go around and catch one on the starboard side to push her to the dock with you," Gary told the captain of the other tug.

"Sounds good, Cap."

Slowly, the tow crabbed toward the dock while *Progress*'s engine rattled through her stack, echoing in the slip between the warehouse and the big trolley structure that looked like a roller coaster which sat on the opposite pier. Once the tow lay against the wood fenders on the cement face of the pier, Clarky caught a line from the bow, making it fast with stiff fingers, then ambled along the hatch as we began to tie up each barge.

"We've got to break it in half," the voice of the *Miss Elizabeth*'s captain crackled over the radio.

"What's he say?" Clarky demanded.

"He says we've got to break the tow in half."

"Why?"

"Didn't say."

"Ask him where."

I did as bidden and got a barge number from the captain.

"They've all got to be put to dock in a special order. I've got a list here," he said.

"God damn! I hate and despise LASH barges," Clarky fumed.

I was soaked through from my shoes to the knees of my jeans and stood for a moment, feeling as though enveloped in a giant oyster, soggy, cold, seaweedy. Together, Clarky and I unlashed the barges freeing one section. Although it was seven-thirty and the deckhand had been asleep for less than two hours, Gary had gotten him up to send him out on the barges with us. While he moaned about Gary's heartlessness, he acknowledged that the overtime pay would help with the second-hand Cadillac he had just acquired.

"Nance, you two go with *Miss Elizabeth* and help them break them apart and Clarky, you come on back," Gary shouted over the decks. "The steering's gone out."

Swearing, Clarky trudged through the snow to climb aboard while the deckhand and I stepped onto the section of tow that the *Miss Elizabeth* was preparing to haul around the face of the pier and put into the next slip. In the harsh glare of the floodlights on the corners of the warehouse, we all looked like zombies, the black outlines of our clothes surmounted by white faces with hollow eyes. The mists clung to my hair and face, and I began to feel chilled to the bone, stamping as I worked to keep the circulation in my feet. It was not until eleven o'clock that we had finished loading the LASH straps aboard *Miss Elizabeth* and stumbled across the dock to *Progress*.

After climbing aboard, the deckhand disappeared in the direction of his cabin and I ducked into the chilly galley for a mug of coffee before dragging myself up the ladder to the wheelhouse. Flopping into the chair, I gulped gratefully at the mug. Slowly, it dawned on me that the wheelhouse was as raw as the night. Gary, who had been rummaging through the cabin, appeared at the top step to enter something in the log book.

"Have you been leaving all the windows open again?" I asked, sipping at the lukewarm coffee.

"The heat's off," he said as he ran his finger down a list of barge numbers.

"Swell."

"Good God, Kiddo. Are you as wet as you look?" he cried, when he finally looked at me. "Get down there right now and get some dry clothes on!"

"Let me finish my coffee."

"No. Now!"

Obediently, I stripped out of my clammy clothes and changed into his downy, insulated coveralls. After draping my wet socks and pants over the cold radiator, I went below for another cup of coffee. All nature seemed to conspire with the machinery to make life difficult. Clarky stomped into the wheelhouse where I sat with Gary and rubbed his perspiring head with a bandanna.

"I need a new coil."

"No spare?" I asked, knowing that the answer would be a sour no.

"Owners don't believe in a lot of spare parts lyin' around."

"I'm getting ready to call Jerry. You got a part number?"

"Yeah. Here," he said, handing Gary a smudged piece of paper.

Maliciously, the stove had joined the cabal of malfunctioning machinery and despite my coaxing and Clarky's impatient tinkering, refused to muster more than a dim flame. By the time we entered Tangier Sound bound for Salisbury with a loaded barge on the hawser two days later, the beast coughed up no more than an indifferent warmth. We had replaced the carburetor in Baltimore, hooking up the new one to the pipes projecting from the stove and leading back through the bulkhead to the fuel tank, turning it on with an altogether unwarranted confidence, only to discover that it did not allow enough fuel flow for a roaring flame. We had made do with less than toasty heat, but once the other problems set in, it seemed the stove rebelled in sympathy and the breakfast in Tangier consisted of limp bacon, loosely scambled eggs, and tepid coffee. While everyone grumbled inwardly, nothing was said. The atmosphere aboard was bleak, but the stark beauty of the Wicomico in late winter helped to sustain us as we crawled around the jackknife corners of the river, now pushing the hopper barge loaded to the gunwales with tree trunks. The last of the geese lingered over the marshes, flying in the undulating

V pattern and honking in the still morning air. Ducks flew up out of their tiny protected puddles in the reeds, quacking loudly at the interruption of their domesticity.

We had picked up the barge in pushing gear in the basin just before entering the river, pumping *Progress*'s bow down in order to drop the fender to the low level of the barge's stern, then plowed up the shallow, mercurially changing channel. At Quantico Wharf, the air was acrid with the odor of creosote, and the clanging trolleys that ferried loads of telephone poles through the processing machines moved continually. Gary pushed the barge into the slip which was little more than a halfheartedly gouged hole in the riverbank, being careful not to nudge the already disintegrating bulkheading. This was representative of many of the piers and bulkheads where we had tried to dock barges. Often they are dangerous in that much of what you see is not what you got. Sturdy-looking boards are rotten and loose, falling away like so much pie crust at a touch.

Once we had tied to the bulkhead, Clarky went below to swear at the heating, leaving Gary to search the Salisbury hardware stores for a new coil. Meanwhile, I set to taking the stove apart and cleaning out a five-gallon bucket load of hardened cinders from the firebox, clearing the fuel feed with a bent coathanger. Free of congealed fuel, the exit pipe began coughing black soot, dropping it into the soot box beneath the stove and covering the galley with a fine dusting of powder as it fell. With blackened face and arms, I shoveled out buckets full of cinders then scrubbed the stove parts and began to reassemble them. Almost as an afterthought, I replaced the new carburetor with the old one, hoping that whatever spirit had moved the springs to go in the first place would be placated by reinstallation. Finally, I was ready to light it. Opening up the valve on the carburetor, I watched as fuel streamed into the firebox at the bottom, waiting until it had accumulated an inch in the trough before stuffing in a flaming piece of paper towel. The towel lay just above the diesel, burning away to ash. A second towel landed in the damp, not enough to douse it but enough to coax a spark, then poof! and a black cloud of smoke followed the small explosion. The fuel caught. I backed off, waiting a few seconds as a steady stream of sticky smoke poured from the mouth of the stove, then replaced the three broken pieces of lid and turned on the blower. It was done. The stove wheezed happily and little by little, the monster warmed. Within ten minutes, it was glowing inside, the difficulties with the carburetor forgotten. An hour later, I made the first pot of genuinely hot coffee we had drunk for two days.

Grease-covered, Clarky leaned into the companionway. I poured a mug of coffee and filled it with sugar and evaporated milk before handing it to him.

"Well, how's it comin'?" I asked.

He stepped into the galley and slumped in his seat.

"Gary's not back with the new coil. That's got to be it. I've cleaned and checked everthing. That's got to be the last thing," he said, sipping at the coffee. "Got her runnin', I see."

"Yeah. I cleaned it out and put the old carburetor back on."

Clarky shook his head with a rueful smile but said nothing. With the return of hot meals, we began to feel more a part of civilization again. And then there was heat! Halfway down the river, Clarky had replaced the coil and worked whatever magic had been necessary to persuade the heater to return. Showers! Hot tap water! Bliss! I leaned out of the companionway, watching as we rounded the bends, savoring the scents of fried chicken and apples as they blended with the cold grasses and salt of the river.

As the stove toasted my back, I marveled at Gary's nerve, sliding around the curves, pulling a wildly fishtailing light barge whose high sides acted as sails, slewing her around the corners and skimming past the docks with only a few feet to spare. She was tethered to our stern on a short hawser and strained to be free. As we rounded the tightest curve on the river, I stepped out of the galley to watch the barge. The tug had entered the bend and turned steadily, bringing her bow through the channel center, but the barge, taking the tug one better, had veered toward the dock set on the outside of the turn, careening toward the defenseless collection of sticks with determination. It obscured the dock, and I waited to hear the crash. Above me, the wheelhouse door squeaked open, and Gary stepped out on the landing. On the fantail, I saw Clarky

127

lean out on the starboad side, transfixed. For several seconds, the barge hung there, the only sounds the engine and the rushing water.

Then I saw a piling, then another and another until the dock came back into sight, intact. The wheelhouse door closed and Clarky wandered out of sight. Better thee than me, I thought as I glanced up toward the wheelhouse.

I had stayed aboard for the entire two weeks of this trip, assuming each day of the second week aboard that I would be relieved by the errant deckhand. Each time we checked in with Jerry, he had heard nothing. After we got home, we discovered why. The deckhand had gotten his cast off and two days later had drunkenly run his car under a tractor trailer on the highway, breaking his jaw. Now, though he was without a cast, his jaw was wired together. He had been lucky to escape with his life.

Our two weeks were up once we had delivered the barge to Norfolk and steamed north to change crews in Wilmington. This time, however, there was no relief in getting off, for the Coast Guard hearing was ahead of us. Gary's hearing had been rescheduled for the Monday following crew change, and that morning we found ourselves sitting in a courtroom in the custom house, waiting for the judge to enter. Jerry, who now owned the *Progress* alone, had retained one of the best maritime lawyers in Baltimore for Gary, and sat beside me in the back of the small room.

What the lawyer had assumed would be a short hearing turned into two gruelling days of trial, including witnesses, cross-examination, and testimony while the two young lawyers from the Coast Guard continually impugned Gary's competency. Jerry and I listened as the judge tried to understand the basic nature of the work as well as the circumstances surrounding the case. Although David had been subpoenaed for the prosecution, he had sat with us in the lawyer's office before the trial, trying to remember everything of value to Gary's case.

As the first day wore on, it became clear that this was not a hearing but indeed an inquest and that the Coast Guard were out for pelts. Dismally, the judge appeared to have no understanding of the realities of commercial water life, and repeatedly stopped the proceedings to question the basic nature of tugboating. As I sat watching the evident malice of the lawyers and Gary's growing frustration, I became more and more discouraged.

David, who for the entire two days was forced to sit on a bench outside the courtroom, had been recalled twice. Ostensibly, he was witness for the prosecution but gradually helped to make Gary's case, answering questions evenly and each time giving Gary an encouraging nod as he left the room. At the beginning of each day, the judge took Gary's license from him and spread it out on his desk. It sat throughout the trial in full view but tantalizingly out of Gary's reach at the judge's fingertips. Gary sat on one side of the room at a table with the lawyer, watching everyone in court and working his hands unceasingly. Now and again, he glanced at me then away. Toward the end of the second day, his patience had ebbed. Had he been on trial before the Supreme Court his nerves could not have been more frayed. These men who had obviously no notion of what it was like to cope with the physical hardship and danger of tug life, who had never lived in the position Gary had, who had never been asked to make the decisions he had been asked to make in his job, were now trying to prove he was unfit for his career and as a final blow, take away his license to practice his livelihood. Control of one of the most important aspects of his life was out of his hands. I sat wondering how we would earn our living if the worst came to pass.

Finally, the prosecution called Gary to the stand. Gary had bitten his tongue valiantly throughout the proceedings but now was hard-pressed to keep from giving the lawyers a piece of his mind. Trying to catch his eye, I willed him to stay calm. The prosecuting attorney smirked and wandered leisurely across the room to confront Gary in imitation of some celluloid trial. Seeing the belligerent determination on Gary's face, the man returned to his table to leaf through his pages of notes.

"Captain Robson, why did you neglect to post a full-time radio watch? Wasn't it negligent of you to leave the radio unattended?"

Livid, Gary rose from the chair, his hands gripping the arms.

"Listen, no one does when they're shut down. The generators were shut down and then the radios don't work. What the hell would you do?" he cried in exasperation.

"What I do is not the issue here."

"Listen, I'm a good captain. I'm not incompetent and I'm not negligent. I had the office call the dispatcher at the canal. I called the Philadelphia Coast Guard. Dammit! They all said there were no restrictions! How am I supposed to know they don't know?"

Nonplussed at his outburst, the lawyer sat for a moment, then decided he had no more questions to ask. Gary's lawyer stood and asked in a calm, mellifluous voice about his previous experience, bringing in references to his character and ability. Once Gary had returned to the table, his lawyer asked the judge to dismiss the case against him. Without hesitation, the judge refused. The lawyer pointed out the fact that the Coast Guardsman who had written the restriction order had been unable to locate the geographical environs of his restrictions on the chart. Still the judge refused to dismiss.

It was later that we were told that this judge had never ruled against the Coast Guard in a dispute. The judge announced that he was entitled to deliberate for six weeks before delivering his verdict.

The remaining ten days at home were overshadowed by the anxious waiting for the verdict. Trying to forget the worry, we had told virtually no one of the hearing or the potential devastation it represented to us and instead huddled by the fire, split wood, planned the garden, and did chores.

The deckhand was still unable to return, so I got back aboard for two more weeks in March. By that time, news of Gary's tribulations had traveled the length and breadth of the Chesapeake. Commercial water traffic is a tiny, roiling community, more like a small town, where news flashes over wires and through gossip in galleys.

We met the *Michael Keen* to make up a LASH tow and push it in tandem down the Delaware River, through the canal to Norfolk. Once we hooked up, Donald came over to visit, invited by the smell of freshly baked cookies. He had come not only to pass the time, but to pump Gary for information about the hearing and to offer moral support. All the way down the Chesapeake, familiar tugs passed, calling to ask how things had gone, wanting to know what exactly the Coast Guard wanted of everyone. Working a never-ending stream of LASH tows, we plodded up and down the bay without enthusiasm.

The weekend before we got off, we had a LASH ship to work, often a gruelling detail as the ship's crews work round the clock. LASH means lighter aboard ship, the lighter being the barge itself. A LASH ship is designed to carry eighty-eight barges. A huge gantry crane straddles the deck of the ship and creeps out over the stern to lift one barge at a time out of the water and cart it over the deck to stow it in the ship's hold.

The sight of the gantry crane overhead lowering its heavy quadrangular mounting of hydraulic lifting gear toward the barge which the tug holds against the rubber fenders at the LASH ship's stern never ceases to fascinate me. The lifting gear consists of four large cups which fit overtop the pyramid-like lifting pads on the barge's four corners. The cups, held rigidly in place by fat pipes that make a giant, rusted tinker toy on wires, descend on the barge in an ominous squealing of rusted sheaves and gears to land with a leaden clatter in place. Once the deckhands direct the placement of the barge at the stern, we clamber back on board the tug while Gary or David holds the tug steadily against it. At the last moment before the lifting cups drop into place, the tug must jump back out of the way, but a moment too soon, and the barge moves as well and must be repositioned. Invariably, the ship is docked so that its clawlike stern sticks out past the docks, making both wind and current an additional problem in maneuvering the barges into place.

Because the barges are loaded with all manner of goods for diverse ports, order of loading is important, and often we would have to spend an hour breaking a single barge out of the middle of a gang crushed into a dock's corner. The work on deck is almost nonstop, the only relief being the fifteen or twenty-minute runs between ship and dock to deliver a barge or collect another.

That weekend, Loveland had contracted to have two tugs working the ship in addition to the *Progress*. The company had

131

hired *Michael Keen* and a little twin-screw tug, which spent the better part of the operation cringing in a corner with one or another of its parts malfunctioning. While there is only one black crew on tugs that I have seen, many of the shoreside line handlers are black. This is only significant when one is confronted by the unrepentant racial prejudice on the water. While I had a tough time dealing with the remarks that would lump all black people into one category, much as all women would be lumped into another confining category, I could see instances where the prejudice was only reinforced.

Clarky and I were breaking one barge out of a group and scrounging to find enough mooring lines to secure those barges we were leaving. Finally, reduced to tying together the four- and five-foot scraps that littered the hatches, Clarky's patience had gone.

"Dammit! Where are those line handlers? There's supposed to be line handlers here with line for these things," he cried in exasperation.

As he spoke, a heavy-set black man sauntered up to the dock, hands in pockets and wearing a Cheshire cat smile.

"Where the hell you been?" Clarky demanded, his jaw stuck out in anger, and his brow beaded with sweat.

"Ah stayed home to watch the fights," the man laughed as he watched us struggling with a job he should have been doing.

"God damn son-of-a-bitch! You're supposed to be out here working!"

Unperturbed, the man dropped a line on the dock and strolled off.

"That fat-ass bastard gets sixteen dollars an hour!" Clarky informed me with venom, breaking his usual rule against swearing in front of me.

My eyes widened.

"You know what you get? About eight today since it's Sunday double-time."

The injustice of this was hard to swallow. Nevertheless, the backbreaking labor seems to go on and on. Each barge must be shuttled to the ship's stern sideways in pushing gear, making the job a tendon-wrenching, exhausting affair for the deck crew. The cables are strung out longer than usual to accommo-

132

date the sixty-foot spread of the barge. One thing that does ease the work a bit is that because they are uniform in size, the cables may be set, one dropped onto a lifting pad without adjustment and the other let out a minimum amount to diminish the strain of hauling it back in with the deck winches. Even with this shortcut, the straining and lifting quickly takes its toll.

Because there were three people needed to work the ship at any given time, one in the wheelhouse and two on deck, I usually acted as swing crew, staying up this time through Gary's watch, then through David's and again through Gary's until after thirty-eight hours of work, I had still not been to sleep. Even for those off watch, however, sleep is difficult if not impossible. The gantry crane has a fire siren on it that howls each time the crane moves, and the hydraulic lifters clang a bell as soon as they go into motion. If this cacophony is not enough to chase sleep, then the crashing and jerking of the tug as she yanks a barge free of a cluster, drags it around, backs and fills her way into position at the ship, then jumps back while the lifting gear comes smashing down will generally finish the job. What results is an unsatisfying series of cat-naps during the short runs between ship and dock.

By the time we were pushing a LASH tow north on Monday, I had decided that perhaps if Gary got into another line of work completely it would be the hand of Providence. I was not at all sure I would survive the rigors of tugboating.

133

E I G H T

I GOT HOME bone-weary and grey-faced, certain I could not endure a full-time job as cook-deckhand. The twelve-hour-plus shift, the physical hardship, the emotional strain, had all united to exhaust me. Furthermore, a love of cooking and eating had combined with a lack of exercise and willpower to add fifteen pounds to my frame, an additional burden in decking. Like it or not, I had seen firsthand evidence of the fact that a female body is not equal in strength to a male body. Although I stand three inches taller than Gary, he could toss a deck line higher and farther than I through sheer muscle. I could manage the work as well as and better than some of the men I had met—chronic drinkers whose stamina and strength had long gone, overweight, underambitious men, wraithlike boys—but when pitted against a man my age and size, the differences were sobering. Gary's insistence that I get my license and get into the wheelhouse where muscle mattered much less than skill, had begun to make more sense to me. At home, I curled into the sofa cushions and nursed my aching joints.

Then the notice came. Gary had been cleared by the Coast Guard judge! The lawyer who called to tell him the verdict announced in a tone of disbelief that it was the first time in memory that that judge had found against the Coast Guard. He had stopped just short of completely vindicating Gary and contented himself with a slap on the wrist but in no other way penalized him. Gary's vocation was intact, his record un-blemished. Likewise, his plans for me remained the same.

134

However, I spent two weeks at home in blissful ignorance of the deckhand's plans for continued recuperation. It was not until I had planted the garden, laid down the mulch, and worked nonstop on the house that the deckhand called to ask if I could go back on the tug the following morning. Despite my antipathy to the labors of washing clothes in the sink and turning over my garden by hand (Gary being averse to buying anything so newfangled as a washing machine or rototiller), I had looked forward to two weeks of working at my own schedule. Getting up after the dawn instead of in darkness, cooking for one instead of five, few dishes, and time to ride my bicycle, all had beckoned me home. With the last minute phone call, the enticements of the tug reappeared, and I could not bring myself to turn down the work.

Whatever reluctance I may have felt at returning was offset by the pure exhilaration of crew change. The tug was in the Delaware with a tow, headed eventually off the coast. We were to meet it via crew boat near Brandywine Light at midnight. After driving to where we all trooped aboard the crew boat which was used to meet ships in Bigstone Anchorage, to deliver groceries, crew, pilots, or to run errands, we all settled down to be ferried out to the *Progress*. Under a yellow-tinged moon that smiled at its brood of glittering stars, we flew out to the tug at a spectacular thirty-five knots. It felt as though we were soaring; I had never moved so fast on the water.

Once the crew boat captain spotted the *Progress*, towing a half-loaded hopper barge on the hawser, the skipper trimmed our speed to match the tug, and slid toward her. As we approached, we all came out on the deck to sort through the baggage, preparing to make the transfer. When the two vessels ran rail to rail, we began to pitch suitcases and duffle bags over the gunwales, trading our load for that on the tug's deck like jugglers throwing Indian clubs in the circus. Gary sprinted up to the wheelhouse to relieve Freddie. As Gary's bag started toward the tug, the boats took a slight jog apart, and instead of landing on the gritty deck, the bag plopped unceremoniously into the water. The heavy oilcloth resisted sinking, and it floated half out of the water, drifting aft. David raced to snatch

135

it out of the water, but missed by a frustrating inch as it danced past his outstretched fingers and headed for the bow of the barge.

The crew boat skipper dropped us back and began to chase the bag but was thwarted by its proximity to the oncoming barge. He had been forced to hang back while we watched the bag's inexorable progress to the raked bow. Certain that it would be swept under the prow, we waited. The bag contained Gary's license, wallet, binoculars, clothes, boots, glasses. At the last moment, it skittered around the side, pushed just out of reach by the small bow wave, and bounced partway along the hull of the barge where we rescued it. By this time, it was three-quarters full of water, but had floated just long enough.

It seemed a short three hours before David leaned into Gary's cabin to call me to make breakfast. Drained, I dreaded beginning the arduous routine for another two weeks.

While oddball trips seemed to be fast becoming our specialty, I think it was more perceived than real. Off-the-wall trips had begun to seem more the norm than the exception for commercial seamen in general. However, the run to Bermuda at the start of hurricane season was unquestionably out of the ordinary for a vessel like old *Progress*.

The regular run of supplies to the Naval Air Station at St. George's was usually made by a small container ship that had run into some bad luck and sunk. The company, anxious lest they lose a lucrative contract, had hired a tug and barge to fill the gap temporarily. As though by the hand of Fate, that tug had broken down and Cappy Loveland had stepped into the breach with an offer the company could not refuse. The offer included the *Progress*.

Gary and I had returned only hours before, worn from another sailing expedition, when Jerry phoned. I was making pickle.

"What equipment is *Progress* going to need for a trip to Bermuda?" he demanded without preamble.

Gary laughed, thinking the question was a joke.

"I mean it," Jerry insisted impatiently.

"Well, let's see. You'd need another license in the wheelhouse for offshore, two AB's . . . then there should be a single side band, a Loran C . . . Hmm, let me think."

"We've got all that. Dave gave me a list. I just wanted to see if you could think of anything else."

"Oh."

"Can you be in Norfolk in five hours?"

"It takes me five hours to get there and I've got a few things to do before I leave," Gary said, taken aback at the suddenness of the proposal. "It would be more like eight."

I had been listening to the conversation, dipping pickle into sterilized jars with my heart in my throat. A six-hundred-mile trip out and back at the end of August in a thirty-six-year-old tug with a single engine that had seen much better days seemed like a flirtation with suicide to me. Gary put his hand over the receiver.

"Curl won't go," he said. "Jerry wants to know if you'll come instead."

I gulped. I thought for a second about Gary's going down without me and what my life would be without him.

"If you're crazy enough to go, I'm going with you," I told him.

"She'll come," Gary said into the receiver.

He hung up, a peculiar smile over his features, a mixture of embarrassment and disbelief.

"Well, I guess we're going to Bermuda," he said, staring at me for a moment before clicking into gear.

"Yeah."

My mind churned. I was half-convinced we would go down en route. The whole thing seemed full of bad omens. Nonetheless, we began racing around the house, packing our bags, shouting instructions and questions to each other while the cat cowered under a table in the living room.

We arrived at Norfolk at midnight and drove up to the railway where *Progress* sat on the ways, looking like a beached walrus. As I climbed the ladder with my gear in tow, I wondered if I had made the right choice. Why was I going? Two young strangers met me at the top of the ladder and took my bag while introducing themselves, their bloodshot eyes scrutinizing this woman crew member.

These were the two AB's (ablebodied seamen who hold certificates to that effect) whom Jerry had hired out of the union hall. Thinking that the *Progress* in question was a twin-screw, three-thousand-horsepower tug belonging to another company as well as another era, they had signed aboard, only to find this battered old DPC atop the rickety railway in the harsh floodlights of a scroungy shipyard. Still not convinced they were staying, they were carefully sizing up each crew member as he arrived, holding in reserve the right to back out at the last minute.

David Gray, who had run for the first time as captain for the past week and a half, was in the wheelhouse, going over the charts by flashlight.

"Glad you could come, Nance," he told me amiably when I stepped through the door.

"Thanks, Dave, I am too, I think."

We had spent many enjoyable times together talking, and had developed a brother-sister relationship of sorts.

"I did the shopping so I think you'll be okay," he said, obliquely referring to my choosiness about the provisioning.

"Great. You, I trust." I smiled as I headed below to take inventory.

Once I had taken enough sausage from the freezer for breakfast, I began going through the cabinets and refrigerator. As though out of another world, a bronzed young man, naked to the waist and bedecked in a profusion of gold chains, hung in the open companionway. After gazing into my eyes with what I imagined was his version of an hypnotic stare, he smiled.

"Nancy Robson," I said, sticking out a hand.

"You the cook?" he asked lazily, running an appraising eye over my disheveled form.

"Yeah."

"You better not make anything fattening," he said patting a well-muscled belly. "My girlfriend'll be mad at you."

"Really?" Like I care.

"This is some tub!" he continued, casting his black eyes around the deckhouse.

138

Without warning, I felt a surge of motherly protectiveness. It was as though a stranger had insulted my child.

"She's done a lot of good duty," I retorted, liking him less and less.

"Well, she better keep it up is all I can say. I've worked on some of the best."

I studied him, a recent graduate of one of the academies, with little time in his life for much experience.

"You get seasick?" he wanted to know, an evil glint in his eyes. "I've got a stomach like iron."

I had heard such a boast before. Another man, a cook who had spent two days tied up beside us regaling me with his years of tribulations through storms and seas, had left and subsequently spent the next three days of running down the coast on the floor of his cabin throwing up. I looked at this tanned young man and wondered.

Harry lumbered up the deck and poked his head into the galley, graced by a smile that would have lit up Broadway. Harry Truitt is a soul all his own. After thirty years in the navy, he had retired to a fifty-acre homestead but been enticed aboard by his neighbor, Freddie Carter, who was by now Jerry's partner. Having begun as a deckhand, he had worked his way up to engineer, gradually gaining more knowledge of the engine to supplement his years of electronics experience in the navy. He and *Progress* were of the same era and for the most part, it was a happy marriage with only an occasional quarrel. Obviously delighted at our good fortune to be going to Bermuda, his old stomping ground, he was wreathed in smiles. Harry is nothing if not an enthusiastic shipmate.

"Hey, Nance. You're coming too, huh? Great! Ah, Bermuda! Where's Honch?" (his term of endearment for Gary).

"Wheelhouse, I think."

"Roge."

Harry wandered up the deck toward the wheelhouse with the mate's eyes on his broad back.

"He's something, isn't he?" he smirked.

"There's nobody like him," I scowled, packing my own groceries into the dark recesses of the refrigerator.

It was the last I saw of the mate for two days. He spent the first part of the trip alternately lying in his bunk and hanging over the side. No matter how hard I tried, I could not stifle a gleeful satisfaction.

Finally, the hoses slithered to the ground, the railway was set in motion, and *Progress* slid down the ramp, tethered to the continental U.S. by four small dock lines. By daybreak we were headed east toward Bermuda, a dot on the vast pale blue of the charts. It looked like a small target.

Despite my fear, the trip out was glorious. A following breeze nudged waves into a never-ending series of gently rolling hills that pushed us farther and farther out to sea with a tender hand. Because of the distance offshore, the watches were changed to four hours on, eight off, making meals at a far more civilized interval. I rose at seven to make breakfast, lunch was served at noon, and dinner at seven-thirty. Without the constant drudgery of LASH barges and decking, the trip seemed more like a cruise, interrupted only by the minor tasks of cooking and washing dishes.

Having borrowed Harry's sextant, Gary and David took sights as an adjunct to a quirky loran and a minimally reliable single side band radio. Deciding that this would be an ideal time to teach me celestial navigation, he had me on the landing outside the wheelhouse on the second evening out, holding the sextant as I braced myself against the rail.

"See up there?" he said, pointing into the deepening blue of the sky overhead. "That's Venus. I want you to take a sight of it."

I looked at him blankly.

"Look. It's not that hard. The main thing is to try to stay steady."

My eyebrows came up and I looked over the side at the froth that swirled along our rolling gunwales.

"Just do your best," he said in response to my apparent skepticism. "Here. Hold it like this, and then—here, give me your hand—there. Move this until you have Venus split exactly halfway by the line of the horizon. Do you see the line I mean?"

I nodded.

"Okay. Then move this gradually until you find the star and then this second adjustment gives you the fine tuning. You get it so it just touches the horizon. Then when you have it exactly where you want it, tell me, '*Mark!*' and I'll take your time for you."

Obediently, I fiddled with the instrument, finding the star as she lay in the folds of satiny azure and dragging it down to touch the horizon line of the sextant.

"Mark!"

"Do it again."

"Okay, *Mark!*"

"Now, let's try another," he said after taking his sight of Venus.

"You need a three-star cross so we'll take Jupiter, Venus, and Sirius. There. Jupiter should be about there."

He checked his star chart and then came out in the balmy breeze that swirled over the deck to stand beside me and point up at the sky. After taking his sights, he gave me the sextant so I could take mine, then took the notations over to the little piece of plywood used as a desk for the logbook and opened up the sight reduction tables. I gazed dreamily at the brightening stars and drank in the sweet salt air.

"Come here," he said, breaking into my reverie. "I want you to do your own so you can see how well you took the sights."

"What?"

"Well, how else are you going to learn?" he demanded.

It was a valid point, but I knew that inside that innocuous looking brick-colored book lurked column upon column of figures set in a thicket of decimal points. He was talking to a person whose checkbook was considered balanced if it agreed with the bank statement within fifty dollars. Reluctantly, I came across the wheelhouse to stand beside him and stare at the blur of numbers on the pages.

"Where did all these numbers come from?" I asked.

It all seemed like the conjurings of some ancient alchemist, a magical incantation that miraculously resulted in a finger pointing to the chart and saying: "You are here!" No matter what I thought of the process, once Gary had decided I

141

was going to learn something, I generally learned it.

"Nat Bowditch worked them out," he said impatiently.

"Really? With the equipment he had? That's amazing!" I burbled, still trying to postpone the inevitable.

"Yeah. Now look here. This first column is your body," he began, undeterred by my smokescreen.

My body? I thought. No, Nancy, keep quiet. He'll explain it. He didn't.

"Yeah. Now first you figure how far off the water your body is," he said, scribbling furiously.

"About eighteen feet?" I ventured.

"You don't know."

"I don't?"

"You have to go to the tables to find out."

"How do the tables know?" I demanded.

"Here. They're all worked out. Look," he pointed. "Here's the time you took and here's the mark on the sextant. Now you go through the columns to find the distance of your body off the water."

"But isn't it about eighteen feet?" I asked again, thoroughly confused as to how a book could tell me how far off the water my body was when it did not contain calculations as to the dimensions of *Progress*. For that matter, would not David's body, which was four inches taller than mine, be farther off the water? At least as far as the sight of the sextant was concerned. How could it possibly take that into account?

"Why do you keep saying eighteen feet?" Gary asked in exasperation.

"Well, just look over the side. How far does that look to you?"

"Babe, I'm not talking about *your* body. I'm talking about *the heavenly* body!" he said, looking at me as though I had left my brain at the sea buoy.

"Oh, that explains a lot," I mumbled.

While I had seen porpoises before, dodging around the tug in search of a human audience, I had never seen such a spectacular show or such a large troupe of performers as the school that

142

crossed our path on the third day out. About fifty adults, babies, and teenagers came loping toward the boat, jumping up by the galley and enjoying our excitement at the sight. Mothers and babies, swimming in easy synchronization, ran alongside, keeping pace with the lumbering tug and tow. A group of about a dozen juveniles played tag with the bow, jockeying boldly for position close enough to the bow to touch their tails to the stem. One show-off swam around the tug in circles, impatiently pushing amidst the thick group at the bow only to dart out again and jump up beside the galley door, peering into the dim interior curiously. Bolder than the rest, he soared out of the water just beside the bow to jackknife back into the crest, cutting down beside the fender. When he came up again, the spectators applauded, shouting encouragement and spurring him on to greater feats of acrobatics. Moving farther away from the tug into clear water, he surged up and executed a graceful half gainer, coming down into the waves with hardly a ripple. We yelled happily. Once again he came out of the water, this time to do a complete back flip, swinging his glistening body over in a stiff somersault before submerging again. More shouts from the gallery. Then he performed a series of comic surges, shooting out of the ocean like a missile, only to flop back down with all the grace of a big-footed clown. Guffaws from the audience. None of us had ever seen such an obvious display. Finally, having run through his repertoire, he bored of the game and after a couple of halfhearted leaps, chased off in search of new audiences to dazzle, new worlds to conquer. Soon we were alone again, accompanied only by the occasional squadrons of flying fish who took off over the crests of the waves, fluttering translucent wings in a frantic effort to escape a predator.

The evenings were magnificent. The tug was awash in the crimson glow of sunset. Soft breezes played through the open doors and portholes. Birds soared by, blinking keen eyes at the few inhabitants of this curiously isolated being. On the third night, just before change of watch, I sat in the wheelhouse with David while Gary went below for a cup of coffee. Without warning, we heard a cry. I dashed below, scanning the waters rushing by our hull for signs of a man overboard, only to be met at the galley companionway by Gary, naked to the waist and wearing a sheepish grin.

"Was that you?"

"Yeah. Come on in and have a look at this," he said, standing aside.

On the tiled deck of the galley lay a flying fish, its gills gasping wildly.

"He flew right in the door and hit me in the back. Scared me half to death," Gary laughed.

"I can imagine."

I bent down to look more closely at the fish, at the iridescent colors that still played over the slick body. Gossamer wings were folded over his spine and his black eye was fixed on us in horror.

"What do you want to do with him? Do you think he'd be any good to eat?"

"Are you planning on getting hit by about ten more of these?"

"Not enough meat, huh?"

"I'll cook him if you want to eat him, but I'd rather throw him back."

"Okay."

The two of us stood for a moment before I realized that Gary had no intention of touching the poor creature. Coming toward him slowly, crooning, I wrapped both hands around his body, trapping the wings.

"Be careful. Some fish can raise their dorsel fin to cut you," Gary said as I picked up the slimy body.

"Thanks."

Slowly, I moved toward the door, then stepped outside in order to drop him back in the water. He stayed motionless, seeming to understand I meant him no harm, until the last minute, when he lost his nerve and wriggled through my fingers. I just managed to stretch out to the rail to let him fall free of the tires, to be eaten by another predator, no doubt, but one who needed the food more than we.

144

At first, the island was a barely perceptible line glimmering on the horizon. Gradually, it swelled until it lay like a poached flounder on a platter of gelatin. As we approached Bermuda on the fifth day out, the tug came alive with our plans for a Friday night out in paradise. When we had come within range for the VHF radio, Gary hailed the agent and asked him to arrange for a pilot to meet us. Although the channel into St. George's harbor is a straightforward run, we were required to hire a pilot. The agent, after burbling something incomprehensible about wearing two hats, two hats, explained that since it was so close to sundown, we would have to wait outside the coral reefs until morning.

Crestfallen, our excited plans in pieces, we settled down to wait. Harry shut down the engine and while we drifted, we all took turns swimming off the side. Then, we puttered in lazy circles until after breakfast when the pilot finally motored out in a small skiff.

St. George's looked to me like a fairyland with its pink and white stucco houses dotted amidst a lush growth of palm and avocado trees. The harbor opened like a secluded lagoon, the blue of its waters mirroring the bright sky. The crumbled remnants of a church sat atop a hill behind St. David's almost camouflaged by the profusion of banana groves and thickets of variegated green that embraced its pale walls. On the left was the naval base, a collection of drab boxes scattered over the golf course green of the land.

We dropped the bridles, picked up the barge on the hip, and crabbed her into the dock beneath the crane. Once we had moored the barge, we tied to the cement quay and patiently awaited the British customs officials. We did not have long to wait. Two men dressed in starched white shorts and short-sleeved shirts climbed aboard, settling down in our galley after a cursory inspection of the tug.

Once past the formalities, I cooked up a buffet lunch and supper in anticipation of a night out ashore. It was not to be. The crane choked to life while the immigration and customs men were still checking our papers, and after a whirlwind grocery tour of the town, we were headed back out of the

145

harbor barely six hours later. Meanwhile, David had boarded a plane and had been replaced by a wholly inexperienced King's Point graduate who took in the wheelhouse with wide-eyed innocence.

As I stirred and sliced in the heat, slapping out the supper, I could almost taste my disappointment. Dinner that night was subdued. The night was calm, belying reports of a tropical storm blowing up in the Caribbean, and we coasted along with a gentle following breeze. Now installed in the captain's cabin together, Gary and I slept under the heated ministrations of the fan which whirred overhead. Having gone to bed at eleven, we were soundly asleep by midnight when suddenly, the two of us were jolted awake by the smell of smoke. Gary snapped on the light, and studied the fan. It turned unhampered. He went to the after port.

"I think it's coming out of the stack!" he said tersely as he yanked on pants.

He sprang out of the cabin while I dressed hurriedly and followed.

"Slow her down and head her back for Bermuda!" he told the mate as he darted past him in the dark.

I followed on his heels down the deck and was confronted with grey smoke billowing from the engine room.

"Good God!" he cried, rushing past the companionway to Harry's cabin. "Harry! Get up! I think something's on fire in the engine room!"

Coming back to the door where I waited chewing my fingers, he tried to step inside the door.

"Go tell him to take it out of gear and get me a towel. I've got to shut her down!"

Racing back up the deck, I did as instructed, and returned with two dampened towels. Harry, in shorts and shoes, stood beside Gary and took one of the towels from me. While they descended the ladder blindly, I sat on the rail and waited, my heart pounding. I knew that should the tug be afire we would have little choice but to stay and fight it. I shivered as I listened to Gary and Harry shouting at each other in the hold. The engine stopped. I counted thirty seconds before seeing them at

146

the top of the engine room landing again, spluttering and falling out of the door to gulp fresh air.

"You guys okay?" I asked, patting both slick backs as they hung over the side, gasping.

"Yeah. The engine's overheated. The place is filled with steam. We can't tell what else is going on, but it doesn't look so far as though anything's actually aflame," Gary told me between coughing fits.

One of the AB's ambled up the deck.

"When's the last time you checked those gauges?" Harry cried.

"I don't know. Not too long," he replied.

"You're suppose to go down every ten minutes, dammit!" Harry retorted.

"Where's your friend?" Gary asked.

"He's sleepin', I think."

"Nance, go count bodies. We've got to go back down and shut down that generator."

"For God's sake be careful and stick close enough to see and touch each other," I said nervously.

Partway through my flashlight bed check, the generator stopped. The tug bobbed eerily in the darkness. Footsteps now echoed through the metal decks. The sounds of water slapping the sides of the hull were audible. The tug felt dead. Visions of the *Mary Celeste** ran through my head. I saw someone atop the wheelhouse tying down temporary lights. Everyone was safe. When I came back to the engine room door, Harry and Gary sat on the waist together, talking.

"What do you guys think?" I asked.

"We can't tell anything right now," Gary said, shaking his head. "We've got to wait till the steam dissipates some so we can see what we're doing."

"All I can figure is the water pump, Honch," Harry said, returning to their conversation. "It might have a loose piece of

*The *Mary Celeste* was an old sailing ship found abandoned in a calm with meals still on the table. It floated along like a ghost ship with no apparent reason for the absence of the crew. The cause was never discovered.

147

packing in it, or a piece of metal, or something. I just wonder if it's got metal in it, where it came from. I don't know."

We floated aimlessly for twelve hours as the tropical sun streamed across a bright sky. An airless day contrasted with the latest weather report of the gathering hurricane. I sat on the rail, trailing my feet in the water while Harry and Gary periodically checked gauges and discussed possibilities for repairs, finally deciding against taking the pump apart for fear of having to repack it. There was no more packing aboard, and few replacement parts.

"What now?" I asked Gary as he passed me on his way to the wheelhouse.

"When Harry cranks her up, I'm going to try to get us back to Bermuda and get Jerry to send us another pump," he said.

"Do you think we'll make it back?"

"All we can do is try," he replied calmly.

Harry came up from his latest check.

"Well?"

"She's cooled enough to start, Honch. I'll just have to stay down and watch what she does."

"Okay, Harr. I'll go on up. Nance, go get up one of the deckhands."

I obeyed, keeping my fingers crossed that our luck would hold. First the generator roared into life. Then the tug shook as Harry cranked up the engine. Gary eased the throttle into gear and slowly moved forward, stretching out the slack hawser which had dropped beneath the glassy water. I heard the engine increase in volume as Gary edged the throttle up to half speed. When the deckhand arrived at the engine room door, I sent him below, then joined Gary in the wheelhouse. He had been trying to raise Bermuda on both the single side band and the VHF without success. We were completely isolated. Should the engine quit, we apparently had no way to contact shore, and no one would be expecting us for four more days. With each passing minute, though, I began to feel better. The fact that the engine was running, that we were closing the distance between us and Bermuda, lifted my spirits. After an hour, Harry dragged himself up the forward ladder, his naked chest and back glistening with sweat.

148

"What's she look like so far, Buddy?" Gary asked out of the open window.

"So far so good, Honch. I came up to tell you to pick her up some and I'll keep watching it."

"Okay, Harr," he responded, pushing the throttle lever down.

The tug picked up speed, increasing the size of the bone in her teeth. We all stood for a second, holding our breath. Then, after wiping his face with a bandanna, Harry turned to plod below, returning to the hundred-and-twenty-degree heat of the engine room. An hour later, we had still not raised the island, but Harry was reasonably satisfied that the engine's temperature would hold, and installed both AB's at the gauges in order to catch a nap.

It was not until we were within clear sight of Bermuda that the radio finally raised anyone, and we were ushered into the harbor in the afternoon to wait for the arrival of a new water pump. This time, we had time to play.

Two mornings later, with yet another King's Point graduate who had come to replace the chain-bedecked Adonis, we chugged out through the gap between the hills and headed for the States, all with nagging doubts about the integrity of the machinery to which we were entrusting our lives. Despite fears, the ride home was a joy. The weather held, picking up a brisk easterly breeze which pushed us back into the Chesapeake channel in four and a half days. By 0220 on the twenty-fifth of August, we steamed into Norfolk harbor, jubilant.

It was in Bermuda that I signed on *Progress* full time. Jerry had bought another tug, a sister ship to *Progress*, and was therefore shy of crew, grabbing at every warm body in sight. David was now permanent captain on the other watch with Clarky and a new mate, while Gary, Harry, the cook-turned-deckhand, and I were on the opposite crew.

I was filled with a mixture of excitement and dread. I loved the water, and I loved being with Gary and sharing our lives so completely. Additionally, I enjoyed the idea of doing something so few women have had the opportunity to do. But I was scared as well, scared of the physical danger, of the ravages of the heavy labor and the atmosphere on my body, scared of

149

being pressed into the two-week-on, two-off schedule in addition to being a fill-in. I had obligations at home. I thought of the hostility and the veiled threats I had met with on occasion. The knowledge that Gary had seen the same sort of prejudice from men who had grown up on tugs and resented his "book learnin'" did nothing to assuage my fears, but it did help to put them in perspective. At the back of my mind was the thought that I could quit if the job proved overwhelming, though Gary's disappointment in me would be acute, I knew. My folks had always told me: "All you can do is your best." This I held firmly in mind.

"You can do it!" was Gary's cheer.

NINE

JERRY BOUGHT the *Nanticoke,* another DPC of the same vintage as *Progress* which had been owned and run by a couple and their six daughters. Frank had run as captain with Debbie, his wife, as mate, and usually two or three daughters as deckhands at any given time. Tired of the nonstop drudgery of running a tug without a relief crew, they sold it to raise horses instead. While Jerry had managed to find crew for the opposite watch and enough to run the *Nanticoke* at least temporarily, he had left Gary without a mate until two days before our next trip.

Raiding the King's Point graduating class again, Jerry produced a young man whose ambitions ran to maritime law, but who needed a job to fill in the time between college and law school. While he was intelligent and pleasant, he had had virtually no experience of the water and was understandably terrified of the hulk of machinery which was now under his dubious control. Between a fear of the equipment and a vague sense of the damage he could inflict with it, he was unwilling to learn maneuvering of any kind, dragging Gary out of bed at all hours to get the tug to the dock and away again, with or without barge. Although he was happy to deck, his nervousness in the wheelhouse developed into a phobia, and he would toy endlessly with his food in order to postpone yet another six-hour stint at the helm. He was unable to bring himself to divert his attention from the helm long enough to read the chart and would keep the deckhand in the wheelhouse for the better part of the watch reading the chart for him.

The last day of the second two-week trip aboard, he ran the tug full-bore across Pooles Island Flats, despite suggestions from both me and the deckhand that he crack her back to keep the sludge from frothing over the fantail as the propeller sucked down into the mud. We finally came to a bone-jolting stop on North Point Bar just outside Baltimore Harbor. When we changed crews at midnight on the Naval Academy bulkhead in Annapolis Harbor, he solemnly shook hands all around and declared that he had enjoyed sailing with us. The next morning, he called Jerry and quit.

The November trip brought a new mate, this time a more experienced boat handler who had owned a tug in Florida until, according to his story, he had been muscled out of it by the Mafia who had used it to smuggle drugs. While he was also willing to deck, he had the disadvantage of being only about five feet, two inches tall and weighing, perhaps, a hundred and twenty pounds fully clothed. One evening as we were making up alongside a barge, he offered to go out on deck while I did the dishes, saying he needed the exercise and fresh air. Grateful for his gallantry, I washed and stacked plates, but had not finished clearing the galley before he returned, fuming, and poured out a mug of coffee.

"Are we off already?" I asked in surprise.

"Harry's doing it on his own," he growled.

"Oh."

I knew how possessive of the deck Harry could be. While he was happy to have me aboard cooking, he had difficulty with my decking beside the men, and would often take a line out of my hands to throw it himself. It was something he did out of his generation's idea of womanhood, something I understood without condoning, and although he and I got along quite well, something that had produced a certain number of tense moments between us. However, Harry's feelings about the decking encompassed more than just women, and as I watched the mate gulp coffee, scowling, I began to wonder exactly what had happened.

"I had a line in the air and he grabbed it and threw it again himself," he almost shouted, his hands waving in exasperation.

152

"Oh. He did that to me once. I wanted to hit him at the time."

"I *did* hit him but I don't think he even noticed. I told him if he had to do it all by himself I wasn't going to fight him over it."

"Just as well," I said, hoping to smooth understandably ruffled feathers. "I'm sure it's not anything personal."

"Personal, hell. He made me feel like an incompetent fool!"

"He didn't mean to," I said quietly, sitting down with a cup of coffee beside the still-angry man.

I had felt exactly the same way when Harry had snatched a line from me, one that had been thrown and was on its way to the deckhand waiting on the fantail of the tug beside us, only to recoil it and throw it himself. And yet, when I had roared up to Gary and complained in virtually the same tone this man was now using, Gary had given me the same soothing speech. It had not helped much at the time, but I had known there was no malice in it. That was just Harry's way. I knew also, that had I ever needed him, Harry would have gone to the wire for me, and that kind of love was enough to override the differences we had with one another.

Although on occasion I had felt like hauling off and punching someone, I knew that physical violence was one barrier I dared not cross. There would be no going back, and ultimately it would accomplish nothing save a fleeting release of steam. I had enough barriers that had to be crossed in order to do the job without stepping over the line between verbal and physical abuse.

One pair of Tennessee hillsmen, brothers who had sailed together until they had begun to fight so brutally that the owner of the tug was forced to separate them, had their own ideas of what my boundaries as a woman were. While I remained in my territory, the galley, they were polite, even deferential. However, once I had stepped outside my "natural" place, I was fair game, and whatever obscenities and nastiness they could conjure up was simply part of the deal. I did not belong on deck in their scheme of life, and they seemed to feel obliged to prove it to me.

One of these brothers had for some time had a large numeral thirteen tatooed on his forehead, but, out of boredom one day, burned it off with a smoldering cigarette butt while he sat in the galley. On another occasion he came to have a cup of coffee in our galley before making up a tow. His ear was swathed in a large bandage and as he lit his cigarette, he scratched it.

"What did you do to yourself?" I asked while stirring soup.

"My wife did it," he said matter-of-factly. "She thought I was running another woman and she emptied a six-gun at me. Missed mostly but she was so mad when she didn't kill me that she bit part of the lobe away."

Horrified, I ducked my head and kept stirring. I later learned that he had been sleeping with his brother's wife and when found out, had nonchalantly admitted to his adultery, declaring himself without remorse. Knowing him, I assumed he considered it his right. His brother, meanwhile, had cheerfully beaten his wife within an inch of her life before divorcing her. While those two brothers were more flamboyant than most of the men on the tugs, they were not atypical. A cousin of theirs informed Clarky one cold night while working a LASH tow that his uncle had gotten him out of the state after he had been convicted of murder. Clarky sidled up to me to relate this interesting piece of news, and the two of us spent the rest of the night side by side on our rounds.

To men like these, I was an anomaly and a threat. I had stepped over a line, disrupted the orderly chain of life, and deserved to be punished. For that reason, I carefully watched who I worked with alone and avoided them whenever possible.

In November, we had driven to Cape Charles in a cold rain to climb aboard the tug in late afternoon. A flat barge sat at a bulkhead some distance away, loaded with huge cement pillars which were bound for a construction site on the Hudson River. As I stirred the turkey tetrazzini, pouring in plenty of sherry and sour cream, I peered through the screen of grey drizzle at

154

the barge. Its cargo looked like pieces of Stonehenge. There was something thrilling about being part of the building of America's bridges and highways, shifting coal for industrial furnaces, transporting steel and stone and lumber.

The wind howled across the ocean from the northeast, with a bleak chill spray that carried hints of the Arctic. Having decided to go north via the bays rather than setting off into the teeth of an ocean storm, we plowed out the channel and turned up the Chesapeake looking at the last of a pink-grey sunset. As we cleared the channel, we were hit full force by the gale that screamed down the length of the bay, whipping its waters.

Forced to close the galley, I sat in the booth after serving supper, chin in hands, and fought the rising nausea. The combination of exhaustion, diesel smoke, and the shuddering pitch of the tug all acted on me, and as I concentrated on getting through each minute, I could feel the familiar hot then cold flash down my back and perspiration start on my forehead. My queasiness was exacerbated by the frightening sound of the metal bulkhead at my back giving with each successive wave. The old metal reeled at each blow of the waves, then sprang back to take yet another blow. The booth flexed and snapped uncomfortably, and I thought of the age of the tug. Spray spurted through the wiring in the overhead.

Struggling with my stomach, I washed the dishes, stacked them still wet into their bins, and then fought my way to my bunk. As I lay down in my clothes and pulled a blanket to my chin, I began to realize that the tug had taken on a peculiar motion, an abnormal diving to windward and a strange pause before righting herself. Having gone down the decks to discover the cause, Gary had found that one of the crew on the opposite side had bolted a rubber flap over most of the starboard scupper and now it impeded the flow of the seas off the deck, producing a swimming pool on the stern that sank her fantail too deeply into the waves.

Unable to correct the problem, Gary scurried back up the deck. I lay in bed when he jumped into my cabin just ahead of another wave and stumbled across the blackness to kiss me goodnight.

"You in here, Kiddo?" he called, his voice forcing cheerfulness.

"Yeah. Here's my hand."

After groping to my bunk, he climbed in beside me and lay down.

"You okay, Love?" I asked softly.

"Rocky," was his terse reply.

"We going to be okay?"

"Sure. Are you worried about the motion?"

"Yeah."

"Somebody's covered the starboard after scupper. There's nothing I can do about it now, but I'll keep an eye on things and we'll get the Goddam thing off in the morning."

I wrapped my arms around him and held him close, unwilling to let him leave the safety of my cabin. Once he was out the door, I would not be sure he was still aboard until morning.

"You warm enough, Babe?" he asked.

"I'm okay."

"Here," he said, reaching into the locker and pulling out several sheets. "Wrap up. Your hands are like ice."

"Thanks, Love. Listen. Hang on tight, huh?"

"You betcha!"

I could hear him grin in the dark.

"I'd better get back up. Harry's got it."

He kissed me briefly and went to the door. As he cracked it open, a gush of water lapped up over the sill and splashed down onto the cement decking. In the dim light outside the door, I could see Gary's blocky figure, head bent in concentration, waiting for a space between the waves. Without another word, he jumped over the sill and slammed the door behind him, hastily dogging it down before leaning over the side to be sick. As I listened to him heaving, hanging onto the bitts, I thought how much I admired him. He just grits his teeth and hangs on, doing his job regardless of the obstacles, his sense of humor helping to alleviate the misery.

By the time I awoke to make breakfast, we were rolling gently in the more protected waters of the upper bay. Before breakfast, Gary attacked the flap covering the scupper and, with a fierceness I had rarely seen, pounded the fasteners off.

156

The weather had moderated and we churned down the Delaware Bay and up the coast with the last warmth of the autumn sun splashed over the salt-encrusted deck. In the bright November sunshine, the streaked arms of the Statue of Liberty sparkled. We rounded Manhattan to steam up the Hudson River, cloaked now in her more subdued hues of bronze and gold, washed over with a muted vermilion. The hills looked purple in the distance. Burnished veils of vegetation covered the land, stopping only at the deep blue river. It was like an Impressionist painting, the colors all bleeding subtly one into the other.

As I kneaded bread, gazing out at the blur of colors, I thought that without having endured the first miserable day, I would never have experienced this magnificence. Puritan by nature, I believed then and now that nothing comes without payment. The discomfort and the fear were a price I was willing to pay to share this treasure. Joyfully, I drank deeply of the rich scents of autumn.

Having by now had several opportunities to taste the exhilaration of running the tug, I had slowly begun to consider sitting for my license when I had accumulated enough time aboard. Moreover, I found myself thinking for the first time like a mate when we brought a pair of hopper barges into the tiny canal known as Newtown Creek which is off of the East River. Newtown Creek actually consists of several miles of narrow waterway lined on either side by crumbling cement bulkheading, and supported in some places by the vessel moored to its side. It is a clogged marine alleyway, littered with fishing skiffs, brightly colored barges, and half-sunken day sailers. Because the turns in this canal were too short to make the barges up end to end, we had made them up side by side on our nose in pushing gear.

Gary sent me out on the bow with a hand radio to act as his bifocals. As I raced back and forth across the bows, checking on the clearance between the barges and the sides of the canal, I suddenly began to think more clearly about how the job should be approached from the wheelhouse. I found myself plotting ahead, figuring how to squeeze the two hundred and eighty feet of tow around the corners, which way to hold the rudder, how soon to begin a turn. Instead of feeling overwhelmed, I was thrilled at the idea. Gary and I worked in tandem, me on the bow, him in the wheelhouse, as he shoehorned the barges into the creek, backing and filling around the final, hairpin turn. Once we had tied them to the deserted docks and shut down, Gary came out on the barges.

"Good job," he said, patting me as he passed by, checking the lines.

Never extravagant in praise, I felt as though I had been knighted.

The mate left us that trip, moving on to a larger tug which ran closer to his home, and leaving Gary once again without a mate. It was with relief that I met the new mate on New Year's Day, 1980. Having nearly exhausted the King's Point graduating class, Jerry this time had raided another company's rolls, and hired a young man who had worked for five years in the James River and Norfolk harbor pushing sand barges. Doug Brown was a lean young man with an engaging smile and a crop of dark hair who shyly introduced himself to the motley crew who tramped aboard the tug in Norfolk. It was not until some months later that I discovered the description he had been given of the tug over the phone coincided very little with the reality of *Progress*. However, at the time, he gave little indication that it was all a shock.

Doug had spent his working life on twin-screw boats, and, after having achieved a level of mastery over that machine, was now reduced to learning the most basic maneuvers anew, much like a jet pilot learning for the first time the peculiarities of an old biplane. Gary gave him the helm, and to Doug's distress, he had trouble in simply getting the tug away from the dock. Then, once clear, he fought to get it back to the pier to his satisfaction, frustrated at the new dance steps involved in crabbing the old lady fore and aft to a dock. In addition to being faced with a new mechanism, he was confronted with the prospect of learning the waters outside the Norfolk-Richmond area, as well as having to size up a completely new crew. After shaking hands all round, we cast off.

158

Two hopper barges waited for us at a pier farther out of the harbor, and it was pelting snow mixed with sleet by the time we started to dig their lines out from under the previous week's frosting. Despite the radar's antipathy to snow, we dropped hawser bridles on the two and plowed out of the harbor. As we passed Old Point, Douglas looked wistfully at the last familiar marker he was to see for some time.

Then he was in the twilight zone. The blizzard obscured the visibility and the radar showed large blank patches while disembodied voices over the radio sounded threatening by their very unfamiliarity. Although the first run up the Chesapeake was a headache for Doug, he was loathe to admit defeat and at each watch struggled on with the charts and the equipment, dancing around the wheelhouse among the radios, radar, and chart. His first relaxed moment came at the approach to the Chesapeake and Delaware Canal when the snow cleared and the clearly etched vista of the Elk River opened into the low string of buoys that lead to the entrance of the canal. As we slid under Reedy Point Bridge at the other end of the passage, carried through by a fair current, Doug remarked that he would be fine if the snow continued to hold off. As though nature had heard him, the skies opened again, and we were encased in a white glove as we rounded the congested turn.

Traffic converged on the canal from all directions, tows and ships coursed through the waters to and from Philadelphia in an uninterrupted line. The deckhand and I took turns staying in the wheelhouse with Doug, listening for place names over the radio and matching them to the chart, helping to spot vessels. His dilemma was complicated by the fact that often tug captains will identify way points by their colloquial rather than chart names, making their whereabouts a mystery to the uninitiated.

At the end of each watch, Doug went below and collapsed into a dead sleep until he was wakened for the next bout. As we tied the two-barge tow to a dock in Philadelphia, he expressed the hope that he would have a chance to get to know the Delaware by running in it for a while. Having already seen what his hopes produced, he should not have been surprised to learn that our next tow was a run back down both bays and into the Inland Waterway to North Carolina.

The Inland Waterway is equipped with a different set of challenges which range from silted channels to bridges with all the clearance of a Playtex Living Girdle to buoys absent at strategic turns. In an effort to let Doug have as much of his watch in daylight as possible, Gary swapped watches with him, jockeying the hours around so that he got up at about eight in the evening and stood until dawn.

In making this decision, Gary had remembered our scrape caused by an absent light on a boat delivery down the waterway some years before. Without a chart of the section just before Albemarle Sound, he and I were running in the wee hours, going by a combination of his memory and flashlight. A missing light on a stake on a spit of land had nearly sent us up overtop the shore, and thoughts of stranding three hundred and ninety feet of barge on the same spit had prompted Gary's caution.

It was midmorning when we approached the Coinjock Bridge, a narrow, hapless link between two low-lying highways, which still bore the signs of its recent mugging by another tug and barge. I had brought Doug a milkshake and stood in the doorway, watching his rising agitation as we skated toward the open bridge.

"How much clearance you reckon we got?" he murmured, his eyes glued to the narrow gap.

"Chart says about seven and a half feet on either side."

Doug snorted as the cement and wood began to disappear behind the looming presence of the barge. While Doug alternately stood behind the wheel and dodged out the door to hang over the rail, I leaned out on the starboard side, watching him gingerly thread the brittle needle's eye with the blunt-nosed barge.

"How're we lookin' that side?" he called across the wheelhouse.

"Lookin' good," I said encouragingly, chewing my lip as

160

A tight fit. Photograph by the author.

the metal slid closer to the fender system, taking on a more skewed angle.

"Can you oooch her a little your way, just sort of shove the tug's fanny over?" I said, adding a little switch of my own posterior as an illustration.

His concentration on the bridge, he flung the wheel port for two swift turns, stopping it with his palm and immediately swinging it back to correct the sideways slide, handling the motion as though he were part of the tug. Despite his faltering self-confidence, I could see that he had a natural feel for the boat and, when necessary, his instinct could carry him past his inexperience. We cleared the slot without a scratch, gliding past the splintered wood with ease.

"Phew!" he exhaled, his eyes bright and a relieved smile showing even teeth.

"See? No problem!" I grinned.

Although Doug complained the whole way down that he had her on the bottom more than not, his distress was a common one, made more acute by the constantly changing channel. As the commercial traffic passed over the shoals, their propellers, thumping close to the bottom, perpetually rede-

Michael Keen pushing a light hopper barge down the Ditch to Aurora, North Carolina. Photograph by the author.

fined the lumps and holes, making each passage an adventure in Braille.

We spent two days watching steam shovels gulp bites of phosphate from the sandy acres of the plant at Aurora, and load them into a chute to pour into the hold like a fine sifting of grain. For Doug, it was two days of rest before the run back up the Ditch, this time with two hopper barges made up stern to stern. When we rounded the last turn before Norfolk harbor, scraping by the fertilizer docks past the bend at Gilmerton Bridge, Doug breathed more easily.

February was one long series of runs outside, going between Philadelphia and Norfolk by way of the coast since the entire upper bay was clogged by ice and the C&D Canal was impassable. March was worse. Although the ice had broken up by then, leaving huge icebergs floating like the lingering cubes in an old-fashioned, the winds had picked up and blustered ceaselessly, piercing the cabins with needlelike fingers and coating the inside of the wheelhouse window with frost.

We left Norfolk in a strong northerly wind that was predicted to rise to thirty knots. Loveland's largest tug and barge were coming up from Puerto Rico, loaded to the gunwales with raw sugar bound for Baltimore. The tug, *Little Dan*, was low on fuel, and, rather than chance their dredging up the sludge at the bottom of their tanks, we were assigned to relieve them of the tow and continue up the bay. The *Little Dan* turned twin screws at 1800 horsepower while the *Progress* boasted only 750 horsepower at the best of times. With a barge like the #3001, forty-three feet by three hundred and drawing eighteen feet, the *Progress* could hope to tow her at perhaps half the speed of *Little Dan*.

By the time we reached *Little Dan* and the tow off Cape Henry, the seas had been steadily rising with the winds, and it was almost too rough to make the transfer. The barge had permanent bridles to which the *Little Dan* had attached a four-hundred-foot piece of ten-inch (circumference) hawser. Then they had shackled their sixteen-hundred-foot hawser to the intermediate piece of nylon rope. When we were about forty-five minutes away, they began to take in their main hawser, stopping the four-hundred-foot piece off in order to unshackle their hawser and attach ours. The tugs were jumping wildly in a nasty chop and all hands on both tugs were turned out to help in the transfer. Doug lassoed the *Little Dan*'s quarter bitts, then he and the deckhand on *Little Dan* doubled the line, cinching the two tugs together. It was too rough to hold. The vessels crashed up and down against one another like two unbroken stallions clawing for freedom in a deafening crunching of metal and tires.

"We can't do this!" Gary shouted from the wheelhouse window. "Doug, let 'em loose! We'll have to hold on station!"

Doug and the other man fought the line free, and the two captains shifted the tugs apart a few feet, trying to hold them in place while the rest of the crews worked. Harry, the deckhand, and I were on the fantail, unshackling our bridles from the hawser thimble in preparation for handing the end of the hawser over the gap to be attached to the four-hundred-foot section of intermediate hawser.

"Get a line in the thimble, and we'll take that across!" called one of the deckhands on the *Little Dan*.

I tied a deck line into the hawser's eye and made ready to heave the deck line across. The tug jounced unpredictably.

"We can't get this shackle into this damn thimble, she's too small. You got a shackle?" another of the men cried over the din after they had tried unsuccessfully to wedge their heavy shackle through the eye in our smaller hawser.

Harry and I scrambled to the milk crate full of shackles, pawing through them with our rumps braced against the towing bitts.

"I've got one here!"

"Look out! The stopper line's slipping!" one of the men yelled.

The line which had held the intermediate hawser against their towing bitts, a makeshift rig to enable the men to unshackle their hawser and shackle in ours, had begun to give way. With the thrashing of the gear, a sudden escape could be fatal.

"We've got a shackle that'll fit. Get it in there!"

Three men pounced on the lines.

"Come on, you son of a bitch, get in there!"

"Look out! She's comin' free!"

"Get that pin in there!"

"Get me a hammer!"

"*No!* It's comin'"

"Look out!"

"I got it!"

"Here, get it wired!"

"Okay!"

One of the men stood back and released the slipping stopper line, and the others ducked out of the way. The transfer was made. Our hawser replaced theirs, and they were free to slide out from under the gear and run for cover. Once the hawser had dropped clear of the propellers, we let out more scope in order to cope with the rising weather conditions.

That done, we all scurried for the galley and a hot mug of coffee. The winds had long since passed the thirty-knot mark and continued to climb, thundering down the bay and pounding us on the nose. I had baked biscuits and potatoes, reserving a spot in the refrigerator for both them and a medicinal jug of Coca Cola. I lurched around the galley, shut tight against the seas that hammered the already dented forward deckhouse. I heard the engine slow and, after a few moments, Doug hopped into the galley, slamming the door behind him.

"Holy cow, Nance. How do you stand it in here?" he cried.

"Got no choice," I smiled wanly.

"Got any Coke?"

"Yeah. Hang on."

I poured a stream of brown cola over several ice cubes, listening to the sound of the ice crack and thinking of cool spring days in the back yard. The tug dove into another wave, sending the frying apples skittering across the stove.

"Listen, if you can't eat dinner, I have saltines in here," I said, pointing to a cabinet, "and I'm cooking potatoes and biscuits and I'll stick 'em right up here next to the Coke. Even if you're sick all night, you've got to eat something. Stuff a few of those in your pocket when you come down for a refill."

"Thanks, Mom," Doug grinned despite a grey face.

I smiled in answer, feeling increasingly nauseous, and stood behind him while he made a dash for the after ladder, ready to slam the door again. Although the rest of the crew habitually used the after ladder in rough weather, I had long ago decided to take my chances on the bow. One night, halfway through climbing to the top deck, I was flung to the quarter bitts, nearly going overboard. Better to get there in a wet heap than not get there, I had decided.

Dinner was an ordeal with the vegetables sliding across the plates and the entire contents of the galley in clattering motion. Once I had washed up and crammed everything into corners, checking the lines which held the second shelf of the refrigerator in place, I crawled to bed through the icy waters deluging the decks. Doors now dripped icicles and moved sluggishly on half-frozen hinges. A glossy layer of ice coated the inside of the doors and the heating could not cope with the penetration of sixty-five-knot winds.

The tug slogged up and down at a knot and a half. At every other wave, the propeller surged out of the water, leaving the

165

straining engine whining at the sudden exposure, only to drop it back down again into another black trough. I had seen Gary but briefly at supper during watch change when he came down for a drink of Coke and a brave kiss administered with blue lips.

Once I lay in my bunk, hearing the straining of the engine and thinking involuntarily of the last crew's close call, the engine having quit suddenly, due, they surmised, to the water in the fuel. Under normal conditions, the water stayed at the bottom of the tanks, but in this chaos, who knew what mix was going through the old engine. Did we have a hole in the bottom? If so, this pounding could only open more of a gap. Each time I heard the propeller whine out of the water, I remembered Clarky's irritated pronouncement that if she over-loaded suddenly, the engine would stall.

With the ice building up along the deckhouse, clinging to the rails in a sharp-clawed grip that fairly dragged us under, I resigned myself to dying. I knew this time Gary would not brave the bitter wind and slick deck to kiss me goodnight. For a trip to my cabin, he could easily lose his life. Having grown superstitious about asking him if we would make it, I was convinced that if I did not hear those words from him when I needed them most, we would die. My toes and fingers ached from the cold and I felt numb, unable even to pray.

For hours I lay there, listening to the ticking of the alarm clock. The tug's motion had become more and more sluggish with each passing hour. The ice was building up on the house, sending her swaying back and forth in a retarded, top-heavy roll. Lying there, cold to the bone, scared beyond reason, I wondered what it would be like to die. The cold would prob-ably numb me quickly, I thought, perhaps a wave would just suck me under and blank out consciousness. I hated the thought of not seeing Gary's face once more. Completely alone, I was unable to conjure even the Twenty-third Psalm which had carried me through so many other sleepless nights.

When the alarm went off, I was still awake and dragged my still-clothed body out of the bunk only to fall onto my knees on the slick cabin deck. The wind had stopped whistling through the gaps in the door sometime in the night but the up and down, the sickening weaving of the overloaded deckhouse had worsened. Anxious to see another human face, I tried to open the door. The dogs stuck, resisting even the kick of my booted foot. Finding a piece of pipe, I pummeled the levers open, but still the door would not move. Several kicks and punches availed me nothing and I suddenly realized why the wind had stopped coming through the gaps. There were no longer spaces. The ice had sealed everything in the night. In my mind's eye, I saw the claw marks on the cabin doors of the *Bill Mather*, that death tug that had drowned three crews, and began pounding the door with my fists.

Dammit! I am *not* going down on this thing! Shouting now, I threw my body against the door frantically, laying my shoulder into the ice-covered metal. Finally, I saw a crack of sunlight, then, redoubling my efforts, opened the door wider until it swung free and I half-fell into the water and ice of the deck. The handrail was merged with the deckhouse and I clawed my way to the galley door on my knees. Harry lurched into the galley behind me and slumped heavily into his place at the table.

"Mornin', Harr," I whispered, barely able to control my stomach.

"Mornin'," he replied, for the first time in my memory greyfaced and haggard. "And how are you this fine morning?"

"Rotten," I said, too tired to bother with bravado. "I was gonna do biscuits. I don't think I can manage sausage or bacon this morning, Harry," I apologized.

"No problem," he said, watching me stumble around in an effort to make a fresh pot of coffee.

I poured last night's grounds down the sink, then sifted some more into the strainer without bothering to measure. Filling the pot with water, I retied it to the stove and leaned back against the sink, gripping the edge for balance. After a few seconds, I went to the refrigerator, intending to retrieve a couple of rolls of refrigerator biscuits, preparing to snatch them out as soon as I popped open the door.

As I opened the latch, the tug pitched forward, sending me crashing into the table. Before I could close the door, the butter plate leapt out and glued itself to my chest. It was the last straw. Fumbling for the door, I scrambled to the side and hung

167

over the bitts being sick while Harry held onto my jacket. By the time I climbed back into the galley, I was soaked.

Determined to put at least *some* food on the table, I opened the refrigerator door again and while Harry braced himself against one side, rooted through the congealed mass at the bottom until I found the biscuits. Once I had gotten them into the oven, I went to the door to suck some air through the crack.

"Want me to cook some eggs?"

"Don't bother, Nance."

"Good. I'll do 'em if you want though, Harr. I can."

He shook his head.

"Just some coffee."

"Roge."

As I was pulling biscuits from the oven, the deckhand came in the door with Gary close on his heels.

"The hawser board's come loose," Gary gasped. "We'd better get it now. We can bring it in and thaw it out before we try to put some new strings in it."

Silently, we all skidded out the door and made our way to the fantail. Oddly, in the relative protection of the afterdeck, I felt safer, watching the stern leap and dive wildly beneath a grey sky. It took four of us to manhandle the sodden, frozen hawser board onto the deck and up into the galley to thaw. Gary took ice picks to the holes, driving the broken pieces of line out of ice-packed holes and pushing the new pieces of nylon in place.

Discovering that we were all still aboard, that we could all still work, if barely, was a tonic for me, and in spite of the fury of the storm, I knew now we would survive. We ran for cover in the Rappahannock, finally crawling into the protection of a hooked finger of the shore more than six hours later. By then, the stove pipe had backed up, filling the galley with a sticky mass of smoke and leaving me twelve hours' scrubbing to do. Nonetheless, we had made it.

When Doug came in for supper, casting his eyes around the blackened interior, he wrinkled his nose.

"I don't know, Nance. I'm not sure we get paid enough for this."

168

Above, Harry beating the ice off the bitts with a sledge hammer and, *below*, ice-encased forward ladder and deckhouse. Photographs by the author.

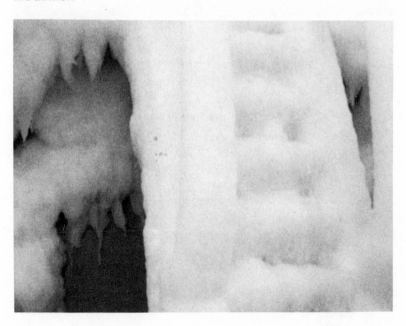

AN INDIFFERENT affection for feminist thought formulated through an innocent conviction that my only limitations were personal shortcomings had been gradually hammered into a more militant posture through the hostility and sometimes outright sabotage I had encountered over the years in "men's work." I had, before acquaintance with the world at large, dealt with a father whose faith in my capability was expressed in permission to use tools, a thirty-foot sailboat, and various vehicles at an early age. It came as a shock to recognize that others would slap limitations on me purely because of my sex. However, while I was becoming more accustomed to dealing with male prejudice, I more and more resented the energy it took to do so. It became increasingly difficult to smile blandly, restraining an acerbic remark to people like the line handler in Norfolk who watched us bring in a tow, then interrupted my swing of a line with the remark: "Your husband should keep you barefoot and pregnant." I longed to climb up on the dock and punch the guy, but instead referred him to the occupant of the wheelhouse.

However, with few exceptions, problems of this sort were restricted to people outside our immediate crew. Aboard, there was a family feeling, or an esprit de corps that bound us together despite personal differences of temperament. Harry, who did not agree with the idea of a woman decking, risking life and limb beside a man while hauling frozen lines around barges, nonetheless accepted me and offered an unflagging friendship that I have treasured over the years. The deckhand, a solitary sort whose warmth was reserved for his immediate family, rarely betrayed any personal preference one way or the other. Gary, who wanted me there, assumed that if it was okay with him, it should be okay with everyone else. It was Douglas who, rather than having to be persuaded that my presence was acceptable, seemed to look on it from the first as a pleasant novelty, one he would enjoy rather than fight.

Gary bent over backwards to keep from playing favorites with me, and he demanded the same devotion to work, regardless of the obstacles, the conditions, or the hour, that he expected of everyone else. In exchange for this, he took every opportunity to demonstrate his faith in my ability, sending me out on barges to help him dock via radio and conferring with me as an equal. Douglas handled the prejudice of outsiders in other ways.

During one afternoon of shifting LASH barges in Baltimore in order to make up a tow, a group of longshoremen who were loading some of the barges treated me to an uninterrupted libretto of obscene remarks, commenting on my parentage, probable sexual preferences, and anatomical makeup. Although I ignored them, I was nonetheless forced to work on the adjacent barges, my silence adding fuel to their banter. Fed up with the abuse, Doug several times demanded that they stop, and finally in exasperation, traded places with me, going out on the deck while I was installed at the helm. His apparent confidence in me silenced them, but often the difficulties were not so clear-cut.

In between a lunatic fringe which heartily wished me harm and those whose self-confidence produced a marked tolerance for a woman in that job fell a wide range of attitudes. When we returned from Bermuda, our crew was pared to four—Gary, a new mate whose confidence in his own ability stemmed from an apparently infinite wellspring of self-delusion, Harry, and myself. Because we were short one member, Harry and I split watches together so that I monitored the engine room and pumped up fuel in addition to cooking, and Harry cooked in addition to working in the engine room. To my surprise, I found myself as possessive of the galley as Harry was

171

of his bailiwick, giving him as little discretion at the stove as he gave me at the work bench. However, despite our jealousy of our own territories, each respected the other's conscientiousness.

The temporary mate, however, reigned in the wheelhouse with a benign neglect that defied understanding. Although he had never before been in the Chesapeake, he blithely ran the LASH tow up the bay without consulting the charts, weather reports, or crew. When I came up to warn him of an impending squall and suggest we shift position, he brushed me aside like a troublesome fly. Indignantly, I reiterated my warnings, this time less tactfully. Again he waved me away, suggesting I stir my pots. It was not until Gary burst out of his cabin and verbally laid me out that the mate realized anything was truly amiss. Gary, assuming I had been aware of the approaching squall and the necessity for repositioning the tug, was infuriated at what he considered my neglect. The mate, happy to duck responsibility, appeared unfazed by Gary's outburst, assuming it confirmed his own opinion of a woman's incompetence.

The spring thaw brought milder weather, and in May *Progress* was scooting up the coast without a tow, bound for Portland, Maine. After ducking into Buzzard's Bay out of an easterly swell, we entered the Cape Cod Canal. Recovered now from our March slog to Baltimore, Doug bubbled over with enthusiasm. Lashing his tape player to the loud hailer microphone, he played Jimmy Buffet tapes to the delighted picnickers along the high banks of the canal.

"God, Nance. Do we really get paid for this?" he crowed, prancing around the wheelhouse with a milkshake in his hand.

I grinned, enjoying his infectious high spirits and remembered his words in the shelter of the Rappahannock: "We don't get paid enough." Tugboating is a series of contrasts, a feast or famine deal. For every brilliant ride through the Cape Cod Canal, there are two drizzling days in Yonkers. For every meal of fresh-caught lobster, there are three biscuits forced down to fight nausea. If sensual experience constitutes living, this is living with a vengeance. Often, it is a clear test of plain old grit, but to those who love it, it offers up the sweet taste of survival against odds and joy in the glories of nature.

We moored to a seaweed-draped pier in Portland, scaling the pilings in the ten-foot tides to drop the loops overtop. Armed with a twenty-dollar bill and a hunger for some lobster, I wandered along the docks searching the clusters of scoop-prowed fishing boats which were laden with lobster pots. The Maine blue laws forbade lobstering on Sunday, and if there were any entrepreneurs whose proclivities ran more to the pocketbook than the conscience, they were nowhere in sight. I stumped along the deserted waterfront enjoying a crisp wind which lifted the hair on my neck and carried the sharp scents of blood-soaked fish piers and drying seaweed.

At the last pier in town, a large fishing vessel disgorged its cargo onto a conveyor belt while several booted men stood by, inspecting their catch. Squaring my shoulders, I marched down the dock to peer at the assortment of fish floating from the hold to the warehouse on the pier. One man in a ragged, navy blue sweater came over to stand beside me.

"I was looking for some lobster," I told him.

"Not today. They don't go out on Sunday."

"Oh. That's too bad. Could I buy some fish from you?"

He grinned as though at some private joke.

"See anything you like?"

"What's that?" I asked, pointing to a large silver-blue fish as it flopped up the conveyor belt, tail-first.

"Haddock. Like it?" he smiled more broadly, poking a hammy hand into the broad gills.

"Yes. It's beautiful. How much?"

I began digging in my pocket, but the man waved aside the offer of mere money for this magnificent specimen from the deep.

"Hold up your hand."

I held it up as though ready to pledge the whole truth and nothing but, and he dropped the open red gills overtop my hand, sliding the fish down until it hung there, leaking. A cold stream of blood ran down inside my shirt and soaked a dark blotch in the elbow of my sweater. It must have weighed fifteen pounds.

"It's really beautiful!" I said again. "It'll feed us all for days."

The man smiled. Some of the others in the warehouse had ceased their soft chatter and had turned to the two of us beside the conveyor belt.

"This is your livelihood. Let me pay you something for it."

"No. Nothing. You take it home and enjoy it," he assured me with a swift, dismissive wave of his hand.

"We certainly will!" I said. "Thanks very much!"

He nodded, and I could hear a gentle ripple of laughter run through the warehouse. Turning with the fish still dripping blood off my elbow, I trudged the two miles back to the tug. I wondered in passing if they had played some sort of fisherman's joke on me, if the fish was magical and would turn from devoured to devourer, or if they simply enjoyed the small things in life like the incongruous sight of someone lumbering along the waterfront carrying an unwrapped fish, like a picture of a homemaker in a far-gone era.

After chopping off head and tail, I could barely manage to wedge the fish into the oven catercorner, it was so large. Dressed in a sauce soubise and fresh parsley and lemon, we feasted on the creamy flesh for two days.

Instead of being sent south immediately, the barge was delayed, and we were able to do some work on the tug. Gary used the installation of a new main engine water pump as the excuse for a shakedown tour through some of the scores of islands that dot the chill Maine waters. Craggy lumps tufted with wild grasses and flowers, they sit cheek-by-jowl with one another like the myriad stones in a giant riverbed. As we wound slowly through the narrow cuts between them, we could see bright sprays of lilac just coming into bloom beside a weathered house or hopeful patches of rock gardens in the shelter of toolsheds and scrub pines. As we coasted along, we came upon an old man pulling lobster pots and paid the shrewd fisherman retail price for his small catch in order to feast that night.

It was during extracurricular sight-seeing tours that I most appreciated the family atmosphere aboard the tug. Gary, both from a sense of responsibility and a natural disinclination to sightsee, usually refused to walk the town with me. It was not until Harry and I had explored the hardware stores, stopping at one of the delis for lunch, and Doug and I had ransacked the gift shops for presents for Doug's girlfriend, Kathy, that he agreed to join me, and then reluctantly. Harry was a delight on these occasions; an enthusiastic explorer unable to pass up a bargain, he would often return to the tug laden with brass hurricane lamps, wooden salad bowls, and pictures in addition to the coils and springs needed for the tug. Gary's enthusiasm for shopping runs only to food in its primitive state, but his energy is inexhaustible when hunting down lobster, scraping mussels off tide-washed rocks, or shucking a five-gallon bucket of razor-edged scallops.

We changed crews in Portland at a small airport which offered little in the way of solace to a reluctant traveler. Being in the habit of anesthetizing myself before flying with several healthy Bloody Marys, I wandered into the airport bar at eight A.M., only mildly embarrassed by the hour. The bar was empty, and the breakfast counter displayed no Bloody Marys.

"Excuse me," I whispered to the woman behind the cash register. "Is there any way I could get a double Bloody Mary?"

She betrayed little surprise.

"Is it an emergency?"

"Well, uh, no, I suppose not," I stammered, taken aback at the idea of a belt at breakfast being a necessity.

Sobered, both at the notion of flying out of that small airport in full possession of my faculties and at depending on a drink to get me through something many people find pleasant, I paced. After several laps across the lobby, a man in black trousers and white shirt approached me.

"Are you the double Bloody Mary?" he asked softly.

"Yes."

"Come with me."

He led me into the bar out of view of the rest of the lobby, and mixed the drink. As he shoved it over the counter to me, he leaned across to confide: "You know, I don't like to fly either."

Ironically, each crew change after that for several months was by air.

"Someone up there wants you to learn how to do this," David had commented to me at one airport.

After a long, bumpy airplane ride to Providence, I was relieved to be back on the water and headed for Philadelphia. At first the two weeks looked to be a peregrination between Baltimore and Philadelphia with one guano-smeared barge after another. However, on the sixth day out, that changed. After leaving a barge at New York, we left Sandy Hook Entrance light tug, and headed for North Carolina.

The weather was glorious—bright, with a gentle June breeze and clear nights. The only one aboard who was less than enthusiastic about the trip was Douglas who, by this time, was totting up monthly telephone bills to Kathy in the neighborhood of two hundred and fifty dollars. They conversed on ship-to-shore radio at all hours of the day and night. The two-day run meant that we would be out of VHF range for the better part of the time, and although he agreed it would be a needed rest for his bank account, he was loathe to be incommunicado for so long.

As we wove through the waves toward Morehead City, Doug began writing Kathy a letter and sent me below for a bottle in which to post it. Amused and delighted with the romantic spirit this piece of whimsy portrayed, I washed out a ketchup bottle and returned to the wheelhouse where Doug was putting the last lines to his note.

"When's the last time you tried to call in?" I asked as he stuffed the letter, twenty-five cents in change, and a cover letter to the finder into the bottle and then heaved it over the side.

"I should do one about now," he drawled, coming back to take the microphone off its hook.

"Tug *Progress*, WB 2594, to Beaufort marine operator," he said offhandedly.

"Beaufort marine operator to tug *Progress*," a soft drawl answered. "Go ahead, *Progress*."

"Yes, ma'am. This is tug *Progress*. I'd like to make a marine call."

"*Progress*, is there a Doug Brown aboard?" she responded.

Doug and I both stared at one another for a moment before he answered.

"Yes, this is Doug Brown speaking."

"Doug, Kathy's lookin' for you," the operator said. "She wants you to call her."

Doug's face lit up, and he let go an involuntary laugh.

"Did she give a phone number, operator?"

"Yes, she did, Doug. Do you want me to try it? She gave me one for work and one for home."

"Uh, I have to call into the office first, operator," Doug said while I chuckled in the background.

"Oh. All right. What number do you want?"

After apprising the office of our continued existence, Doug placed a call to Kathy. Reluctant to leave in the middle of the story, and without a direct request from Doug, I sat in the wheelhouse sipping tea and trying to look inconspicuous. At the end of the conversation, the phone clicked over the wires as Kathy hung up and Doug hung on to sign off with the operator.

"Tug *Progress*, are you through?"

"Yes, thank you for that, operator. This is tug . . ."

"Doug, are you gonna be makin' that call to Kathy tonight through the marine operator?" she broke in sweetly.

Nonplussed, Doug grinned.

"Uh, no, operator. I'll be callin' from a land phone."

"Oh. Okay. I just wanted to be sure I'd be here at ten if you were gonna call through here. Sometimes we close up kinda early."

The two of us laughed as he signed off, and he shook his head.

"What do you think about her comin' to meet us when we get to Morehead City? Do you think Gary'd mind if she stayed on the tug?" he asked finally after I'd stopped giggling into my tea.

" I can't see why, so long as she's willing to get off whenever we have to go."

"Okay!"

What he did not say then was that Kathy's VW was unroadworthy for any but the most favorable road conditions. Leaving in the dead of night would have been an impossibility. We logged in the dock at Morehead City at 1445 on the twenty-ninth of May. One of Loveland's barge-chasers met us and directed us to a fuel dock. From there, we all sprang into action. Gary went grocery shopping with me, Doug dashed to the telephone to call Kathy, and the deckhand and Harry loaded fuel.

Once we had lugged fourteen bags of groceries over the docks, we found that Douglas had indeed persuaded Kathy to drive the two and a half hours from Hatteras in her beat-up VW as soon as she got off work. Meanwhile, Fred, the bargeman, took Gary, Doug, and me to have a look at the load we were to take to New Orleans.

After one glance, Doug muttered from the back seat: "I wouldn't give you two cents for that tow."

Fred only grinned. At the dock sat what looked like a three-story condominium welded to a flat barge. Its upper story overhung the barge by a good ten feet, making the tow appear ominously top-heavy.

"What is that thing?" I asked.

"It's the superstructure of a seagoing dredge," Fred chuckled.

"Can that get through the bridge?" Gary asked skeptically, referring to the narrow drawbridge across the harbor.

"According to specifications, she can get through," Fred replied. "We've got the *Evelyn Doris* coming to help you."

"Good."

We sat for a moment, staring at the tow, later to be compared to a giant typewriter as she scudded behind us on the long pull across the Gulf.

While Kathy and I stood beside Fred on the dock watching the tow squeeze through the drawbridge, and listening to the nervous banter back and forth between Gary and the other captain, I decided that if they indeed made it through the bridge, the rest of the trip would be easy. Late that afternoon we cast off, easing the cumbersome tow into the channel while Kathy stood on the dock. A slim figure with dark, waist-length hair lifting on a warm breeze, she had one hand poised wistfully in the air as we ebbed away. It had been a bitter pill for her to watch Doug sail off on an adventure she would have gratefully shared.

178

The weather was clear and warm with a steady easterly pushing us sideways and lifting the hull of the tow with each rolling wave. When I took a milkshake up to Doug one afternoon, he expressed a qualm I had dared not voice as I peered out at the large slice of daylight visible under the hull of the barge.

"She sure looks easy to dump, doesn't she?"

"What would happen, Doug?"

"Well, it wouldn't be bad here. There's enough hawser out that it would just be like dropping anchor and we could act as mooring buoy until they could raise her, but the Gulf is different."

"Do you think it would pull us under?"

"Yeah. I reckon so. You know where the ax is, don't ya?" he grinned.

"Yeah," I murmured, wondering whether, spurred by fear's adrenalin, I could chop the thick nylon hawser in two before the tow could pull us down.

Doug by now was convinced that Gary was a crazy man, willing to take anything anywhere. I had seen Gary refuse only one tow, and that one because the vessel was not only not seaworthy in his estimation, but because it contained a repair crew who lived aboard and who would have worked at welding jobs while we towed. The responsibility was more than he was willing to undertake. Otherwise, he looked at each new adventure as a welcome test.

When we turned the tip of Florida and ran before an already hot wind, the tug became almost unbearable. The deckhand rigged up a hammock on the afterdeck in which he slept to escape the sweltering heat of his cabin, and Doug had taken to dragging his mattress out of his room directly behind the galley stove, and laying it over the collection of LASH straps on the top deck. The rest of us suffered in our cabins.

Crew change day was nearing, and by Gary's calculations, we would be changing at Key West. Late in the evening after passing Miami, he tried to call into the office, apprising them of our location and his speculations as to the best place to change crew. He had a suspicion that the exhange would be delayed.

The flood of Cuban refugees had reached its peak, with boat loads of the released occupants of Castro's prisons clogging the waters along with countless families looking for a better life.

Having kept close tabs on the worsening situation, Gary had learned that the government had placed people in his position in a Catch 22 situation. By the law of the sea, a captain must aid any vessel in distress, as many of these were, to the point where it endangers the lives of his own crew. However, by edict, any captain caught bringing in Cuban refugees, for whatever reason, would have his vessel and license seized. Understandably, Gary wished to avoid any contact.

It took almost an hour to pierce the haze of telephone conversation on the wires and make his connection with Loveland's office. Their verdict was that, rather than risk navigating the small harbor with our oversized tow and inviting damage, not to mention the possibility of encountering a half-sunken vessel loaded to the gunwales with refugees, we should keep going. Harry and I had been sitting in the wheelhouse with Gary, listening to the pronouncement, and disappointedly realized we would be subjected to the inescapable heat for another five days. We had little time to complain before the marine operator hailed us.

"Tug *Progress*, you have a call on channel twenty-six."

Gary turned the dial to answer.

"Maybe they changed their minds," Harry brightened.

"Tug *Progress* standing by for a call," Gary said into the microphone.

"Yes, is this tug *Progress* WB 2594?" the operator asked.

"Roger, WB 2594."

"Stand by, Captain, we have a telephone call for Doug."

"Nance, go out and wake Doug up quick!"

Tripping over the layers of plywood and sheet metal stacked on the afterdeck, I came out to Doug who was sprawled out on his bare mattress in swimming trunks. The roar of the engine through the stack almost drowned my shouts.

"Doug! Douglas! Wake up! A phone call for you!" I screamed above the rattling din.

Having thrashed in the heat until the sun had gone down after eight o'clock, he raised his head dazedly and mumbled.

180

"Doug!" I shouted, coming closer to his ear.

"What? Are we goin' down?" he asked, propping himself on his elbows to look around.

"No! You've got a radio call!"

"Oh, no!" he cried, springing up from the mattress.

I came back into the wheelhouse to hear Gary confirming that Doug was ready to take the call. When Doug stumbled into the wheelhouse, Gary handed him the mike.

"I don't know what it is," he said.

"Yeah, this is Doug Brown," Doug muttered groggily.

"Doug? Is that you?" Kathy's voice filtered into the wheelhouse.

"Yeah. What is it?" Doug asked, rubbing his face to restore the feeling.

"Oh, Hayell!" she moaned. "You're not on watch now, are you? Did they wake you up?"

"Yeah, Kathy. What is it?"

"Oh, Doug, I didn't want them to wake you up," she said in dismay. "I just wanted to give Gary a message for you before you got out of range."

"Well, I'm here now, what is it?" he asked gently.

"I just wanted to tell you something."

"Okay, Honey. What is it?"

"I just wanted to tell you that I love you!" she burst out.

Doug blushed mightily while Gary and Harry barely suppressed guffaws.

"Is that Gary laughing?" she wanted to know.

"Yeah," Doug chuckled good-naturedly.

By this time, the three of us were struggling to keep from dissolving into hysterics.

"It's okay, Kathy," Doug assured her, a smile on his face.

"Oh, Hayell!" she cried. "Is he laughin' at me? Tell him to quit laughin'."

Doug chuckled with the rest of us, not having the heart to tell her that the only one to have missed the conversation for fifty miles was the deckhand asleep below.

"It's okay, Kathy. I love you too. Is there anything else?"

"No, I just wanted Gary to tell you that I love you," she repeated miserably.

"Okay. I'll call you as soon as I can," he promised before signing off.

Harry stared tactfully at the stars, pointing out the bright ones. Doug waited to hear the operator terminate the connection.

"Doug?" a soft voice came on the line.

In the background, laughter could be heard.

"Are you and Kathy finished?" she sniggered.

"Tug *Progress* finished with that call, thank you, operator," he replied before tromping back to his lumpy mattress.

Once resigned to the disappointment of the postponed crew change, we struck out across the Gulf with a certain relaxed inevitability. While we had passed several small boats loaded well past capacity with Cuban refugees, some of them holding fishing lines as they drifted toward the shores of the United States, we skated by without incident.

The Gulf of Mexico looked like a big pond, an uninterrupted pool of blue whose flat surface was broken only by a leaping fish or a school of porpoise. The porpoise, particularly, were like visitors from another world, tamed by their contact with the vessels which ply the Gulf waters regularly. They invariably searched out the human occupants, circling the tug until they found a live audience, then performing lazily while they studied these poor landbound creatures. Our habits seemed to fascinate them, and often while I was cooking, they would rise and dip beside the galley door, peeking into the shaded recesses at the gangly being who moved so awkwardly on two legs while they, with gleaming grace, moved fluidly from one game to the next.

The birds likewise seemed interested in contact with humans, stopping not only for an occasional morsel of bread but for the edification of acquaintance with an alien habitat and creature. As I kneaded bread one sticky afternoon, a small bird, no larger than a mouse, flew in the open companionway and lighted on the table within easy reach. He stood with little feet splayed apart, balancing against the tug's gentle roll, and watched, cocking his head to see better what this peculiar process would eventually produce. When I pulled a scrap from the dough and pushed it toward his nose with one finger, he

182

snatched it eagerly in his beak but spit it out almost immediately with a look of unfathomable perplexity. I could imagine his wondering: "Bugs, Woman, do you really eat this stuff?"

Despite our culinary differences, he decided to stay, flitting to the ledge of a porthole to watch our comings and goings. During lunch, he leaned out over the rim of the port, inspecting the plates of sandwiches, and listening to our conversation. He appeared to be more interested than fearful and left only after he had spent sufficient time for an accurate report to his clan.

For four and a half days, the Gulf was still, the tug a noisy, incongruous intruder in this pristine scene of sea and sky. Despite the ease of the crossing, it was not without a sense of relief that we spotted the South Pass of the Mississippi. Loveland had hired a small local tug to assist us upriver, guiding Gary and Doug through the complex etiquette of river traffic. The tug was manned by a Cajun captain who spoke in the soft, nearly indiscernible patois of the bayous, and a nearly bald, white-haired wizened cook who pitched lines onto the flat deck while we tied them to the barge's side. We made up along the starboard side, sandwiching the huge tow between the two tugs and then made for the bottleneck of the South Pass.

In this region, not only is the language on the radio a combination of French, mulched with a Brooklynese richly slathered with Deep South, but the dance steps between the vessels are done to a completely different tune. Instead of holding to one or the other side of the channel, upriver traffic runs from point to point, keeping tight to the bends while the down-bound traffic swoops out into the curves, carried by the racing current. As if that were not enough confusion, the signals for overtaking vessels and meeting vessels are exactly the opposite to what we were accustomed to in what now appeared to be the sedate North.

In the late afternoon as we threaded our way through the bayous and reeds, I brought Doug a milkshake and sat in the wheelhouse for a few moments. The river ahead seemed to narrow conspicuously and I could see the prow of a large ship peeking out from behind a clump of trees.

"Douglas, are we gonna be okay with that guy?" I asked

after waiting as long as I could for the situation to resolve itself.

"I sure hope so, Nance. It's gonna be close," he replied with more agitation than his manner had betrayed. "He says he wants to pass on one whistle and I just don't see how he's gonna make it."

I looked again at the ship's growing size, the lines mildly blurred without my glasses, and thought that Douglas was taking the crisis rather well. The ship could easily plow us under without leaving so much as a trace.

"Uh, do you think maybe we should move over?"

"I asked him a couple of times, and I asked if he was sure he wanted to see us on one whistle, and he keeps sayin' yes."

"There's not enough room between us and the bank for him to pass, is there?" I asked a bit nervously.

"I don't see how, but he's committed now," Doug shook his head.

I chewed my nails and thought of the high accident rate on the Mississippi where barges, casually moored, sometimes broke loose in the current and ran down unwary pleasure craft, and where the ships occasionally ran over crew boats on their way from the oil fields.

"Are we gonna be okay?" I asked finally.

"Yeah, we should be okay, but I wonder if he's gonna be up on the bank," Doug murmured, glancing out of the window.

Suddenly suspicious, I followed his gaze.

"What are you looking at?"

"The guy comin' up on us on two whistles instead of one," he replied, pointing.

I peered out of the window aft, and saw a tug pushing a tow with a curled bow wave as she skidded by our assist tug with little more than ten feet to spare.

"God! I thought you were talking about that ship up there!" I said, pointing out the forward window.

Doug laughed.

"Put your specs on, Nance. He's docked. You can just see the dock comin' out now."

"Oh."

It made me question whether or not I could handle the wheelhouse. Perception was everything. Then I remembered

184

the story Gary had told me of the pilot who had followed what he thought was a string of buoys and, instead, crashed into a bridge, having been following the headlights of the cars.

Sleep was impossible in that heat. Once we had turned into the pass, the mosquitoes, untamed ancestors of the domestic variety that had plagued us in the Ditch, gnawed at us through sheets, clothes, and hair. Having baked breads and pies and made casseroles, I shut off the oven, determined to serve up nothing but cold meals for the duration. After removing a tin of muffins, I wandered up to the wheelhouse for a moment to get a breath of air and sat dripping perspiration onto the cement deck.

"Nance, why don't you go on over next door and sit in their galley awhile. They're air-conditioned," Doug told me. "I slept there."

"No kidding? They didn't mind?"

"No, they were real nice about it. It sure felt good, I can tell ya."

I thought a minute. Aside from Doug's ability to charm people with his natural southern friendliness, I wondered if their reaction to a woman might be quite different from their reaction to a man.

"Do you think it would be okay for me to go over alone?" I asked, knowing he would understand the implication of my question.

"Yeah, I think so. Go on over and introduce yourself to the captain and see what you think. He's real friendly. I couldn't understand half of what he said, but he smiles a lot," he grinned.

"Okay. Sounds good."

After washing my face and running a comb through my hair, I strolled across the barge with a half-dozen blueberry muffins as an offering. As I cracked open the galley door, a rush of cold air hit me. Although no one was inside, I stepped in, shut the door behind me, and sat down for a second. The sudden contrast between the sweltering outdoors and the chill galley raised goosebumps on my wet arms. My shirt clung. The deckhand stepped out of the passageway and closed the door behind him, exhibiting no surprise at my presence.

"Hi! Come to visit?" he smiled, his bright blue eyes twinkling.

"Yeah, if it's okay with you. I just wanted to cool off for a bit."

"Sure. Here, let me get you some coffee."

"Thanks. I brought you some blueberry muffins."

"Boy, I love blueberry. My favorite. Name's Red," he told me, pulling a warm muffin from under the napkins as he sat down.

I refrained from glancing at the snowy fringes of hair left on a head roasted pink in the Louisiana sun.

"Nancy Robson," I replied and stuck out a hand.

"Pleased to meet ya," he said, shaking my hand vigorously. "You don't meet many ladies on tugs."

"No, I guess not. I thought I might see one or two down here with the tradition of women on riverboats and all."

"I don't know nuthin' 'bout that, but I ain't seen any wimmen out here. You like tugboatin'?"

"Some days more than others but on the whole, yeah. A lot," I returned his grin. "I came because my husband wanted me to be with him and I got to enjoy it."

"Who's yer husband?"

"The blond man with the beard."

"Little guy? He's captain?"

"That's him."

"Oh. He likes you out with him, huh?"

"Seems to. You wouldn't want your wife with you?" I grinned.

"Hell, I ain't got no wife. Not no more. I can't live wif nobody. Been married five times in my life and I'm fifty. Five times in thirty-five years," he mused, taking a gulp of coffee.

This worn-out gnome was only fifty? Stunned, I looked at him again. He appeared to be at least seventy. His blue eyes were lodged in a face of pink wrinkles that looked like an unmade bed, and he walked in a stooped crawl. What would I look like in twenty more years of this?

"You're not married anymore, huh?"

"Naw. Dey none of 'em could stick to me," he shook his head. "Now I live in de bayou and fish off ma porch. Dat's all ah do except come out here. No woman wants to live in a shack in de bayou wif me. You ever been divorced?"

I shook my head.

"You like bein' married?" he wanted to know, leaning forward to better hear my answer.

"I like being married to him. He's pretty tough, but I like him."

"Dat's good. Dat's good," he decided.

"I've got to get back and finish my chores," I said finally. "You want to come to supper? We've got plenty."

"You kiddin'? An' leave dis air-conditionin'? No thanks."

"Well, the offer's still good if you change your mind," I laughed at his bluntness.

Stepping out on deck was like immersion in a sauna. That night was one long nightmare of swatting mosquitoes, packing, and scrubbing. It was the first time that I looked forward to a ride on an air-conditioned plane.

IT WAS NOT without a sense of loss and regret that Gary and I decided to leave old *Progress,* a decision made more difficult by the fact that we were fully aware the rapport we all shared aboard was rare. However, one thing that tipped the balance was the age of the tug coupled with the trips she had been called on to make. Several, the Bermuda trip included, could easily have been much more hair-raising or even final given a slight change in weather. When we saw the damage she had sustained on the return across the Gulf from New Orleans, we began to think we were tempting the fates too much.

During a brutal pounding in a northeast storm, her forward house had been badly crushed with the result, we felt, that the integrity of the vessel had been seriously compromised. Perhaps she would carry on the same way for ten or more years; perhaps she would hit an unlucky storm the next time around Hatteras and go down without a trace. There was no way to foretell.

Additionally, Gary felt that he could further his career in another job. He wanted to upgrade his license, an effort which would offer him no advancement aboard *Progress,* and he wanted to work some larger tugs. Finally, he had decided it was time for me to stop decking.

With more than his usual bluntness, he informed me that the job had aged me fifteen years. I thought of Red in the bayous of Louisiana. I looked at my permanently grime-seamed hands, the nails broken and the skin around them split and raw.

Studying the grey lines on my face, and the grey in my hair, I realized that Gary had spoken the truth. I had added at least twenty pounds to my frame, and indeed felt old. Despite a nagging fear of a life without the adventure we had shared aboard *Progress*, I agreed. Gary gave Jerry a month's notice in the beginning of September.

Coincidentally, Harry did the same. During the past several months, the continual battle against the demise of aging machinery had sapped Harry's enthusiasm for the job, and he had been talking more and more of going ashore full time to his wife Betty, and their fifty acres in Delaware.

Our last run on the *Progress* was a steady shuttle between Savannah, Georgia, and West Palm Beach, Florida, with the #3001. Free of ice now, and tied to a dock in West Palm Beach where she was taking on raw sugar, she looked innocent enough, nothing like the crystal palace that had threatened to anchor us all in the lower Chesapeake the previous March.

We had boarded yet another plane and arrived in Florida on a sweltering day. Because the loading required constant shifting of the barge under a fixed chute, David had stayed

Loading the #3001 at West Palm Beach, *Progress* in the foreground. Photograph by Douglas M. Brown.

behind in the wheelhouse until Gary climbed the ladder to relieve him, staying only long enough after our arrival to pull a shirt over a back glistening with perspiration, and to express regret at our decision to resign. The rest of us made languorous preparations to leave. That evening, as the sun splattered brilliant shades of orange and crimson over a clear sky, we picked up the #3001's pennant, a chain bridle which was fixed to either side of the barge's bow. Once it was shackled to our hawser, we cast off from the dock.

The little inlet at West Palm Beach is cozy, to say the least. It is coronary material, to say the most. Million-dollar homes sprawl along shores which encroach on what little harbor space there is. These houses sit primly on their verdant bibs of lawn, daring a five-thousand-ton barge to plow through their living rooms. Pleasure boaters, many feeling the effects of numerous tropical punches quaffed in sun and fun, thread their unpredictable ways through the middle of the narrow channel, darting in and out like so many moths at a flame. There was little to be done save blow the horn and pray.

Loveland had hired an assist tug whose small wheelhouse peered over the barge's hatches, looking like a duck peeping over an enormous lily pad. Gary's immediate concern was to retain control of the barge which had begun to slew around awkwardly in the eddying currents of the inlet, despite the efforts of the other tug to hold it steady. The barge followed badly, like a skittish colt, forcing Gary to crab the tow out. Unfortunately, in that crammed piece of waterway, our path looked as erratic as some of the waterskiers, alternating between yanking the barge away from the riprap along the southern shore and short bursts of throttle which steadied the tug up in an easterly direction. To those who sipped cocktails in their air-conditioned living rooms only a hundred yards from where Gary struggled for control of the beast, it must have looked as though we were being overtaken by Moby Dick.

"Your ol' man's crazy, Nance," Doug said to me as we watched him dance between the windows and the wheel. "I'm glad he's at the helm, not me."

As soon as the tug had cleared the jetties, the Gulf Stream, which runs by the mouth of the inlet, took her north, skewing her sideways to the tow. Gary pushed the throttle down hard, fighting to keep her off the beach where hundreds of people still sunbathed in the setting sun. Finally, she was safely past the congested channel and the assist tug was turned back into the inlet.

With the barge loaded to eighteen feet of draft, our only hope of making any way was to stay inside the Gulf Stream until the last possible minute when we would angle off toward Savannah. The Gulf Stream announces itself with a fanfare of aquamarine, a sharp contrast to the deep, clear azure of the southern ocean waters, and adds about three knots to a northward journey. Without the extra push of the current, our speed would have been halved.

We let the hawser out, then settled down to watch the last glow behind scores of pastel-colored mansions lining the Florida beach which differed so markedly from our grubby, inelegant existence. After three and a half days, we entered the Savannah River at dawn.

Once past the jetties, the channel winds through the grassy fens where clouds of mosquitoes turn out to welcome all available flesh. As we rounded the final turn, the town suddenly appeared, a surprise of renovated colonial shops and warehouses planted firmly on the swamp. Having combined the best of the eighteenth and twentieth centuries, the waterfront presented a face worn with the character lines of age, yet still vigorous. From the muddy eastern end of the waterfront where a group of tugs lay tied to a crumbling quay, a new cement bulkhead sprang up, a bulwark between the freshly bricked parks of civilization and the ancient river. Then, as suddenly as we had come upon it, we were past the row of restaurants and shops, and back to the workaday world of rusting covered sheds where lived hulks or half-mended ships, barges rammed onto the banks of the opposite shore, and bare-metal tugs in the process of construction. Pipes and grime and heavy equipment littered shipyards along the shore. A welding torch flashed.

Farther upriver, man's encroachments dwindled, and opposite the sugar refinery was a lagoon where overhanging trees sheltered families of ducks and fish flapped out of the water

191

chasing flies. The refinery squatted at the far end of a vast parking lot, and on a bulkheaded quay sat a crane, dangling its clawed bucket over the barge as we pushed her to the dock. Unlike West Palm where the barge had to be shifted under a stationary loading chute, here, the barge remained stationary while the crane trundled back and forth, chewing the cargo from her holds. Therefore, the tug was released from duty for the thirty hours of off-loading.

Savoring our unexpected freedom, we headed back down-river to dock at the waterfront where women in freshly ironed sundresses strolled arm in arm with their beaux. We tied the disheveled *Progress* to the dapper brick bulkhead, determined to enjoy our last time together.

Douglas, who regretted our parting, was also mildly spooked at the idea that it was simultaneously to be the last trip for three of us. Worried that the fates would take grim delight in scuttling our plans, he made a halfhearted attempt to dissuade us from going.

"At least get off one at a time!" he pleaded.

His anxiety notwithstanding, the return trip to West Palm Beach was glorious as we scooted along the shore. However, the sustained good weather only served to convince Doug that Mother Nature had a particularly nasty surprise in store, and in spite of soft breezes and the occasional visits of porpoise and birds, he continued to chew his nails.

As the *Progress*'s wheelhouse is too low to see over the light barge which loomed like the Chase Manhattan Bank before us once we were made up alongside, we towed the barge in with the aid of the same assist tug. The tug had collected Doug and put him up on the barge to catch lines and hand others down to us. Once inside the turning basin, we broke around and made up heads and tails to the port bow of the barge and the two small tugs put her to the dock.

As we prepared to take the barge out again, a delegation of two from the local pilot's association arrived. They insisted that Gary was obligated to take a pilot with such a large tow. Gary smiled at them and excused himself to look up the rules and call the Coast Guard. Returning, he told them he was in no way obligated. Degree of danger of the cargo, not the size of the

Leaving the Savannah River with the tow. Photograph by Douglas M. Brown.

barge, was the determining factor. They cajoled. They threatened. Gary phoned Loveland to have him double-check. Under the law, he was not required to take a pilot.

The two men stood on the dock, their threats ignored, while we eased the loaded barge away from the dock and dragged her back toward the inlet with the assist tug made up behind.

"You'd better not make 'em too mad," Doug advised, looking back at the angry faces on the edge of the bulkhead. "We've got to get back in here."

Gary chuckled devilishly.

"Not me. At least not for a couple of months. If they can prove it's the law, they can come next time. They just thought they'd pick up an extra fee. Business must be slow."

Doug glanced back at the barge as she slewed sideways in the current, surrounded by the fragile figures of speedboats and daysailers.

"Better not make any mistakes."

"You're right there, Buddy," Gary replied cheerfully, clearly exhilarated by the challenge. "How does she look?"

"She's close, Gary," Doug replied, staring as the barge narrowed on the riprap by a pillared home. "Let me go out back and see."

He trotted along the top deck to stand at the after controls, calling his perceptions forward to Gary who darted around the wheelhouse. I could see Doug felt we were just asking for trouble.

Although we were treated to a variety of oaths from the pleasure craft, we cleared the last fisherman on the jetties without incident. Some months later, another tug with the same barge would not be so lucky. Inwardly, I drew a breath, assuming that if the pilot's association did make trouble, their case would be considerably less credible with Gary's successful departure. The late afternoon sun gleamed over the water and beat down onto the hot metal decks. Our sunburned skin smelled like old leather. We had slowed to let out the hawser, and the entire crew was scattered about the fantail. Harry sat on the waist, gazing off toward the shore wistfully. The deckhand and I stood behind the towing bitts on the port side, bathed in the setting sun while Gary leaned over the upper rail at the control station. Doug had come back out of the wheelhouse to stand beside Gary.

Mark, the deckhand, waited for Gary's order to cast off the wraps of hawser from the towing bitts.

"Okay!" Gary shouted from the upper deck.

"Hang on just a sec, Mark. Let me get across into the shade," I said, touching his arm to be sure he heard me.

"Sure."

"Hey! What the hell do you think you're doing, Woman! Get the hell out of there!" Gary cried, not having heard me speak to Mark.

Assuming I had thoughtlessly chosen one of the most dangerous moments to cross the deck, he let fly at me with a stream of epithets seldom heard from him. Startled at his vehemence, the others could not decide whether to come to my rescue then or try to comfort me later. Everyone fell silent on the afterdeck.

"Kinda rough on ya, wasn't he?" Mark said quietly after we had let out the hawser and secured the hawser board. "I heard you. I wasn't going to let it off until you got clear."

194

"I know. It's okay," I replied, mildly surprised at my own calm. "He's only like that with me when he's worried. He was afraid I'd done it without thinking and would get hurt."

At the bottom of his explosion, I suspected, was as much apprehension at leaving familiar surroundings and faces, as fear for my safety on this final trip. When I stepped into the wheelhouse, he was primed for another salvo.

"Haven't you got more sense than that?" he cried.

"Gary, I asked Mark to hold it for a second so I could get across. I wouldn't do that without saying something. You just couldn't hear it from where you were. Give me a little credit."

Defused, he came over to put an arm around me.

"I worry about your getting hurt," he said finally.

"I know."

Although we had set out in fair weather, it quickly deteriorated into a northeaster. Grey clouds of misty rain enveloped us and a steady wind, blown down from the Hebrides, produced a jolting, broad roll. Doug had watched the storm clouds gather with a conviction that they were a forecast of doom, plodding up to the wheelhouse each time with all the enthusiasm of a man climbing the last steps to the gallows. By the third day, the seas had increased so that every chore was an effort. Simply staying in a seat was a strain.

I plopped myself in the wheelhouse chair while the chicken Francine and muffins browned below, and peered over Doug's shoulder to the blurred horizon. All the windows were open, despite a constant drizzle, and Doug braced himself against the wheel, staring out grimly. The chair had been lashed to the radiator with a piece of nylon line, but every now and again, a lurch sent me grappling for an additional handhold.

"I wish you guys weren't gettin' off," Doug muttered after a silence.

"I kinda wish we weren't too," I said.

"No, I mean, I wish all three of you weren't gettin' off together," he insisted, glancing at me. "Aren't you afraid we'll go down just because it's your last trip?"

"I hadn't really thought about it," I lied.

"This weather wasn't predicted like this," he continued.

195

"It was supposed to be one rainy day and then turn good again."

I looked at him, his profile turned toward me. He was genuinely unhappy. Loath to admit my own irrational superstitions, I thought suddenly of the foreman on the last LASH ship we had worked who had made a special visit to our galley to inform everyone that there was a dead man aboard the ship.

"No one will blame you if you don't want to work until his body's taken off," he had said.

At the time, I had been more jolted by his assumption that it would make a difference. Now, I would have been less sanquine.

"Doug," I began rationally, "this is a nor'easter. They always last three days. The weatherman should know that, but even if he doesn't, you do. Besides, if we survived that trip up the bay last March, we sure as hell are going to make this one. Gary's just got luck. I'd count on his luck any day."

"Yeah?" he said, turning to study me for a chink in my armor.

"Yeah. I'm honestly not worried," I said, feeling more convinced as I went along. "It's the plane ride home that's got me spooked."

He grinned.

"Okay, Ma."

Returning his smile, I remembered autumn evenings in my youth coming in from a day-long sail chilled to the bone to sip homemade soup by the fire. With that memory, I could only look on a northeaster as a friend. Just above the wheelhouse window, I saw Mark's shaggy head at the top of the ladder. As he came around the deck, the tug fell into a wave. The lashing which held the chair snapped. The chair pitched toward the open door, while I fell, grabbing for a hold. The tug careened wildly onto her side and as I fell, I looked over the rail to see the murky ocean coming toward me. Mark stepped into the space, only to be hit by my body, wrapped around the chair, and the plywood chart table which I had snatched on my way out the door. As he fell back against the rail, the tug began to come back up again, and he stood me on my feet. Then he helped me jam the chart board back in its chocks, and retie the chair. Doug looked at us balefully.

196

"You okay?"

"Yeah. I'm fine," I said, profoundly grateful that Mark had chosen that moment to block that door.

"Good luck, huh?" Doug asked.

"I didn't go over, did I? Thanks a million, Mark."

"No charge," he smiled.

We were lumbering up and down the waves like a clumsy albatross looking for a place to light. At sea, the relationships between human and beast alter. Out of control of his environment, man becomes a more vulnerable creature, struggling like all other wild things to come to terms with the elements. We all become fellow creatures, fascinated by each other's ability to cope. By now, we were eighty-five miles off the Georgia coast, rolling along as though we were the only live thing in the world.

We had been visited by birds before, one or two intrepid hunters, who chased their quarry of bugs through open doorways, gripping the sills with scrawny feet and watching in curious silence the creatures that populated this moving oasis in a wide ocean. This time, we had acquired a troupe of about twelve who flitted around the decks. Perhaps it was their numbers that made them bold, or perhaps some empirical intelligence. Whatever the cause, we began to notice some definitely exploratory advances toward some of us by some of them.

While standing on the fantail with my arms at my sides, absorbed in watching Gary and Harry haul a dolphin aboard, I became aware of a soft brushing against my hand. I looked down and was startled to discover a little warbler, feathers all puffed out, staring unafraid into my face. Still later, we were witness to a more touching display of intuitive trust.

I had wandered up to the wheelhouse to enjoy a better view of the birds' foredeck acrobatics. Gary and Harry stood at the windows, energetically discussing navigation. When I turned to read something in the logbook which lay open on the shelf at the back of the wheelhouse, I was astonished to find a little female sitting in quiet bewilderment atop the book. Although I leaned back to give her ample room through which to exit, she held her ground, chest pumping mightily and eyes

Warbler surveying the seascape. Photograph by Charlton A. Gunter.

wide with fear. She seemed paralyzed with fright. Gradually inching my fingers toward her chest, I tried to calm her, speaking soothingly and then extending my open hand for her to sniff and examine. When my hand was beside her, I lifted an index finger and gingerly stroked her heaving breast feathers. She submitted to this in frozen silence, eyeing my finger and me suspiciously.

When it became apparent I was making no progress in calming her, I withdrew my hand and stood back once again. This seemed to provoke a frenzied attempt at escape through a fixed window at the back of the wheelhouse. She flew against the glass, futilely battering herself against the pane while I tried to capture her in a cupped hand. Just as suddenly, she stopped and fell back onto the book, panting. I retreated and watched for an opportunity to aid her release.

For several minutes, she sat looking the situation over, and finally made another attempt, thrusting herself up against a pane of glass very near Harry's shoulder. Jolted from their conversation, Harry and Gary stared uncomprehendingly at the bird's frantic endeavors. Then, Harry wrapped a hammy

198

hand around the quivering little body and slowly pushed it out of the open window in front of him, opening his fist to free the bird.

Instead of taking flight, she stood in his large palm, blinking curiously at Harry who stared back in delight. She hopped around his hand, peering over the side at her friends below, then turned to study us from her new vantage point. She stood there for some time, confident in her return to freedom and in our benevolence. Eventually, she heard a loud *chirp!* from one of the other birds. At that, she rose and fluttered down to supper.

On our last night out, I stood at the galley door as the sun descended behind the opaque screen of rain, dimming the grey light little by little until darkness seeped in upon us. Stew bubbled in a pot on the stove. I sat in the doorway, staring across the folds of ocean, admiring the starkness of nature. In the distance, I thought I saw something jump. Then a little closer, the water glistened in the dark for a second. Finally, I could make out a pair of small porpoises, leaping with exuberant abandon to fetch up beside the galley door and keep pace, close enough for me to reach out a hand to touch them. Their delight at seeing me was enough to lift my flagging spirits, and I whistled to them, listening for the tiny whistle in response as they surged out of the water. Porpoises seem to smile all the time, and I envied their carefree attitude, their unfettered enjoyment of something so simple as watching me watch them. And then they were gone with a twist of the tail that shot them forward effortlessly as though after keeping pace with the halting steps of a child, they had chosen to stride on. I waved goodbye, calling out as they joyously searched newer diversions.

Despite the undercurrent of tension, the trip was without serious incident. The engine ran smoothly, virtually nothing leaked, and the stove worked with a politesse I had not realized she possessed. It was as though everything was on its good behavior the better to say goodbye. We slid into the mouth of the Savannah River at dawn and were witness to one of the most spectacular sunrises I have ever seen. An indigo and slate-colored circus parade of clouds marched triumphantly across a deep rose sky. The water glowed golden in pools where the dawn spilled down to its edge, and now and then a pelican soared over the dark shapes of the land, diving for its breakfast. I felt an ache in my throat at the thought of leaving that beauty.

After docking, packing our gear for the last time, and stacking our bags on deck, we took pictures of the crew. We were a disreputable looking lot, hair slicked down wet from the shower, clothes ragged at the edges, hot, and exhausted. We stood together on the *Progress*'s pitted foredeck and smiled while one of the barge-chasers snapped the shutter. Then, without ceremoney, we all traipsed across the barge, hauling our bags, and drove to meet the other crew at the airport.

Saying goodbye to the tug was harder for me as I had no illusions about my job opportunities. I knew they would be infinitely more limited than Gary's. He had been promised a job elsewhere and was busily studying the rules of the road for the Great Lakes where he would meet a 2200 horsepower tug. As far as I knew then, I was going home for good.

We met the other crew in the lobby as they stepped off the plane at eleven that morning and exchanged the usual information and gossip, laced with stories of the trip. The deckhand, the same one whose place I had taken for the four months before, stuck his face into mine and breathed bourbon all over me.

"I'm glad yer gettin' off," he announced drunkenly.

"Why?" I demanded, my temper barely reined.

"Because women don't belong on tugs. Nothin' against you or anything. You just don't belong on a tug."

My swift rejoinder, a masterpiece of repartee, was a Bronx cheer. Had I been a man, I would have decked him. But had I been a man, I would never have been the recipient of such a charming confidence. Unfortunately, I knew his attitude was more prevalent than acceptance of the idea of a woman aboard a tug, both among deckhands and owners alike. I was fully aware how fortunate I had been in the crew on the *Progress* who, for the most part, had treated me with friendship and respect. I quaked at the thought of having to talk someone into giving me a chance elsewhere, knowing only too well that Gary's presence alone had won me this job.

While I was distressed at bidding farewell to such a happy working situation, in some ways, I was relieved to be home. Every muscle in my body ached. My hands were indelibly marked with tiny black lines. I looked haggard—in the words of a friend: "Rode hard and put away wet." Sadly, I did look older than my years and I was no more happy than any other person, man or woman, at being mistaken for ten years my senior. Therefore, I had made plans to settle back for some reading, a desultory stab at the housework, and a good, long sleep.

Gary had other plans.

He was not home a week when another tug owner called to hire him onto an old tug that ran between Tampa and Houston. Unable to turn down even a temporary job, he agreed to go for three weeks, and eight days after getting off *Progress* for the last time, Gary was on a plane bound for Florida. It was the first time I had been alone in two years, but rather than revel in my freedom, I found I had grown accustomed to his face, accustomed to the fact of his constant presence. Three weeks stretched into five, and just when I had begun to give up hopes of seeing him for Thanksgiving, he telephoned.

The owner had proposed a deal. He would let Gary off if he would go to Mexico to run a supply boat for a month. Gary agreed to go if I could come also. I agreed to go if I could spend my wages, without argument, on a piano. The deal was sealed.

Although Gary could have physically left the tug and come home without the owner's say-so, he had several reasons for not doing so. Firstly, he did not like to leave anyone in a bind for crew, even someone who made little effort at replacing him. Secondly, the commercial water community being so small, one's employability depends on reputation. His reputation had always been one of willingness to work, honesty, and capability. Thirdly, he cannot stand to throw away money. As long as he's paid, he works.

The owner let him off five days early in order to help me get the firewood in, seal the house, and pack. As an afterthought, we wrote out our wills.

T W E L V E

AT FIRST a trip to Mexico sounded exciting, even romantic. At the time Gary agreed to go, one of the owners assured him that everything aboard the supply boat was in working order. It was not until the twelfth of November when he was driving us to the airport that this man first muttered something about the air-conditioning needing some new parts. Knowing that the temperature was still ninety-two degrees in the shade and that the supply boat had virtually no ventilation, I asked what part was needed. The condenser. Oh. The part that makes it work. Right. Fine.

After a few more miles, he mentioned something about keeping the engines running until the first of the year when the boat was due back for her annual inspection. What do you mean, keep the engines running? No problem, it's just that she's running on seven cylinders [of the twelve] on her port engine. No problem, there's always the other. Without pause for any more elaboration, he remarked that he assumed we had enough cash on us to pay for the plane tickets from Merida to Carmen where the boat was based. Not given to carrying much cash, we began emptying our pockets and wallets, and finally pooled enough money to pay for the two tickets with five dollars to spare. The trip had begun to look definitely more exciting than romantic.

Although at least half our crew changes on *Progress* had been by air, I had still not reconciled myself to flying on the large commercial jets with copilots and backup systems, let alone on some of the crop dusters we had boarded. However, none of them had prepared me for the run between Mérida and Ciudad del Carmen.

We had flown a jumbo jet to Miami, then transferred to an old commuter plane to Mérida, Mexico. As I sat in the Mérida airport, watching the various aircraft take off and land around us, I debated whether to stay or flee. Through the windows which surrounded the lobby, we could see all manner of flying machines taxiing along the cement. As I watched the traffic, a dapper little Lear jet cruised up to the doors in front of us and stopped. She looked pert and self-confident.

"I can handle that," I told Gary.

"I don't want to disappoint you, Babe, but I don't think that's ours," he said, patting the shoulder he held securely.

"No?"

As we spoke, a battered old 1938 troop carrier lumbered up to the side of the building and spluttered to a halt. The wing nearest us had a jagged scar across it. A man in uniform propped open the hatch with a stick as though it were the hood of a vintage Studebaker.

"I think that might be it," Gary said softly, taking a firmer hold of my shoulders.

"What? No! No, it couldn't be!" I cried. "I'm not getting on that thing! No way. Look at it, Gare. It's got to be eighty years old!"

"Now, Nance, it can't be eighty years old," he said reasonably, trying to calm what he could see was a brewing case of hysterics.

"*Look* at it, Gare. That's the sort of thing they flew in *Twelve O'Clock High!*"

"Nance, they fly this route every day. It'll be okay!" he soothed.

"You've got to be kidding! We got off the tug because we were afraid it wasn't safe and we're getting on that thing? It's older than *Progress*, and she didn't have to fly! You've got to be crazy!"

A voice came over the loudspeaker announcing our flight.

"Come on, let's get our bags," he said, taking me by the hand and leading me toward the doors.

"Gare, I don't think I can do this."

"Look, Babe, You've got to go. I'm going. We haven't got any more money. What do you think you'd do here? You don't even speak the language."

I felt trapped. He knew that unless I was certain through whatever intuition I trusted that we would die en route, I would ultimately succumb to reason. We stuffed our bags into the compartment under the rusted belly of the plane as though boarding a Trailways bus for Hoboken. As I climbed aboard, I peered down the interior which was filled with pipe racks and seats, and began to cry. Having heard somewhere that the after section of a plane is the safer, I slid into a window seat behind the port wing. The rusty seat belt refused to adjust and I was forced to settle for a loose approximation of secure. Gary flopped into the seat beside me and put his arm around my shoulders again.

"Strap up your seat belt," I told him abruptly.

He did.

"Don't they have any drinks on this thing?" I asked with an irritation born of panic.

I looked around to find the stewardess, a lovely, dark-haired mestiza who was pouring measured doses of beer into cups that looked suspiciously like the things I had seen on trays in hospital corridors.

Once meagerly fortified with several specimen cups of Mexican beer, I settled down to stare out of the window and wait for the inevitable takeoff which never failed to unnerve me. The pilot, a lean man of indeterminate years who wore a pair of thick, horn-rimmed glasses (whatever happened to vision requirements?) climbed into his seat and strapped in. There was no copilot. Once the fourteen passengers were aboard, the pilot turned the key and pumped the throttle. The engine coughed and shook the plane, then stopped. I looked at Gary with wide-eyed terror. He smiled grimly and tightened his grip on me. Studying the wing while the pilot again tried to pump the engine to life, I suddenly realized that the exhaust pipe, which came out through the wing, was held in place by several layers of duct tape. When the engine fired up again, the duct tape came loose to allow the pipe to flap cheerily in the

204

commotion. The engine died again. The pipe fell back into place, its unstuck duct tape curled at the edges.

"Listen, there's still time to back out," I said, hoping that Gary's nerve had finally failed him.

"It'll be okay," he said without conviction. "Drink your beer."

Eventually, the pilot prodded the engine to an asthmatic roar and we took off, rumbling down the runway with every rivet rattling in the fuselage. Once we were airborne, however, the engine ran with only sporadic heart-stopping hesitations for the entire half-hour flight. Resigned, I took pleasure in the landscape that rushed past beneath the landing gear. When we screeched to a fishtailing stop at the Carmen airport, I was certain that the worst of the trip was over. Grabbing my pocketbook, I bolted out the door into the wet, subtropical night.

There was no one from the crew to meet us. Instead, the deckhand had dispatched some friends to pick us up while the supply boat ran back out to the Campeche oil fields for an undisclosed period. Having been traveling for fourteen hours, I longed for a shower and a clean bed. It was not to be. After a meal at the Mexican equivalent of McDonald's, an open-air taco stand where the proprietor cooked ribs and tortillas while we looked on, we were deposited at the darkened gate of the Ugland Company.

Unbeknownst to me, the owners of the supply boat had some sort of arrangement with Ugland, and we were subsequently installed in a room adjoining the office. The room boasted two twin beds, a window with a large hole in what used to be screening which let in mosquitoes and bats, and a continuous parade of black rats the size of our overfed housecat.

A sleepless night gave way to a hot, hazy dawn and, still without a chance to bathe, I rose and dressed. In a small kitchen at the back, a battalion of cockroaches, each as big as my thumb, conspired to empty the contents of the pantry with the efficiency of the SS. Groggy, tired, and dirty, I felt as though I was in a technicolor nightmare.

While the Norwegian manager of Ugland's Mexican headquarters was friendly, he was not enthralled with uninvited weekend houseguests, and tried to make arrangements for our immediate transfer to the supply boat. However, nothing in Mexico is immediate. We spent a day and a night biding our time. Captain Andreas checked every available crew boat for a passage out and tried unsuccessfully to locate the supply boat. Finally, faced with the prospect of our residing in the office over the weekend, he had another suggestion.

"Perhaps we get you on a helicopter. Dey take you up and fly around 'til dey find de boat," he said, picking up the telephone.

"Helicopter?" I gasped.

Captain Andreas looked startled for a moment before adding: "It iss all right. Dey lower you onto de deck in de basket wid your bagss."

"They what?" I shrieked.

By this time, tears coursed down my cheeks. Gary had come over to put an arm around me solicitously.

"It's okay," he told the captain. "She always does this when she has to fly."

"Well, I guess you could stay here until we find anoder way for you to go out and your husband get de helicopter," he offered.

"No, that's okay," I assured him, sniffing. "If he goes, I go."

"You sure?"

"Yes. I'm sure. We've gotten this far together."

Despite assurances that I would do as I was told without argument, the helicopter was not mentioned again. That afternoon we were packed onto a crew boat and spent twelve hours whizzing through the oil fields in search of the supply boat.

The Campeche oil field, tucked into the crooked arm of the Yucatán Peninsula, is nearly the size of Rhode Island. Finding someone in the field involves a series of radio calls that begin with: "Have you seen . . . ?" It was not until after midnight that we pitched our bags over the gunwales onto the afterdeck of the supply boat. We had not eaten since that morning when I had picked two oranges from the tree at the back of Ugland's office. Once the introductions were finished, we set to the dried hotdogs and rice on the stove.

The crew was an interesting mix of characters. Three Hondurans made up the large part of the deck crew, hired less for their skill than their willingness to take half the wages demanded by American seamen. Hercules O'Connor, the youngest at twenty, was the eldest of eight children. Cheerful and willing, he was as honest a man as Diogenes could have wished. Gideon, a man anywhere from thirty to fifty whose face betrayed years of abuse in the form of cigarettes and alcohol, spoke good English and had mastered a certain amount of American idiom which gave a subtle sense of humor full rein. It was only later that we discovered he was wanted for undisclosed crimes under another name and that he was not to be trusted. Clarence, a quiet, slow-moving Honduran of about fifty, acted as engineer despite a basic antipathy to machinery. Not until we were two days from Louisiana five weeks later did he confide to me that he could not go to the United States because he was wanted on two counts of bigamy. The American members, besides Gary and me, were a middle-aged yacht captain whose unceasing whining guaranteed that his arrival would clear a compartment, and a young man whose apparently sole qualification for the work was a willingness to endure heat and discomfort for months on end.

The Mexican bureaucracy is a system of perquisites and power which must be experienced to be fully appreciated. By law, all foreign labor must carry a Mexican work permit which is issued for a set fee at three-month intervals. While the fee ostensibly goes to the government, the bribe, which is an intrinsic part of the transaction, goes to a bureaucrat and appears to be tied to an invisible sliding scale. I was told at the Ugland office that permits and releases for other things cost varying amounts, and that the bribes which were given in the form of color TV's or stereos, as well as hard currency, were routinely budgeted into the operating expenses of the company.

Ciudad del Carmen, an island at the bottom of the Yucatán, had grown into a Mexican replica of a Klondike boomtown. Originally, the island had boasted perhaps five thousand people, but in six years the population had increased tenfold.

Bordellos had sprung up like mushrooms and did a brisk business. Foreign laborers of all kinds, gringoes, Hondurans, and other Central Americans who had flocked to the jobs created by the oil, clogged the streets and cantinas. To the Mexicans who had little benefited from the expanding job market, these strangers were a source of resentment.

Amidst the squalor, decent Mexican families clung to their dignity and their children's innocence in hopes of preserving their way of life through the upheaval. Most impressive to me were the squat women who, despite half-paved streets and ancient sewers which backed up into the shower drains at every heavy rain, always wore dresses and high-heeled shoes, and walked with the proud, upright bearing of their Mayan ancestors. In local schools, their children learned to celebrate the traditional Mexican holidays, commemorating their revolution with a parade, for which they dressed as bandoleros swathed in guns and strings of bullets. Gary and I watched serious-faced children march past their proud parents who held younger siblings, threading a path through painted prostitutes and foreigners wearing Rolex watches who thronged the dust-choked streets. It is difficult to reconcile that Mexico, of the rats and roaches, with the glowing descriptions I had heard of Acapulco and Mazatlán. To me, this was the Mexico that Americans should see, the land of poverty and pride, desperation and dignity.

Marketing in Mexico was a unique experience. With one freezer aboard functioning and that at limited capacity, as well as only one refrigerator which worked, I could not fill the boat to brimming as I had done with *Progress*. Like the local people, I was forced to shop often for small amounts and buy only what one of the Hondurans, who acted as translator, and I could carry in our arms. Bargaining with the stall keepers in the large market was not easy, filtered as it was through Gideon's or Hercules's imperfect English. Additionally, the fact that I was a gringa meant that the prices were automatically doubled or even trebled. Although I could hardly begrudge the natives their opportunism, I was nonetheless limited in funds, it being almost impossible to extract money long-distance from the owners. When Gary and I arrived, the Hondurans, who were paid in cash, had not seen a peso for two months and the grand total of the grocery money was less than a hundred dollars. Only after repeated phone calls did the owners finally wire some cash.

More difficult than the problems with lack of transportation, translation, and money, were the struggles I had with my American sensibilities over picking out dripping slabs of meat and seeing the butchers hack them to pieces before my eyes. The central market was a low-ceilinged cement and wood building with row upon row of stalls. Plucked chickens hung by necks or feet, entrails dangled from hooks, wet carcasses lined the butchery walls. Other stalls held assortments of fruits and vegetables, dried meats and sausages, and baked goods. Out on the long porch facing the harbor were marble slabs of fish and seafood, all covered with a multitude of flies. Gradually, however, I hardened to the practice of pointing out a chicken and having the proud vendor lop it to pieces then wrap the entire bird in a paper parcel and drop it into my bag. Eventually, I could trudge through the streets with blood dripping down my bare legs without so much as a second thought. I even ventured into the realm of sheeps' kidneys and calves' brains to mollify the Hondurans. However, my callousness dissolved at the thought of having to butcher our Thanksgiving turkey myself.

We had been ordered out and faced the prospect of Thanksgiving at sea, so I decided to make a real American spread—turkey, stuffing, cranberry sauce, and all the trimmings—and regaled the Hondurans with descriptions of our repast in order to enlist their help in carting it back. Hercules was the only one interested. The Mexican farmers by this time were aware of Thanksgiving, and prepared for it by descending on the markets like a horde of locusts with their crates of turkeys. As Hercules and I approached the market, I could see several wizened old men squatting beside their stacked crates of birds, all oblivious to the noise. We stopped before one man who sat beneath a tree, one of his seven turkeys tethered to a crate beside him. The bird sat on top of the crate, gazing placidly over the boats in the harbor, and ignored us as we came closer to inspect. The bird's plumage was beautiful, a mottled dove and bronze, flecked with red and a rich, chocolate brown.

"Herc, ask him if I can touch the bird," I said, wanting to check the plumpness of the breast through the covering of feathers.

"He say sure," Hercules grinned, happy to learn the ritual of picking a turkey.

I reached my hands around the turkey, ready to withdraw at the first sign of a bite. Instead of objecting, the turkey laid its head against my hand and rubbed as though he were an affectionate housecat.

"My God, Herc! He's a pet!" I cried in horror.

I could not bear the thought of watching the old man hack the bird's head off or, worse, wring his neck before my eyes.

"He say that's a good one, Nance," Hercules told me as the old man studied my reaction carefully.

"I don't know if I could watch while he kills him," I shook my head. "He's so affectionate."

Hercules translated, grinning at my squeamishness.

"He say he don't kill 'em. You got to kill him," Hercules informed me cheerfully.

"You're kidding! You mean to say I've got to walk this thing through the streets, take him on a crew boat, and tie him up out back alive?"

"Yeah. I guess so. Maybe we could get a cart to take him," Hercules offered, clearly enjoying this.

"But even if we get a cart, I've still got to tie him up and kill him."

"He be fresh," he told me, flashing a dazzling smile.

"Yeah, but I don't like the idea of getting personally acquainted with my dinner," I explained.

It had taken me years to be able to chop head and feet off the geese Gary brought home after a day's hunting. I could not imagine wresting this charming bird's life from him in hand-to-beak combat. The idea of a turkey dinner was losing its appeal.

"I kill him, Nance," Hercules offered, seeing his dinner on the verge of escape.

210

I sighed. I had eaten turkey before. I would do so again. What sort of scruples were these that only balked at the actual deed?

"Okay, Herc. Ask him how much he wants for that one."

Hercules did as I asked. The man's eyes lit up at the thought of a sale. But when Hercules translated, I could hardly believe my ears.

"He wants how much? Hercules, that's almost thirty-eight dollars! He can't weigh more than twelve pounds. That can't be right. Ask him again."

The conversation was repeated and after a fruitless period of bargaining during which the man held firm at thirty-seven American dollars, I finally dragged Hercules away.

"We can't afford to spend that on one meal," I explained.

"I give up taking my pay for another two weeks," he offered anxiously.

"You're not going to get your wages out of this money anyway. We've got to get some more to pay you all. But thanks for the offer."

Disappointed, we dragged our parcels through the streets to wait at the quayside for a ride out to the boat which for unexplained reasons was not allowed into the dock. The dockmaster, who had taken to slapping his pearl-handled six-gun and squeezing me like ripe fruit whenever possible, was nowhere in sight. This time, we found a crew boat to ferry us out to the anchored supply boat before the dockmaster discovered I was within reach.

To judge by our experience, running a supply boat, the dray horse of the oil fields, is boring work. On broad afterdecks, these boats haul oil drums, supplies of groceries, pipe, tools, or any one of a dozen other things needed by the rigs. The oversized tanks carry water and fuel to the generators and watertanks on the rigs. When we arrived, Gary wanted to know if there was a chart of the field identifying names and locations of the rigs. There was none. Pemex, the oil company of the Mexican government, was the employer but its minions ran a surprisingly casual operation. Sometimes, a voice on the radio

211

would direct our movements, other times, we would receive orders through other supply boat captains which were often confused and usually inefficient.

Once out of the harbor, there is little to see save the monotonous blue of the Gulf. Spidery oil rigs dot the waters of the Campeche oil field and for the most part, one rig looks identical to the next. After a five-hour run out to one of the rigs, we would be forced to sit tied impotently to one leg while Gary tried to raise someone on the radio to inform them of our presence below. Eventually, someone would collect whatever we had for them, but there was rarely any rush about it. At one rig, we sat for nearly an hour while Gary alternately hailed the crew on the radio and blasted the horn only to be deluged with the muddy water used for cooling the drill. Furious, Gary pulled out, leaving them to ponder when they would get their next shipment of drinking water and fuel.

One dividend of the interminable waiting at the rigs was the opportunity to fish. With admirable regularity, the Hondurans brought aboard red snapper, grouper, and an occasional shark, all of which ended up in the oven or the pot to supplement our less than inspiring fare. Ironically, one of the best fishing holes was the capped well, Ixtoc, now abandoned, that had burned out of control for the better part of a year.

When we arrived on the supply boat, no one person was responsible for meals or dishes. Each man foraged for himself with the consequence that one man could consume the entire allotment of steaks and consign the rest of the crew to baloney sandwiches. The night we arrived, dishes were stacked chest high in the sink and coated with an assault force of cockroaches. Accustomed to grime but not personal filth, I set to cleaning up the galley and battling the vermin. After scouring the shelving, I sprayed everything with insecticide until the crew pleaded for mercy. Then I scrubbed the pots and pans in addition to the dishes and jars. Finally, I took over cooking for the most part as well since it was something with which I was familiar and the men aboard refused to let me deck when they could stop me. Hercules happily worked alongside me, delighted at making the boat into a home away from home, and swabbed the decks every day.

I had met with hostility on tugs before, but was not prepared for the brand of antagonism I found in Mexico. Men assumed I was a "certain sort" by virtue of my presence there. However, most of my difficulties were in the immediate vicinity of the harbor and the seamen who crowded the docks, and decreased with distance from the waterfront. In the residential areas, I encountered nothing but the friendly smiles of families sitting in their front room windows which opened onto the sidewalk, or a hesitant greeting from a native when we passed one another on the street.

Gary had been given no reason why our boat had been selected to make a trip to Tampico with a portable barracks. After a radio call from Pemex, our boat was ordered alongside a ship to have the boxed barracks loaded onto our afterdeck. Several of the ship's deckhands came aboard to secure the barracks to the steel padeyes that poked up at intervals between the wooden sheathing planks covering the steel deck. According to the initial orders, we were to leave at once, but then the orders were changed to a delay of one day, then two. By the time we pulled out of the harbor bound across the Gulf for the two-day run to Tampico, the weather had turned ugly, blowing a fifty-knot northerly gale that picked up ten- to fifteen-foot seas. In the pounding, the contents of the vessel soon became a rat's nest. Cabins and corridors were wide, without handholds in either the overhead or bulkheading, and the captain's cabin, situated in the bow, the width of the boat, took on the feeling of a tempest-tossed ballroom through which we would free-fall to the bunks. By the time we reached Tampico, I was a mass of bruises.

Both Gary and I had been battling fluctuating cases of Montezuma's revenge since our arrival. That, coupled with a bad case of seasickness which was not helped by the fetid air, kept me in misery for the better part of two days. Half-dreaming, half-waking, I lay in the bunk, too weak from dragging myself to the head and back to brace myself against the chaotic motion. Finally, when Gary struggled across the cabin to kiss me goodnight the second evening out, I flung my arms around his neck and whimpered.

"Are we going down?"

"Oh, Babe. Have you been lying here worried about that?" he cried in a rush of compassion.

"Yeah."

He held me tightly.

"Well, don't. We're going to make it," he told me firmly.

"Promise?"

"Promise. I'm not even worried."

Once fortified with his assurance, I could relax and concentrate on enduring. In the middle of the night, the winds finally began to moderate, and by the time we arrived off Tampico, I was beginning to return to my old self.

Although the channel into Tampico is a straightforward run between two jetties which are the portcullis to a well-marked river, a pilot is required. Despite understandable need for the local knowledge of pilots in many places, in other areas, piloting had begun to take on the aura of genteel highway robbery. We were the only vessel waiting to come into the harbor, yet we were forced to wait for twelve hours within easy sight of the pilot station until a pilot arrived by launch.

"We must not look like we've got anything interesting on board for them, like cases of booze or cigarettes," the American deckhand remarked as he studied the pilot station.

In spite of being kept waiting like an unwanted suitor, we all enjoyed the time to fish and clear up the internal turmoil caused by two days of rough weather. In the warmth of the afternoon sun, Gary spotted a fishing vessel. Instead of the sleek, white, proud-nosed boats along our coastal waters, this brightly painted barque resembled the *Santa Maria*. As she drew near, we could see three blocky men in shorts, the image of Columbus's descendants, scurrying around on deck and sweeping up shrimp.

"Nance, go and see how much money we can spare, and see if we've got anything to trade," Gary said to me. "Herc, go out on the stern and ask what they want for some of their catch."

Gary eased the twin-screw vessel backwards until we were within ten feet of their stern. The crew appeared delighted to do business, flashing gold-toothed smiles and shouting greetings. Hercules, the deckhand, and I stood on the stern, trying

214

to barter over the language gap, Hercules's Spanish faltering with their dialect. I held up a bucket and a fistful of pesos. Hanging off the rope-ladder rigging, one man leaned over the side and snatched the bucket. One of the men held the tiller which threatened to pitch him over the side in the large swells, while the other two topped off the bucket with their hands, digging into the cache in their hold to fill the container brimming. After a quick conference on our deck, I handed them a wad of pesos which they took without counting, and stuffed into pants pockets.

"Good God! Look at these!" the deckhand crowed.

He held up one shrimp the size of a small lobster.

"What else can we give them?" I asked, signalling for them to wait while I scoured our meager larder.

Pulling out two bottles of red wine I had been hoarding, a box of cookies, and a bag of onions, I retured to the stern to pitch them over the gunwales to the merry chatter of the fishermen.

"Muchas gracias! Bellisima!" I shouted between cupped hands as we pulled away, hoping that the appreciation would translate.

The men waved the wine bottles at us then began heaving crabs onto our decks, bombarding us while we scooped up the broken parts for the pot.

In contrast to the bright-eyed openness of the fishermen, the pilot who arrived at dusk wore an impenetrable mask of boredom. Having learned early the differences between the Mexican people and the Mexican officials, we were immediately on our guard, returning to a correct formality which offered tea and sandwiches but no warmth. We had seen some bureaucrats feign ignorance of English in order to eavesdrop on an unwary speaker. They seemed to suck in insults, real or imagined, then take satisfaction in grinding their source through the mill of official paperwork.

Since no doubt every official in Tampico knew of our arrival shortly after our request for a pilot, it was a surprise to find no immigration or customs officers waiting for us on the dock. The pilot trotted off, taking with him a packet of the deckhand's cigarettes. No one else was in sight. A steamy darkness enveloped us, bringing with it hordes of buzzing insects. The only ventilation in the boat came through three doors, one at the back of each of three decks, and the few tiny portholes. After scrubbing the supper dishes and leaving them in the drain board, I sat down at the open companionway and stared at the stars.

At some ports I had seen prostitutes wandering casually along the piers or even, in Baltimore, climbing ships' ladders. Often they were lanky, make-up-daubed teenagers dressed in gaudy, tight clothes and high heels, stumbling up the gang-plank with an adolescent's ungainliness. For me it was a dis-heartening sight, the thought of so many wasted lives, but I was totally unprepared for the open exuberance of the Mexican prostitutes who, with a keen eye to business, brought their wares to the customers at quayside in crowded dugout canoes. As I watched, a group of diminutive woman, ranging in age from late teens to early forties, tied a boat to the stern and poured over onto our deck, faces eager with anticipation of a full evening's wages from the crew.

"Gary!"

He was beside me, leaning out into the floodlights of the afterdeck.

"Holy Christ, no way! Hey! Not here! You can get right back in that boat!" he cried, meeting them partway across the deck and waving his arms as though directing an airplane in for a landing.

The other men piled out the door behind him.

"Wait a minute," came a male voice from behind me, followed by a couple of discreet murmurs.

Oblivious to the men, Gary shooed the women back to their boat while they glanced over their shoulders at the crew who stood in a knot behind me.

"God, I don't believe this place!" Gary muttered as he stepped back over the sill and climbed the steps to the wheelhouse.

A couple of the men had sauntered across the deck to stare longingly at the departing females. Alone, the middle-aged yacht captain stepped back into the galley where I was pouring out another cup of coffee.

"I can't see that! I don't go for foreign women," he confided. "Not that I'm any angel. I mean, when you're away from your family as much as I am, well, I got a good, healthy appetite if you know what I mean. I mean, I've had my flings, but I just don't go for that. You don't know what you'll catch from them."

Far more disgusted at his admission that he had cheated on his wife only with the "right sort" than at the idea of all the single men aboard trading money for sexual favors, I stared at him, open-mouthed. Without comment, I turned my back to busy myself at the sink.

"Of course, it's different for her," he continued, referring to his wife. "We been married since we was twenty. She's a good mother and a good wife."

"Um."

"Yeah. She's always been true to me. I'd never hurt her or nuthin' by lettin' her know what goes on. Women just don't know."

"Really."

"Yeah," he replied, looking at me with innocent stupidity.

"Why are you so sure she's been faithful?" I asked maliciously, wanting to hurt him for the hurts he had inflicted on his no doubt long-suffering wife.

His eyes widened.

"What do you mean?"

"I mean, what makes you so sure she's not doing the same thing you are?" I repeated, angry with myself even as I said it for maligning a person I had never even met and to whom I meant no harm.

"I just know her is all," he said defensively.

"Just like she knows you I guess, huh?"

Feeling nearly out of control of myself, I bolted for the two flights of steps to the wheelhouse where Gary leafed through the charts in the dim light at the chart table.

By the time the customs and immigration officials came, Clarence was the only one still up, solemnly munching a sandwich and playing solitaire at the table when they stepped through the door. Within ten minutes, we were all fidgeting at the opening to the large cubbyhole where the table sat while the two men shuffled through our documents. Once they had

217

worked their way through everyone's passports and work permits, they demanded to see the papers for the vessel, the bills of lading, etc., which had been issued to Gary at Carmen. He brought the wad of papers given to him by the Carmen bureaucrats, who had assured him that everything was in order, and placed it before the two men who sat sipping coffee and eating as they worked. With apparent lack of interest, they flipped through the papers, then turned a mildly inquiring face to Gary and told him in Spanish that he was missing one crucial paper. Gideon translated.

They were sorry, but he lacked an important document. He and I returned to the cabin and the wheelhouse to search through drawers, under bunks, in closets. We returned with nothing.

When Gary informed them, through Gideon, that we could not find any other documents, the officials simply smiled and replied that they already knew we did not have it. They knew he had not been issued the paper in Carmen.

"They knew?" he shouted at Gideon. "Christ! Why the hell didn't they so? Look, the people at Carmen gave me this fistful of stuff before we left to cover the trip," Gary continued, stabbing a finger at the collection of documents spread on the table. "They said it was all we needed. That's all I know. Now why the hell isn't it enough? What do they want?"

Apparently affronted by Gary's exasperatedly belligerent tone, the two officials sat bolt upright and began reassembling their papers in silence.

"Christ, now what?" Gary cried.

Wordlessly, the men rose and made for the door.

"What more could I do? I was told by the people who are supposed to know that I had everything," Gary said as they elbowed their way through the crowded passage.

"Gideon, ask them to sit down again," I cried desperately. "We can get this sorted out calmly."

It was no use. Their Latin pride apparently wounded, they stalked through the door.

"God, now what?" Gary said again.

"What exactly did they say, Gideon?" I asked, hoping somehow to analyze our situation.

Without warning, the officials reappeared at the door and spoke a few words to Gideon who stood just inside, surrounded by the rest of us.

"He says they want our passports."

"What? No way!" I said without even trying to step back and give Gary a chance to decide.

Gideon reached resignedly inside his pocket and handed his passport to one of the men. Clarence and Hercules looked perplexed, caught between me and Gideon.

"They are official people, Nance. If they say they want your passport, you should give it to them," Gideon said quietly.

I shook my head. As far as I was concerned, it was our only protection.

"You must do what you think best, but I'm not giving them my passport and neither is Gary," I declared. "It is not required."

"It is no good to make them angry."

"As far as I can see, it is no good to placate them, either," I retorted.

Silently, Hercules and Clarence handed their passports to the two Mexican officials and the four Americans clutched theirs for whatever good or ill it may have done. Angered at our defiance, the men turned to Gary and informed him that the Americans were all confined to the boat. The next morning, they returned with reinforcements and presented Gary with a summons, a demand he appear at a hearing the following Monday. Confused, exasperated, and scared, Gary and I retired to the wheelhouse to try to work out some plan of attack with the meager resources at our disposal. Our options seemed distinctly limited. The best we could hope for was some sort of rescue in the form of a local agent who would be familiar with the workings of the local bureaucracy. While we sat in the wheelhouse, still uncertain of the charges against Gary or of the penalty, we heard an American voice on the radio, informing shoreside of his impending arrival at the dock just behind us.

"Let's call him and see if he has a single side band radio."

Gary raised the captain of the supply boat whose home dock was one pier downriver. The disembodied voice sounded unconcerned about Gary's plight, but did agree to make a phone call for him. Like many of the other pieces of equipment aboard, our single side band was inoperable and Gary had been unable to get through to the United States in order to apprise the owner with whom he had been dealing of his dilemma. Once the other boat tied up, Gary hot-footed it over the dock in defiance of the dictum of the two officials. The captain of the other boat was a man about our age, a casual sort who had spent many months running the boat out of Tampico with an all-Mexican crew and seemed mildly acquainted with the machinations of the bureaucracy. While Gary was gone, I nervously cooked and scrubbed, glancing out of the doorway at every movement, thinking perhaps he had been spotted and dragged off to an obscure jail. After an hour, I scurried over the cement dock to the galley of the smaller supply boat where Gary sat chatting with the American captain.

Michael, the captain, seemed to take Gary's predicament much less seriously than did we and was more concerned with having a couple of English-speaking compatriots nearby.

"They probably want a bigger bribe," he said matter-of-factly. "You know, it's good to see some Americans and to speak English again. We hardly ever see Americans here. I hope you guys can stay around for a while."

I earnestly hoped otherwise but smiled at the friendly face and kept silent. As Gary and I walked across the quay together, he kept glancing at me, finally putting his arm around my shoulders.

"It'll be all right," he said.

"It better be or I'll come after every damned bureaucrat in this place," I told him with a wry smile.

"That's my Nance!"

T H I R T E E N

THE WEEKEND lay on us like a stone. Michael, the supply boat captain, had tried to coax us into joining him at a nearby cantina for supper and some music, but we still felt restricted by the Mexican officials and remained on board. Instead, he visited us and desultorily played poker, glad of a chance to converse in English. He was alone in Mexico, lured by the adventure and the promise of a steady, well-paid job, but he sorely missed his home.

"You're the first American woman I've spoken to for four months," he told me over a hand of cards Saturday evening.

"How much longer are you going to stay here?" I asked.

"I don't know. I don't know what I'd do if I went home. I'd probably get another job to fill in the time and save some more money until I got back here," he told me with a trace of irony in his voice as he slapped down his cards. "You've won again."

"You let me win so I'll keep playing."

He grinned and dealt out another hand.

"You guys get along really well, don't you?" he asked finally.

"Me and Gary? Yeah. We think so. We have some real ripsnorters, but we like each other better than anyone else."

"No kids?"

"No. I couldn't come with him if we had," I told him, wondering if we could ever make that question in our lives a conscious decision.

"You're lucky," he said without inflection.

"Do you have children?"

He shook his head.

"I've never been married. My sister and brother-in-law have two. I spend a lot of time with them when I'm home. My brother-in-law keeps telling me how tough it is to keep the spark in a marriage when you have kids."

"Maybe it depends on the kind of spark you started with."

"Maybe. You know, it's nice to have you and Gary here. Nice to be able to talk. My whole crew's Mexican. All of 'em."

"You get lonely down here?" I asked.

He nodded.

"Sometimes. The people are really nice. I take out a girl, a Mexican girl who works at the cantina. Her husband deserted her, left her with a little boy. I take some classes at the college when I'm in, but it's sure good to talk with someone from home."

As I studied him, I thought perhaps he and Gary had something of the same drive in their blood.

"You can't stand not to come but you have a hard time here, don't you?"

He shrugged.

"That's why Gary wanted me to come on the tug to start with. He loves it out here, and in most ways so do I, but we can't stand to be apart. Right now, it's the best of both worlds."

"You should get your license," he remarked.

"That's what Gary says but most of the men I've met tell me I don't belong here."

"The hell with them. You've got a good opportunity down here. Use it. You can try running the boat and doing some maneuvering around the rigs. You could hit one—gently," he added with a grin, "but it wouldn't matter here. You don't really need a license to operate a boat here. Gary's overqualified."

Gary trotted down the steps and slid into the enclosed booth beside me.

"Are you sure you guys can't come out to the cantina with me and have a couple of beers?" Michael wanted to know.

"If you've got some chicken, bring it over and I'll make jambalaya for supper. We've got some beautiful shrimp. Eat with us and bring a few beers. We'll all chip in," I said.

"You're on!"

The agent whom the owner had hired to accompany Gary to the hearing on Monday arrived just moments before Gary had determined to leave. Gary and I paced the afterdeck together in the heat, sweat soaking through his clean shirt. Gideon had showered and dressed in order to act as a back-up interpreter. Gary left with the two men, still uncertain of what the charges against him were, and without a clear idea as to the nature of the ostensibly missing document. Additionally, having to rely on the auspices of a stranger from the town, and Gideon, whom he was coming to look on with a certain distrust, left him anxious. After they left, I puttered and fidgeted for hours, pacing the afterdeck in between scrubbing and cooking, drinking glass after glass of cold coffee. Lunch came and went and then the sun began to drop behind the grey rooftops of the warehouses of the fenced-in compound at which we were moored. Images of Gary being handcuffed and spirited to a dank, prerevolutionary prison haunted me. At four, Michael came in from a short job at the rigs and came across the quay. He poked his head in the galley door where I was making shrimp salad.

"Still hasn't come home?" he asked.

I shook my head and leaned against the defunct freezer which was tied in place with a single line looped around its empty middle.

"How about some cards?" he ventured in an effort to occupy me with something other than vain speculations.

We shuffled and dealt the cards, but I could not concentrate on the faces in my hands. Finally, I gave up, and went to pace the afterdeck in the shade of the blue barracks still shackled to the pad eyes. Michael followed me silently.

"Look, he'll be okay. All they want is more money, I'm sure. Once he comes up with that, he'll be back here," he told me as he took his leave.

"Thanks."

"Come on over to let me know when he gets back," he said as he stepped onto the cement dock.

223

"Okay."

I wondered where Gary would find money for the bribe. At the sound of every car engine, I scanned the chain link fence that surrounded the compound, hoping to see Gary's blond head inside. After a lackadaisical dinner, I returned to my vigil. Finally, a car stopped at the opening in the fence where the guard hut sat. The door of the vehicle opened, and I saw Gary step out onto the tarmac, framed by a pink sunset. My heart leapt, but I held my ground and waited for him to come across the compound and climb onto the boat. I threw my arms around his neck and waited for an account of his day. Nothing.

"Well?" I said, leaning back to look at his relaxed face.

"Well, it looks as though they wanted a bribe and that was their way of squeezing it out of us," he said.

"Where did you get the money?"

"The agent advanced it."

"Are we free?"

"Looks like it. You can go shopping in Tampico tomorrow."

"That's it?"

It was an anticlimax, despite my relief.

"I sure think so, Kiddo. There's no way of telling with things down here, but I sure think that's all there is to it," he replied, shaking his head in exasperation.

"I was scared they were going to take you away and it would take me forever to find you again," I said quietly.

"Me too," he smiled, hugging me.

That evening, Gary and I walked with Michael up the muddy streets to a liquor store where we bought three bottles of red wine. In the wheelhouse, Gary's portable radio twanged out the guitar music of a Brownsville radio station, while we drank the wine out of cracked plastic cups. I wondered how Michael stood living in this alien world for months on end. His eagerness to spend time with the two of us bespoke a loneliness which I suspected he buried most of the time. He struck me as a man similar to Gary—basically reserved, ambitious, steady, a person who would endure much to achieve what he considered his ultimate goal. It was a character unlike most of the men I had met over the past several years on the water, and made me homesick for the family we had known on *Progress*.

Over the weekend, a large, anchor-pulling tug had arrived and moored across our stern and that of a Norwegian tug already tied to our port side. Both crews appeared to make a study of debauchery, welcoming boatloads of prostitutes aboard for a party which lasted virtually all night punctuated by the screams of women and the warwhoops of men. By now, Michael knew most of the working girls along the quay and watched wryly as the drunken Norwegian sailors swayed to the music of a large radio that blasted over the forward loud-hailer. Three prostitutes danced with four men, stopping now and again to take a drink from paper cups. As we sat in the window of the wheelhouse, sipping the local red wine and watching, I began to wonder if perhaps this was no kind of life for anyone.

"They get a lot of money from those guys," Michael said quietly, following my gaze to the women on deck, "but they don't like the Norwegians. Those guys get their kicks beating their women up. You see the small one with all the makeup?" he continued, pointing discreetly to a middle-aged woman in tight pants and high heels who was draped over one of the tousled men. "She just got out of the hospital last week."

"Charming. That girl's beautiful," I nodded toward another.

Coal black hair cascaded down a lean, straight back. Her features, a flawless melange of Spanish, Indian, and perhaps Caucasian heritage, were dominated by two large, dark eyes.

"She has two children to support. Her husband left her. It's a good living for her. She makes ten times what she could working in a shop down here. It would cost me a day's pay to spend the night with her. They call me chinchi hombre," he grinned, turning to face me.

"What does that mean?"

"Cheapskate," he laughed.

I laughed with him. I suspected that a hunger for more than a night's sex bought and paid for accounted for his reluctance rather than pure frugality. He had spent every available minute with us since we had arrived.

"I'll really miss you guys when you have to leave," he said.

"You've been a lot of fun," I smiled, neglecting to add that I appreciated his refinement so far as his conversation was

225

concerned. Although he spoke to me of crude things, he expressed himself in a refined way, a nicety not observed by many of the men I had met on the water.

The mate on the tug behind us, a particularly unsavory man who spent large blocks of his time drunk, had shown me a picture of his family, a red-cheeked young wife and three beautiful children, only moments before he began telling me in graphic detail about his escapades with the local prostitutes.

The Honduran cook, a charming rogue who apparently already had two wives at home, fell in love with the regularity of a tree frog and had that morning proposed to a waitress at one of the cantinas downriver. Along with the others, he took full advantage of the here today gone tomorrowness of a seaman's life. The captain of the tug, sensing my repugnance to much of the goings-on, spent his time in the galley telling me of his English wife in a heavy stutter that inexplicably disappeared once he was an anonymous voice on the radio.

The morning following Gary's day-long fracas with the authorities, I coaxed Hercules into accompanying me into nearby Madero. Tampico proper was six miles away but Madero was only a two-mile hike to reach several streets of shops and banks. We must have made an incongruous pair, he, lean and tall, with skin the color of black walnut shells, and a perpetually gleaming smile, and I, overweight, freckled, and sunburned with prematurely greying hair hidden under a borrowed cowboy hat. We passed the shacks which huddled along the river in the grassless aprons of dirt. The huts, crazy quilt assemblages of scrap tin, plywood, and reeds, all slapped together for shelter and privacy, leaned into one another in exhaustion. Here and there a chicken coop sat beside the door, and several fighting cocks, large, arrogant birds tethered by one spurred ankle, strutted in the dust.

Once we turned away from the river and the railroad tracks, the houses began to look gradually more prosperous. They were made some of wood, some of pink brick, and along the residential streets near the shops, many boasted fretwork balconies with hanging baskets of flowers. When we reached the shops, Hercules set off in search of postcards and a post office.

226

Having learned just enough Spanish by now to buy food and make change, I was content to amble along the sidewalks, peering into the open doors and stopping occasionally to put another parcel into the string bag I carried. On the street, people stared, nodding now and again in greeting. Unlike the Mexican bureaucrats, whose enmity was palpable, the shopkeepers were friendly and patient, seeming to enjoy the slow process of translation and the exchange involved in a transaction with a foreigner.

As I trod the cracked sidewalks in pursuit of Hercules, I began to notice that several people who stood farther along the block were waving me toward them. As I approached, they pushed me still farther up the street, urging me toward more eagerly gesturing people. At the entrance to one building, an old man who had been standing and smiling brightly, took me by the arm and led me through the door to point out Hercules in line at the postage stamp window.

"Muchos gracias," I bowed to my ancient guide.

With dignity, he returned the bow ever so slightly and murmured, "De nada," before returning to the glaring sunshine.

"Herc, all these people just led me to you," I marveled.

"That's nice," he remarked, licking his stamps. "People are so friendly."

Surprised at his easy acceptance of this kindness, I realized that this sort of generosity was commonplace in his experience. These people were simply good-hearted folk who were happy to show kindness to a stranger in exchange for nothing more than a smile of appreciation. It was a shock to realize that they were the same race as those haughty bureaucrats whose disdain and undisguised relish at wielding power had proven so unnerving.

We returned to the boat from a shopping trip to Tampico in the late afternoon. Gideon disappeared in the direction of his cabin and his hidden cache of rum which he had been nursing with increasing regularity over the past few weeks. After dropping his load of parcels on the galley floor and mixing himself some iced tea, the deckhand mounted the steps, leaving me alone to stow the groceries. It was not until I was halfway through cooking supper that Gary appeared with an offer to take me out. The deckhand, anxious to escape the boredom on the boat, suddenly materialized again and decided to accompany us on the two-mile walk to nearby Madero to find a restaurant. Although the streets were lined with an abundance of small carry-out shops ranging from indigenous Mexican food to exotic combinations of Mexican-Indonesian, Chinese-Hungarian, and Philippino, we found no proper, sit-down restaurant that was not jammed with customers. Deciding to go into the city of Tampico again, we walked partway out of Madero on the main road, hoping to meet with some mode of conveyance.

The local system of transportation was dependent on a collection of broken-down cars of varying ages and in various stages of disintegration which roamed the thoroughfares. Having already taken a dilapidated taxi into Tampico to shop, we began to question what differences separated the taxis from the coches. Michael's brief description of the coches was: "more crowded and cheaper than taxis."

We walked several blocks past the shops to a conspicuous corner, and then stood keeping a lookout on the traffic that sped past. A small crowd of people collected on the opposite corner under an overhanging roof. We began to notice their interest in us as they pointed, huddled for a rapid confabulation, then stood upright to stare. Finally, one man detached himself from the group and came over to us. Speaking gently in Spanish, he took Gary by the sleeve and urged him back across the street with him. The man's compatriots beckoned us toward them with smiles and gestures, and seemed satisfied when the three of us joined them.

In short order, a wheezing taxi ground to a halt before the crowd and five of the people rushed into the street and crawled into it. With the doors still wide, the car's occupants gestured frantically for us to join them and at their cheerful behest, the three of us squeezed into the dusty interior, crushing ourselves against an assortment of smiling passengers who awkwardly searched pockets for the twenty cents for the ride to Tampico. So this was a coché! Except for the democratic number of people inside, and its minimal cost, it was indistinguishable from its more elite counterpart, the taxi.

Six of us crowded into the back seat. I sat on Gary's lap, smashed against the deckhand who leaned forward in order to be able to breathe. Three other short, blocky people hung onto the seat and door handles to keep from bursting out the doors. A small woman, who sat beside the driver, chirped directions at him which were barely audible over the sound of a huge radio carried by the fat teenager beside her.

As we approached the brightly lit town, the number of riders dwindled until finally the driver stopped at a curb in the center of town, and waited for us to get out. Wrinkled, sticky with sweat, but exhilarated by the spontaneous generosity of feeling, we made our way along the crowded sidewalk. By now, the shops had closed, but the carts of the street vendors still glittered with merchandise and people paraded through the warm evening, glancing at the rows of earrings and bracelets, all laid out with meticulous care for the inspection of potential customers. A mariachi band played energetically in the park.

It was after we had turned the corner behind the market that the scene changed from one of bright celebration to destitution. More battered stalls, slapped together out of the debris collected along the shore or filched from construction sites, were covered with a torn blanket or newspapers to tell passersby that they had closed their business for the night. Two tiny old men sat beside one stand, eating burritos and quietly watching the reflected lights from the center of town. Farther along, an old woman lay on the sidewalk beside a child whose limp body fell slightly off the newspaper that they used as a mattress. The child's face pulled at me and this poor woman's attempt to maintain some dignity and comfort for her charge tore at my heart. Our eyes met for a second, then parted. Guilt at my good fortune in life overwhelmed me, but I passed by without a word.

Not three blocks from this newspaper pallet, the Hotel Ingleses thrust its concrete facade to the stars. In front of the glass-enclosed marble steps sat two large, well-kept potted palms, and inside we could see a gaily lit interior where a clerk, as scrubbed and elegant as his surroundings, pored over a registry. The place shone with unabashed wealth beside sidewalks filled with people whose lives were one long struggle for simple sustenance.

We waited at the docks in Tampico for seven days. During that time, we watched the dock crew unload and reload the blue box, our reason for being there, three times as though unable to decide whether or not to take delivery at all. In the interim, we shifted a barge, puttered with the painting and varnish, and cleaned.

Gideon, whose constant drinking had become a problem, finally refused to work at all and Gary fired him, paying him his back wages and demanding that he pack his things and leave by the next morning. After several attempts to enlist the sympathy of the rest of the crew, Gideon bowed to the inevitable, and stalked up to the bus depot, ostensibly to check out the schedules to his home in Honduras. Later that evening, he returned, tearfully and drunkenly protesting that he had met with foul play. He claimed he had been assaulted and robbed of his money, all his wages stolen, and that he had nowhere to go. Like the little boy who cried wolf, he had told too many lies, and, protests and pleas notwithstanding, Gary insisted that he be off the boat by morning. Clarance, sympathetic to Gideon's pleas, had lent him enough money for a bus ticket home, but woke to discover that both Gideon and his savings were gone.

The owner, meanwhile, was making frantic attempts to ransom his captive vessel from the authorities. Having been told that they planned to keep us idle for two weeks while they sorted through the paperwork, he pounced on the telephone, calling agents in Mexico City, Washington, D.C., Carmen, and Tampico. Gary had been in continual contact with the owner via a telephone in the dockmaster's office, and came back to the boat one afternoon to announce we were leaving that night. Having been assured that the owner had arranged our release, Gary began to make preparations for our departure.

According to the plan, we were to steam northward, allegedly bound for Brownsville, Texas, until we could make VHF radio contact with the owner. At this time, he would order us back to Carmen. All perfectly routine, he said. The scheme sounded suspicious to me, and Gary, not as casual about the idea as he sounded, had decided to leave under cover of darkness.

Disappointed that we were deserting him, Michael insisted that Gary and I spend the last evening with him in the small cantina which opened its doors onto the river just downriver from the cement dock. The cantina, an open-air cafeteria which served beer and mixed drinks as well as a variety of fresh seafood and home-made Mexican favorites, boasted a toilet that was an outhouse which hung over the river and was accessible via one narrow board from which more than one customer had fallen to an impromptu baptism. At nine that evening, while the three of us sat munching steamed shrimp splashed with liberal doses of lime, the deckhand scurried in to retrieve Gary. The local agent, the man who had accompanied him to the hearing, was aboard, and needed to see Gary immediately. Gary rose to follow the deckhand and left me with Michael and the owner, a bright-eyed woman who periodically joined our conversation in heavily accented but lively English.

Gary threaded his way back over the debris to climb the fence that separated the cantina from the docks. The agent stood at his car just outside the gate and after conferring, the two of them sped off into the country, finally arriving at a darkened house. There, the agent roused an immigration official. Leaving Gary in the car, the agent carried on a long conversation on the sidewalk while the official, clad in nothing but pajamas and slippers, yawned and rubbed his eyes. Apparently striking a bargain, the agent climbed back into the car and took Gary back to the gate at the dock where he left him standing in the glaring floodlights.

When I climbed into the galley Gary was sipping a mug of black coffee.

"We're going in about an hour."

"Everything squared away?" I asked, sitting down beside him.

"I guess. We're not taking a pilot this time."

"No? Are you going to be in trouble?"

"Only if they catch us," he grinned.

We drifted out of Tampico River at midnight, coasting by

the darkened pilot station, then Gary turned north at the jetties and headed toward Brownsville. As the dawn came up, Gary tried to reach the marine operator, finally getting a radio telephone call through to the owner at eight o'clock. As promised, he ordered us to turn around and head south to Carmen.

After puttering into the harbor, we rafted to another supply boat while Gary applied for permission to come into the dock to take on fresh water and food. Permission was denied. Not only were we not allowed into the dock, not even to exchange one crew member for another who had flown down, but we were to leave the harbor immediately. Whatever fix the owner had arranged in Mexico City had not extended to Carmen and we were persona non grata.

The supply boat to which we were tied was packed to capacity with fresh fruits and vegetables, and Dee, once she had learned of our predicament, offered a carton of fresh cabbages and fruits as a temporary care package. Delighted, I joined her in the walk-in chilled pantry and sorted through racks of produce while she piled one thing on the next and chatted.

"Gideon's on board," she remarked as we stepped out into the sunshine where Hercules filled twenty-gallon plastic jugs with water from the other boat's tanks.

I stopped and stared at her in surprise.

"Do you know why Gary let him go?"

"He said something about a drinking problem that got blown out of proportion."

"That was the original reason, but when he was fired, he stole all his bunkmate's money."

Dee snorted.

"That wouldn't bother the captain. He's been sellin' all the equipment on board and then tellin' the company it's been stolen," she said. "But listen, don't you tell anyone I said that!"

"My God, Dee! By why don't you all report him?" I cried.

"Well, the mate's got a cut of the cash. As far as I know, the company likes this guy. They don't usually believe a woman. Hysterical, you know," she said disdainfully. "And besides, he carries a gun."

"Oh."

"He told Gideon he could stay here as long as he needed to find another job."

"Well, just be sure you keep your doors locked," I sighed.

"Are you kidding? I've got to with this crew!"

Once we had loaded the water jugs, we separated from the supply boat to anchor by ourselves. Rather than leaving immediately as ordered, we stayed while Gary, Clarence, and the deckhand installed the new single side band radio in hopes of being able to reach the owner. Although we were treated to periodic tirades over the radio from the Mexican officials, the three of them continued to work all afternoon. At Gary's instructions, I made out a short grub list which he then radioed into one of the American ship's chandlers.

"I'm hoping that we can swing by the dock after dark and get this stuff aboard," he told me.

The single side band worked, and Gary put a call in to the owner who, already into his cocktail hour, assured us he could fix it and ordered us to wait it out until they cooled off. Having been through the system in Tampico, Gary was not anxious to try this one as well, but waited until later that evening when another call to the owner produced orders to bring the boat back to Louisiana.

We waited for darkness, watching the last of the rose fade into black on the horizon, and then upped anchor to drift into the dock. Gary had made arrangements with the chandlers to meet us at a sheltered corner of the bulkhead, hoping that officialdom had not eavesdropped on the conversation. As we idled in, he scanned the pier with binoculars. A supply boat was tied to the bulkhead, and beside it, in the dim corner, was a jeep, parked at the edge of the quay. As we eased beside the boat, two figures jumped out of the jeep and began heaving sacks and boxes onto the deck, scrambling over the pipes laid over the boat's stern. The rest of us lined up along the gunwale to grab sacks and boxes. The mate, washed and packed, came running down the steps, his duffle bag hitched up onto his shoulder.

Gary had come out back to help with the food as well as exchange some rapid-fire conversation with the chandler. Suddenly, the dockmaster came running across the dock, brandishing his six-gun, followed by a deputy who shouted and waved his fists.

"Listen, Gary. I'm gettin' off," the mate told him.

Gary glanced up at the two uniformed men.

"They don't want you. If you get off, it's your lookout," he advised.

"Okay!" the mate returned, and flung a leg over the rail.

The chandler scurried back to the jeep and started the engine. Gary bolted up the steps to the wheelhouse and put the engines in forward, pulling away from the dock while the dockmaster and his minion cursed at us. I could see the mate and his relief, whom Gary had left on the dock, race for the jeep and hop into it as it backed off of the dock. The two Mexicans remained on the dock, waving the gun and threatening.

As Hercules, Clarence, and I sorted through the food, I became aware that I was shaking. Sitting down on the door sill for a moment, I sucked in a deep breath and watched as the two wildly gesticulating silhouettes faded into the black background of the warehouses. It had all taken no more than three minutes.

We were headed home!

"Did you think they was going to shoot us?" Hercules asked as he picked up a case of beer that had come aboard.

"I don't know. I guess maybe I did," I grinned.

"I thought they was going to shoot Gary," he told me, a broad smile visible in the dim glow cast by the running lights.

"Well, we made it!"

"I never been to America!" Hercules said gleefully as he stepped into the galley.

"Well, God willing, you're going now!"

By the time I got to the wheelhouse, Gary was embroiled in a radio telephone conversation with the owner over having left the mate's replacement on the dock. Exasperated at his own impotence, he badgered Gary to return to the dock again to collect the man. Without refusing point-blank, Gary repeated his reasoning, once again explaining that the men who chased us away were armed, and as far as he knew, dangerous.

"Damn it, Gary! They weren't going to shoot you!" the owner exclaimed.

234

"Easy for him to say," I remarked acidly.

Cayos Arenos is an atoll so tiny that it does not even merit a dot on the large-scale charts. Having heard the confirmation of an impending gale, Gary rummaged through the Sailing Directions in search of a shelter from the storm. The atoll sat nearly in our path, above the Yucatán Peninsula, and proved to be exactly thirty-six hours from Carmen. The Loran, under normal conditions the modern seaman's answer to dead reckoning, like the rest of the equipment had a personality disorder and refused to print out any but even numbers. This would have been handy had our goal been Texas, but since the atoll was about the size of a large shopping mall, we needed more precise navigation. Gary therefore depended on the sights he took from dawn to dusk on his sextant, and worked out our location as had generations before him. After a day and a half of running compass courses based on the Sailing Directions and Gary's celestial navigation, we spotted a sandspit graced by one slender lighthouse and the corpse of a destroyer which had been brutalized by the seas. This was Cayos Arenos. We had made it just ahead of the storm.

Since that morning, the winds had been steadily increasing, and the sky altered from the azure reflection of the Gulf waters to an angry, mottled slate, the black clouds churning into one another. The wind picked up crests on the darkling waves, sending bursts of salt spray over the surface. The atoll itself was comprised of two mounds of sand that were barely raised above the wide Gulf waves. It had at one time been one long spit, arching gracefully back toward the Yucatán and lightly fringed with sea grass. Now, the waters rushed through a groove cut through the center just south of the lighthouse.

As we ran up toward the meager shelter offered by the hooked islands, we saw a clutter of brightly painted fishing boats bobbing at anchor under the lee of the shore. Without a chart, Gary could only guess at the shoals and depths, knowing at least that the seabed on this side of the island was rocky. Stationing me and Hercules on the bow to take soundings with a jury-rigged lead line, he gingerly poked the boat up toward the shore.

"How's it look?" he shouted, leaning against the sealed

window in front of the controls.

"I can't tell," I yelled back, "The line won't go straight down. The current keeps taking it out back before it hits bottom. We can't see bottom yet, though."

Hercules and I leaned over the side, gesturing with hands, and shouting. After edging up to shore as closely as we dared, Gary let go the switch and the drum on deck beside us spun out the wire which held a five-hundred-pound anchor. Gary eased the boat back, laying out scope in hopes of setting the anchor on the stony bottom. In a few minutes, we swung back against the straining wire, and Clarence shut off the engines. Then we settled back to wait. Uncertain of the anchor in these conditions, Gary sat in the wheelhouse taking bearings off the surrounding shore and the wrecked destroyer. It was not long before he sent Clarence below to crank up the engines. We were dragging. Three times we edged up toward shore to repeat the process of dropping anchor and waiting, only to find we were dragging, more and more rapidly as the winds increased. It began to look as though we would have to stand round-the-clock watches in order to keep us in place.

Our maneuvers had attracted an audience of interested fishermen who sat under gaily decorated canopies in their cockpits. Although their boats jounced crazily, their anchors held fast and they could watch us at their leisure. As we made a fourth run toward shore, we could see three men scramble into a small coracle barely large enough to hold them and set off on the waves. Two sat on thwarts in the boat while the third man stood in the stern, sculling with one oar dropped unceremoniously into a chock cut in the wooden transom. It was several minutes before we realized that they were making their way toward us, rising and dipping into the troughs of waves that threatened to swallow them completely. As we continued our effort to set the anchor yet another time, they chased us vigorously. They were unlikely looking pirates, three swarthy men whose ship was no bigger than a large bathtub. On guard, Gary slowed the boat to enable them to catch us, as Hercules and I prepared to meet them on the afterdeck.

When they climbed over the rail, they betrayed neither

236

friendliness nor hostility. The two larger men stalked up to the wheelhouse while the oarsman stayed behind to hold the boat, standing on the bow and holding onto our rail to keep the two from colliding.

"Herc, you'd better go up to translate," I told Hercules as he watched the straight-backed figures mount the outside ladders to where Gary stood by the wheelhouse.

I had read about piracy, but if this was an example, it was a peculiar approach. Pointing to the painter which was dropped in the bow, I gestured for the oarsman to hand it to me, and walked the dinghy out to the stern where I tied it to keep it from banging. Smiling, he worked his way up over the stern, and leaned over the rail beside me, admiring the way the winds scudded off the tops of the black waves.

Once he had ascertained that his boat was safe, he was ready to join his fellows and by the time the two of us climbed to the wheelhouse, the Mexican captain had directed Gary practically to the beach and instructed that he drop anchor on the sandy bottom. Our anchor set, Gary dispatched Clarence to the engines, and me to the galley to lay out the best buffet our larder could muster. When I returned carrying a tray laden with sliced salami, cheeses, bread, and beer, the three men were spaced around the wheelhouse, gingerly touching the pieces of electronic equipment with looks of wonderment.

The food was greeted by enthusiastic smiles and nods of appreciation, and as we ate, Gary explained the workings of the Loran, using as simple terms as possible to facilitate Hercules's faltering translation. Gary drew a chart from under the table in order to illustrate his explanation, and when the Mexican captain's eyes fell on the clean chart, they lit up.

"He say you have beautiful charts," Hercules translated. "Will you show him where we are?"

"What do you mean?" Gary asked in astonishment. "Doesn't he use charts? How does he navigate?"

Hercules turned to the captain.

"He say he use radio. He bin runnin' the Gulf since many years now wi' his daddy. His daddy teach him."

"Does he mean Radio Direction Finder and compass?"

237

Gary wanted to know, having understood that the location of favorite fishing spots was a secret passed from generation to generation.

In response to Gary's question, the captain let go a flood of colloquial Spanish which Hercules, open-mouthed, tried to follow.

"He say he has no compass. He can tell where he is by what channel's on the radio."

"What? That can't be right. Where's he come from?"

"They say Progresso."

"Progresso! Christ! They couldn't possibly get up here from there with nothing but a radio!" Gary cried. "Ask him again."

Hercules turned back to the fisherman who watched this exchange with interest.

"He say that's right. He tune to a station and that way, he find out where he's close to."

"That's amazing! How could he find this place?"

"Because he knew where it was," Hercules replied when he had translated the question to the captain.

"Unbelievable!" Gary said, shaking his head.

The captain, obviously pleased at Gary's incredulity, merely smiled and nodded his affirmation.

"Ask him if he'd like some charts," Gary said, pulling some of the out-of-date duplicates that were stowed in the table.

When Hercules translated, the man nodded emphatically, his eyes gleaming at the prospect of possessing a chart. As we ate and drank, we learned that they spent weeks at a time scouring their special fishing holes for red snapper, grouper, lobster, shark, and barracuda. Once the meal was finished, we began looking around at each other, at a loss as to how to continue the conversation. The deckhand, the only crew member who smoked, had been carefully hoarding his last few packets of American cigarettes and was only reluctantly persuaded to part with some of them. Each man took a cigarette and puffed on it luxuriously, sending lovingly wrought smoke-rings over their heads. With little sympathy for the poor deckhand's wishes, we prevailed on him to give them two packs, putting him on short rations until we got home. Thanking him for his generosity, the three went below and strode to their small dinghy, followed by our crew.

It was an hour later when they returned. This time, secure in our mooring, they had come bearing gifts of fish, a bag of conch, and two large lobster tails. They were accompanied by yet another man, a tiny bronzed person who, except for the musculature of a grown man, looked like a ten-year-old child.

The deckhand, Hercules, and I greeted them as they clambered over the rail, bright smiles across their faces this time. The captain took the fish, half the size of his diminutive crew member, and held it up for my inspection. Flabbergasted at their beneficence, and chagrined at having little to give in return, I quickly exhausted my Spanish and fell back on Hercules for more superlatives.

Thanking him, I took the fish and started for the galley, intending to put it into the refrigerator whole. One of the other crewmen stopped me, and for a moment, I was afraid I had mistaken their intentions. The black-haired man reached into a scabbard at his side and withdrew a thick dagger. For a second, I froze. With a small smile, he took the fish from me and laid it on the deck. Crouching on the deck he ran the knife blade along the spine, deftly filleting out one long slab of white flesh. As I stood there, marveling at his swift dexterity, he warmed to his audience, and several times stood to sharpen his blade against that of his friend, stroking the bright steels against each other with flamboyant confidence. When he had finished, he stood, the fish frame in his hand, and started to fling it overboard.

"Whoa!" I cried, "Sopa! Sopa!" [Soup! Soup!]

"Ah!" he smiled, nodding approbation at the frugality.

After stowing the fish and passing out the last of our beer, I made sandwiches and carried them onto the back deck where we sat on the grimy pieces of equipment and lube oil drums tied against the deckhouse. The smallest man was dressed in nothing but a pair of tight bathing trunks which revealed a wicked purple scar from knee to hip.

Pointing to the scar, the deckhand asked in English: "How'd you get that?"

The man looked down thoughtfully and ran a finger the length of the mark, feeling it beneath his finger before replying.

239

"He say a shark bite him," Hercules translated.

"A shark!"

The captain spoke.

Hercules listened, then explained to us, "He say he dive for lobster. He go down seventy feet sometimes. He go down without anything on his back."

"What do you mean without anything on his back? Tanks?" I asked.

Hercules spoke to the captain again.

"No, he use no tanks. He hold his breath," Hercules said. "He dive down and hold his breath and find lobster. That's when a shark bite him. Captain say he nearly die."

"Good God, Herc. That's amazing. Tell him we're very impressed."

Hercules translated to the pleased smiles of the Mexican crew. While they finished the sandwiches and the beer, I hunted through the stores to find something special to give them. After making up a box of cheese, yams, some fresh fruit and onions, and our only box of cookies, I searched through the cabinets, trying to think what would be a treat to men who had been on a fishing boat for weeks. Nothing seemed appropriate, and as an afterthought, I added the only watermelon aboard. When I handed the box of food to the captain, he smiled appreciatively and bowed, but when I returned to present the watermelon to him, his eyes lit up. The others gathered to feel its cool skin and tap it for ripeness.

"Captain say it his favorite food," Hercules told me happily.

"Tell him it's mine, too. I hope they enjoy it."

Beaming, the captain took personal charge of the melon, wrapping it in thick, tanned arms and carrying it with the pride of a new grandfather to his dinghy.

After they had passed the precious watermelon over the rail to the captain's waiting arms, he sat bolt upright on the thwart, the melon on his lap, while his fellows descended into the bounding boat to huddle just above the waves. With cheerful goodbyes, they shoved off and made their way back through the chop to their anchored boats.

Early the next morning, we pulled anchor and scooted across the Gulf toward Louisiana. Feeling renewed vigor at the

240

thought of going home, I scrubbed the galley again, putting my nose into the wind outside occasionally in hopes of catching the first land scents on the air. We were less than a day's run from the bayou when the good engine blew up. Gary noticed thick black clouds of smoke pouring through the starboard stack and sent Clarence below to shut the engine off. Fleetingly, I wondered if we were doomed to remain on this trip forever until fate overtook us. While I stood by the helm, Gary, Clarence, and the deckhand searched for the problem. Although written in English, the manual was of little help, so they gingerly dismantled pieces of the engine in an effort to peep inside. The result was a tentative diagnosis of broken rocker arm, complicated by cam shaft dislocation and a nonfiring bank of cylinders. Without the help of the originally good engine, we limped along on the bad one, listening to the ominous coughs and wheezes with foreboding. As we approached the wide thicket of oil rigs that fan out from the Mississippi delta, Gary tried to reach the owner.

The radio was jammed with people wanting to make telephone calls, all holding on to listen for their names as the operator worked through a long waiting list. Gary periodically tuned in to see how fast our name was moving up the list.

Eventually we got through to inform the owner of our ETA so he could arrange for U.S. Customs and Immigration clearance. The officials who met us were friendly enough to the Americans but were decidedly cool toward Hercules and Clarence. Clarence, in agony over being shipped off to an American jail, kept to his cabin, producing his papers, then scurrying back to lie down and nurse a headache. He had informed me only the night before of the fact that he was wanted for bigamy in two states.

"Divorce is so expensive, Nance, you know, and a man need a woman. If my wife and me don't get alone, she find another man, I find another woman. No one hurt. We do not mind what the other do."

"Which wife doesn't mind, Clarence?"

"The wife in Honduras. She the mother of my kids."

"Then how do the authorities know you're a bigamist?"

"I also have wife in Florida and one in Texas."

"Oh. Well, Clarence, I'm not going to say anything."

"Thanks, Nance," he said miserably.

While the immigration officials were inspecting our papers, the customs men were inspecting the larder and Clarence hid, praying he would pass unnoticed through the paperwork mill of the bureaucracy and be spewed out the other side unharmed.

Finally, the officials released the boat, and Gary and I accompanied Clarence and Hercules to the immigration authorities at the airport before catching our own flight north. The man who occupied the tiny office stuffed back in a corridor behind the glitter of the airport lobbies, seemed more like a frustrated commandant than a mild-mannered bureaucrat.

"This is my office, my territory, and no one pushes me around. I do the pushing," he announced.

Clarence was visibly shaken but remained silent. Our plane was due to depart, and so we had to leave the two Hondurans in the clutches of a man who looked as though he had not eaten an unsuspecting visa applicant in weeks. When I glanced back over my shoulder, Hercules was still standing beside the man's desk looking bewildered while Clarence was trying to disappear into a chair.

After five weeks of fighting tooth and nail for honest treatment and the simple right to do the jobs for which we had been hired, we sat in a jumbo jet dusting off the last of the Tampico topsoil, headed for home.

FOURTEEN

WE WERE both exhausted. Aside from the physically de-
bilitating effect of Montezuma's revenge, and the unpleasant-
ness of salty drinking water, we were just plain tired. Gary
especially felt as though he had spent every waking hour in a
battle with either a corrupt bureaucracy or cantankerous
equipment. After settling into the house, we looked forward to
our first peaceful Christmas together since our wedding.

Gary had been promised a job with a large tug and barge
company and had expressed a desire to upgrade his license
before starting work. Realizing that he could study more effi-
ciently under the structure of an organized classroom, he en-
rolled in the Tidewater School of Navigation and, in the first
week of January, began driving to Norfolk, Virginia, and back
each week. For two weeks, he left at four A.M. Monday to drive
the five hours to Norfolk, then returned home late Friday
night. Saturday morning of the second week he lay in bed
complaining about the lonely monotony of the drive. The next
thing I knew, he was totting up my working time on commercial
vessels and announced that I could sit for a second class license.
The license would allow me to run as mate on any uninspected
vessel up to two hundred gross tons (a figure calculated by a
mixture of wishful thinking and voodoo arithmetic, as far as I
could discern), up to two hundred miles offshore. Although
skeptical, I agreed to try. The following Monday, we were
packing the car, colliding with one another, spilling cups of
coffee.

At dawn, we drove across the Chesapeake Bay Bridge-Tunnel. After having seen the sprawl of the bridge-tunnel from the perspective of the water, its entire length arched between the two low, sandy shores, the view from the bridge was an interesting change. As I looked down into the frothy shoals at the eastern end, I could see the feeding grounds for the hammerhead sharks, and in the anchorage on either side of Thimble Shoal Channel, several tankers lay in a wide-spaced group waiting their turn at the docks.

Slowed by the rush-hour traffic, I began to dread the initial meeting at the school. I need not have worried. The two partners who ran the school, Bill Hamilton and Ed Smith, welcomed me as easily as they had Gary. Bill, a former Coast Guard officer, and Ed, former master of ships who had run all kinds of vessels over the years, were patient and encouraging. Between them, their knowledge spanned more that I felt competent to learn, and the time I spent studying there was invaluable.

Gary and I moved into a local run-down hotel near the school, and I spent a good deal of time during fitful nights wondering if one of the entrepreneurs pacing outside would climb the fire escape that was clamped outside an unlockable window. The time spent at the hotel with Gary was not so fraught with paranoia as the time I spent there alone after he had passed his tests and gone back to work, leaving me to drive the distance to stay in Norfolk alone.

After four weeks of learning the Rules of the Road, working with chart navigation, and trying to decipher the Coast Guard regulations as set out in a collection of volumes that rivals the *Encyclopedia Britannica* in size, I marched over to the Coast Guard office, papers and recommendations in hand, to request a sitting. Anxious about the test itself, I had not anticipated opposition to my sitting for a license, despite having had to wrest my seaman's card from the Coast Guard in Baltimore as though I were repossessing their charter. Naiveté soon collapsed.

In spite of a democratic system of first-come-first-served which was organized with the simple expedient of a sign-in sheet, the uniformed petty officer studiously circumvented the list, calling out every name but mine, dealing with the men while ignoring me. This I was prepared to swallow. However, when he had exhausted the complement of males in the waiting area, then sat down with his back to me, I began to burn. Knowing I was dependent on the Coast Guard's goodwill to sit for my license, I opened with a very small salvo. I laid my envelope of papers on the reception desk and cleared my throat. He turned a page. Palms sweating, butterflies in my stomach, I shuffled papers and called out: "Excuse me." He reached for his coffee. While I was gearing up to come around the desk to confront him face to face, a uniformed man with a pleasant face approached the desk.

"Do you need some help?" he asked with a smile.

"Yes, please. I'd like to apply to sit for my tug operator's license, second class."

"Ah, that's this gentleman's department. Mr. Jones?" he said, turning to the hunched form of the petty officer. "Do you think you could help this lady?"

Mr. Jones looked around without moving.

"Oh! I didn't know anyone was there."

Rising, he came to the reception desk and shuffled through my time sheets, the letters of recommendation, and the verification of where and when I had worked. After a surly inspection of me and my papers, he pushed them toward me.

"You can only sit for a second class license. And you'll be restricted to a hundred-mile limit."

Covering rising anger with a forced smile, I said: "I think if you'll look at the verifications again, it states that I served *two* hundred miles offshore and am therefore applying for a *two-hundred-mile* limit."

Clearly irritated at my audacity to question his authority, he snatched the sheaf of papers and dropped it onto a blotter before a man concentrating raptly on eating a doughnut. As I drummed my fingers lightly on the countertop which acted as both a reception desk and a partition, I thought of the man at the Baltimore branch of the Coast Guard who had tried so hard to withold my seaman's card.

At that time worried that an increased crackdown by the Coast Guard on those who worked commercially without proper

245

papers would take me off the tug, Gary had driven me the two hours to Baltimore to get my Z-card (seaman's papers). When we entered the office and laid my ream of documents on the desk, the duty officer rose and sauntered toward us.

"She needs a seaman's card," Gary informed the man.

He looked skeptical. Deliberately, he riffled through the papers, then beamed.

"She doesn't have a certificate from the steward's school," he said delightedly. "She can't get her card without the steward's certificate."

"What's a steward's certificate?" I asked.

"She's not a steward, she's a seaman, ordinary, wiper," Gary replied.

"What? Well, I think she's still got to have a steward's certificate," he growled uncertainly.

"No, she doesn't. She's a seaman, ordinary, wiper," Gary repeated firmly.

"Are you sure?" the duty officer said. "She's got to be a cook."

"I'm her captain. She's a deckhand," Gary retorted.

The man coughed, then returned to the stack of papers on the desk top. As he sorted through my birth certificate, passport, social security cards, and a letter from Jerry confirming that I was gainfully employed as a deckhand, he noted the discrepancy between the two names on my social security cards, one in my maiden name, the other in my married name.

"How many last names you got?"

"Robson is my married name."

"Where's your marriage certificate?"

I shuffled through the stack to pull out a photocopy of the document.

"Where's the original?"

"In the safe deposit box."

A triumphant grin spread over his face.

"I need to see the original."

"But I've got all this! Here, here's my driver's license and credit cards as well," I said, spilling the contents of my wallet over the broad countertop.

"Well, it doesn't matter. You need the original," he assured me.

Gary could see that I was about to explode and stepped gently on my foot, warning me to keep silent.

"If that's what you need, we'll be back tomorrow with it," he told the man icily.

"Can't come tomorrow," the duty officer replied gleefully. "We've got our recruits coming in from Piney Point. I might could fit her in on Thursday."

Infuriated at our own impotence and the man's obduracy, we drove home and returned two days later with the required paper. This time, the receptionist's superior was in residence and seemed to have fewer scruples against issuing a Z-card to a woman.

"Why did you bring the original marriage license too?" the captain asked as he reviewed my documents. "All you need is the copy."

Clutching my hard-won Z-card, I leaned on the reception desk in Norfolk, watching the machinations of yet another frustrated petty officer. He strolled back to the desk with my papers in hand.

"You can come back tomorrow first thing and sit for it," he told me. "You've got to pass the Rules of the Road first with ninety percent. Then you can do the chartwork on Friday if you make it that far."

"Thank you very much," I replied sweetly, feeling one more hurdle pass.

The following morning when I walked toward the testing room door, the petty officer who sat at his desk with a cup of coffee and the newspaper hardly glanced up. Inside the room were several men of varying ages and descriptions, one of them a fellow student at the Tidewater School. Easing myself into one of the desks spaced around the room, I pulled out a handful of sharpened pencils and a calculator. The surly petty officer sauntered in, passing close behind my chair, and stood for a moment at the front of the room surveying the nervous faces. My heart sank. I knew from the descriptions of others who had taken the test that some of the questions were ambiguous and needed explanation by the proctor. If this man were to be proctor, I knew there would be no discussion.

You can do it, I told myself determinedly. Show him.

The door to the room opened again and the pleasant-faced officer of the day before stepped inside.

"I'll be your proctor," he smiled to the applicants. "Okay, how many are sitting for tankerman?"

Several hands went up.

"Now tug operator."

More hands waved in the air. Finally, finished with passing out tests, the proctor leaned against a bookcase on one side of the room and watched the sweating concentration begin. The petty officer, who had wandered through the room while his compatriot was handing out tests, came over to lean against the back of my chair. The proctor, waiting for a few moments, strolled toward the petty officer and with quiet tact, showed him the door. For me, the proctor now wore an aura of knighthood.

At the end of each section of the test, the proctor checked the scores before handing over the next portion. With each of his charges he was sympathetic, but after the treatment I had received from the petty officer, his congratulations at the successful completion of each installment was doubly welcome. Then came the chart problem.

With a large chart of the California coast, and a list of ten questions, I began my practical navigation test. Starting from this point, you travel for so many hours at such and such a speed, allowing for a southerly current of so much. Where are you now? What is off your starboard beam? What are the characteristics of the light you see? There were several lighthouses on the chart, and each new question depended on the correct answer to the previous one. Although everyone was allowed to miss one question, should it be in the beginning of the journey, the likelihood of having the rest of the answers correct diminished with each passing mile. I had approached the chart work with trepidation, but had gained more confidence as I worked, taking relative bearings from my changing location with an ease I found mildly disconcerting. At the ninth question, I stopped. Inherent in the question was the horrifying clue that I was twenty miles and one hundred and eighty degrees off course. Breaking out in a cold sweat, I returned to the beginning of the problem, methodically working through every piece of information, drawing it out on the chart, double-checking my answers. I had returned to within a pencil-point of my original location. A small voice inside began shrieking: "You see! You see! You can't do it! You can't! You can't!" In an effort to calm myself, I worked through the problem one more time before taking the entire chart into the proctor's office and laying it across his desk.

"Either I've hopelessly miscalculated or there is a typographical error in the question," I said miserably when he asked my difficulty.

With a quizzical look, he reached into the files and extracted a sheet of questions and answers. After slowly working through the problem as I showed him how I had arrived at my present dilemma, he reread the question and then the answer.

"Typographical error," he pronounced with a smile.

While he corrected the final portion of the test, I sat in a chair opposite, struggling to keep my nervousness under control. Then it was done. He looked up, a grin on his slender face, and stuck out his hand.

"Congratulations!" he said. "You did it."

"Thanks," I said, pumping his arm. "Thanks a lot. You were a big help."

Handing me the test scores, he told me to give them to the petty officer who, he assured me, would type out my license and swear me in. Overjoyed, I warmly thanked him again and stepped out into the next room where the petty officer slumped over a stack of papers. Trying not to look too pleased with myself, I handed him the piece of paper. Wordlessly, he looked at the scores, then pitched them onto a pile on his desk.

"Uh, the proctor told me you would type up my license and then swear me in," I said, crestfallen that he could still obstruct me after I had passed the tests.

"The secretary's gone," he mumbled.

"What?"

"The secretary's gone. She's the only one who can type up

the license. I don't think she'll be back today. You'll have to come back next week."

"But I live five hours away! I can type. I'll type it up!" I offered desperately.

The proctor had stuck his head into the room in time to hear the discussion.

"You're not allowed to type it up. It has to be done by one of the secretaries and they're both gone," the petty officer insisted irritably.

"She got good marks," the proctor interjected gently.

"Can't be done," the other insisted.

I felt on the verge of tears at the frustration. Gary was away on another tug, unreachable. There would be no one to commiserate with me when I got home.

"Look, why don't you take a walk and come back in an hour and a half?" the proctor suggested, darting a look at the petty officer. "We'll see what we can do."

With hands jammed in pockets and my pocketbook banging against my hip, I left. While I sensed that this postponement was out of the ordinary, I felt helpless to overcome it with reason and so trudged across the mall to the Tidewater School.

Bill and Ed stood in the doorway in conference and stopped when they saw me coming.

"Well?" Ed demanded, a look of happy anticipation on his face.

"Well, I passed," I replied, subduing the little kid inside who jumped up and down and shouted: "Yay! I did it!"

"Great! Let's see it," Ed said, holding out a broad hand.

"They didn't give it to me. The guy told me the secretary wasn't in and she had to type it up. He said I couldn't type it. He wants me to come back next week."

As I spoke, their eyes widened.

"You're kidding! They didn't give it to you right then?"

I shook my head.

"I've never seen them do that before," Ed said. "Do you want me to go over and talk with them?"

"Thanks, not yet. The proctor said to come back in an hour and a half and they might be able to do something then. If not, would you mind?"

250

"Sure. No problem," he assured me.

Despite the stall, by five o'clock that evening, I was waltzing down the fast-emptying mall, clutching my new license. Without being able to prove it, I had a feeling that the proctor had applied enough pressure to the petty officer to produce the desired results, and it was he who read me the oath and swore me into the ranks of wheelhouse people licensed by the United States Coast Guard.

It was not until the drive home that my excitement palled as I ruminated on my real prospects for experience and advancement as a commercial seaman. The license was only a piece of paper that legally entitled me to ask for a job. What I would have to deal with in terms of prejudice and skepticism was another matter. I had been out there long enough to know that the tug industry was a closely protected enclave of male supremacy and that the deckhand who at the airport had so bluntly told me I did not belong had expressed a majority view. I quaked at the idea of convincing a reluctant owner to give me a chance at a mate's job and then finding that the resident captain was so unhappy over a female mate that he would refuse to work with me, or worse, sabotage my work on the tug.

In the end, it was Gary who wangled my first job as a mate. A respected wheelhouse man, he is sporadically asked to fill in spot jobs with various companies. Shortly after I got my license, a small company in Wilmington phoned to ask if he would run as mate on one of their tugs for a weekend, a short job between Philadelphia and Baltimore with two barges. Instead of agreeing immediately, he proposed that they hire me as mate and allow him to accompany me as a passenger. They had no objections. It was in this way that I began to work as a free-lance, fill-in mate.

Having a license, even for the second spot in the wheelhouse, was a distinct advantage over applying for work as a deckhand, especially for a woman. Wheelhouse people were in shorter supply than deck crew, and I could not compete on deck with a young man my size. The wheelhouse offered me a better footing.

The mate's job is virtually the same as the captain's in most companies. The watch is usually from noon to six and from

251

midnight to six A.M., and the mate is expected to be competent to deal with whatever comes his (or her) way during that time. He is expected to be able to navigate, maneuver, and occasionally climb down and deck. As a matter of practicality, the relationship between the responsibilities of the mate and the amount of freedom a captain will give the mate depends largely on the relationship between the two and the trust the captain has in the individual's capabilities.

The security of knowing that the captain is always available in case of an emergency was tempered for me by the dread of leaning too heavily on him and never mastering the skills necessary to do the job well. Since I had had little wheelhouse experience, I was less than confident about my abilities, despite Gary's ceaseless encouragement. I doubt I would have had the chance to even work at the job without his personal advocacy and, in any case, will never know for certain. More important than how I got a chance was how well I did the job once there.

Added to my worries was the possibility of hostility from the captain or crew. The job is a symbiotic mesh of personalities and skills, with some crews more compatible than others. I had heard hair-raising stories of feuds between crew members, some ending in the death of one or both parties. One of the less brutal battles took place between a captain and crew of our acquaintance. A bully and a liar, the captain rode his crews unmercifully and in retaliation was treated by his crew members to massive doses of Ex-Lax administered in the numerous cups of coffee he drank daily. It was not until after a battery of hospital tests to say nothing of weeks of acute embarrassment that the captain discovered he had been the recipient of some relatively mild vengeance.

The hostility I might encounter could take many forms, but I was a target purely because of my sex, something the others had never experienced. Being female made me an easy mark for physical hostility, especially in the confined quarters of a tug. Most of my experiences on the water had been good rather than bad, but where antipathy existed, it was acute. Never having been the victim of direct assault, I was nonetheless cognizant of the possibilities, but worried more over the subtly veiled enmity of an unfamiliar captain.

The man in the wheelhouse can deliberately put a hated deckhand's life in jeopardy, expressing his intent with the mere flicker of an eye, a mirthless smile, or a seemingly casual comment while he "accidentally" crashes into a barge on which the deckhand is working. Harry Truitt had been the victim of such an "accident" while he decked for a man who took a sadistic pleasure in making his life aboard miserable. Harry, loyal to the end and ever-ready to follow orders, a conditioning from the navy which was coupled with a natural desire to please, stood on the fantail beside the hawser waiting for the captain to slow the tug after letting out some hawser. As Harry watched the hawser thrash, faking out the last several coils of the line without any apparent slowing of the engine, he looked up at the captain who stood by the after controls.

"Grab it, Harry! Get a turn on there before we lose it!" the man shouted to Harry.

After a moment's hesitation, Harry called to the captain to slow the boat so that he could get a grip on the hawser.

"Grab it! Grab it!" the captain shouted.

Thinking that there was a problem with the controls, Harry stepped toward the coil of hawser which was still snaking its weight across the deck before racing through the bitts. Reaching out a hand, he tried to flip the line onto the port horn of the towing bitts, almost managing a turn but with the speed of the tug, it flew off again, lashing out and striking Harry across the legs with such force that it knocked him to the deck. The doctor who treated Harry told him he had been lucky not to lose both legs. As it was, he carried the bruises with him for months.

A hostile captain could make a mate look incompetent by deliberately injuring a deckhand on the mate's watch and blaming the incident on the mate's inexperience or inability. While in a rational world this might cast doubts on the captain as well, this life does not foster rational behavior. Long periods spent away from home in the confined atmosphere of a tug more often produce paranoia than perspective.

One engineer, so anxious to escape the tug on which he worked and at the same time retaliate for real or imagined slights by the owner, made a deliberate attempt to destroy the only engine of the tug on which he rode by putting a cupful of bolts and scrap into the water pump and allowing it to work through the engine. His timing was such that the engine seized up in a gale partway across the Gulf of Mexico, leaving the tug to drift in a storm for two days before being rescued. Although the engineer could have as easily gone down with the rest of the crew, he had his revenge. In any case, since I had had so little experience, whatever mishap might occur, the captain's judgement would be the more valid in the eyes of the owners.

With this in mind, Gary and I decided that, initially, I would work only when he was aboard as well, until we could acquaint ourselves with the crews and conditions. Since the companies realized they were getting two crew members for the price of one, they had no objection. We spent a year doing jobs this way with me hired as mate, paid and acknowledged as such, while Gary ran as tutor-in-residence. The captain could sleep undisturbed and Gary could give me as much opportunity as possible to learn to maneuver.

Gradually, as we began to know some of the crewmen and they us, we began to feel more relaxed about the idea of my being there alone. Most came to understand that we were trying to make a life for ourselves together and respected that goal. It was only occasionally that I was forced to deal with the threat of sabotage.

One captain, sitting with me in a small wheelhouse while I guided two barges rafted side by side through the Chesapeake and Delaware Canal, leaned against the window and discussed his years of tugboating. As he talked, I nodded, my attention on the canal and on steering by one of the two electric tillers which were no larger than a man's finger and attached to the paneling just beneath the windows. Suddenly, I could feel the tow veer toward the bank on the starboard side and hastily touched the tiller to port in an effort to correct the swing. The captain had fallen silent and hunched in the corner beside the port window. I glanced up at the rudder indicator affixed over my head and saw that the helm was not answering my pressure on the electric tiller, but had continued to slide to starboard until it was pinned hard over.

"Hey, ya got me!" I cried, realizing that the tiller on the side beneath his elbow was the culprit.

Lazily, he turned toward me, moving only his head. "What?"

"Move! You've got me pinned!" I cried, clawing at his shirt-sleeve in an effort to shift his position.

"Hmmm?"

"I said *move!*"

I finally managed to get a tight enough grip on his shirt to pull him back against the wheehouse door behind him, forcing him to release the tiller pinned under his hand.

"Oh my gosh! I must've accidently leaned on it!" he said.

"Yeah. I guess so. I got her now," I said without elaboration as I watched the tow return to a stable course parallel to the rock riprap.

Without another word, he left me alone. As I worked the few facts of the incident over in my mind, trying to decide whether it had indeed been an accident, I kept coming back to one problem: had he simply leaned against the tiller, it would have swung the tow to port, not to starboard. In order to move to starboard, the tiller would have had to have been pulled. Fifteen minutes later, Gary climbed into the wheelhouse with two mugs of coffee.

"Thanks, Sweetheart. What have you been doing?"

"Listening to the captain tell us about how hysterical you got when he accidentally leaned against the lever and you thought we were going to crash," he said matter-of-factly.

"I wouldn't have said hysterical."

"I didn't think it sounded like you," he remarked.

I told Gary my version of the story and waited for his reaction.

"It might have happened the way he said," Gary said finally, "there's no way of proving it either way. But you'd better keep your eyes open."

"Yeah, I know."

"Listen. You can do this. Just keep him from getting you in a position to do you in," Gary ordered.

"Easier said than done."

"Just do it."

"Rodger dodger," I smiled.

The still-nebulous tiller incident notwithstanding, for the most part the men were good to me, accepting me in a friendly, brotherly way, and the owners seemed satisfied enough to keep hiring me back. Slowly, I turned over in my mind the idea of going without Gary. While to a certain extent that would defeat our ultimate purpose of working together, we decided that the more experience I had and the more people who came to know my work without the crutch of my husband, the more opportunities we might have of working together again. Still, I was hesitant to aggressively solicit jobs. Having become accustomed to run predominantly for one Wilmington company on a couple of their tugs, I had worked into a comfortable niche and was slow to test myself with something new. I liked coming to know the boats and the crews and hung back at the idea of starting over somewhere else. But Gary had other plans.

FIFTEEN

In THE BEGINNING of April 1982, I discovered I was pregnant. That same week, we were hired to deliver a forty-seven-foot sailboat from Summerhill Key, Florida, to Georgetown, Maryland. As always, Gary described the trip to me as a pleasure cruise. As always, I swallowed it hook, line, and sinker despite previous experience. This time, however, we asked two friends to join us which perpetuated the deception that it was to be a vacation.

Doug Brown, Gary's mate on *Progress*, had married Kathy of the long distance radio telephone calls and to my delight, I found that she and I liked each other very much. When I phoned to ask if she and Doug could make the offshore run, she was immediately enthusiastic. After her initial acceptance, pending Doug's approval, she began to think out loud about their one-year-old son, Josh.

Kathy is nothing if not a loving and conscientious mother and was reluctant to leave him for the ten days to two weeks the trip was projected to take. It would mean that they would miss his first birthday, that Josh would see his father for perhaps thirteen hours of the two weeks off the tug, and that she would worry about him the entire trip.

"Bring him," I said naively. "We'll manage."

Gary and I were both anxious to see if we could manage. Having been told so often that a woman can't work on a tug, we were hopeful that we could prove "them" wrong a second time when "they" said we couldn't run with a child. Could we meld our previous life with the new one growing inside me?

Kathy and I worked out the logistics as best we could without having seen the layout of the boat. The boat, a ketch, was part of a fleet owned by a newly formed charter company. We had been hired for the job by one of the partners of the charter company who assured us the vessel was immediately ready to go as it had been chartered all winter. He painted a glowing picture of the company's "southern organization" and its "manager," adding that we would have credit and cash at our disposal for spare parts and fuel. Even so, Gary planned for us to fly to Florida two days early and work through a checklist before the Browns joined us just before casting off.

It was not until I sat at the airport waiting for the flight that I remembered I was pregnant. No Bloody Marys. The ride to Miami consisted of a terrifying collection of creaks and groans and shudderings. However, it was not until we sat on the small plane from Miami to Key West and heard the pilot cheerfully announce that we were privileged to be seated on the oldest aircraft still in commercial service in the United States that I knew real panic.

When we stepped out onto the runway in Key West, we were alone except for the ground crew. There was no southern manager in evidence to take us the final forty-five minutes to the boat. After several phone calls, Gary raised the man the partner had described as the southern manager, but what arrived was a bare-chested beachcomber and his T-shirted wife who stuffed us into a van and took off, only two hours after we had landed.

It was on the drive that things began to disintegrate. Rather than having been chartered all winter, the vessel had, they told us, been delivered from the manufacturer to the bulkhead at which it was now tied and had remained there untouched. There were no credit cards for fuel, lube oil, filters, or spare parts, and the corporate checking account held a grand total of $67.24. When we arrived at the dock, things took a further turn for the worse. There was not a flashlight to be found let alone batteries. The engine and equipment manuals were unopened and it was only later that we discovered that, in

258

spite of careful instructions for hand-starting the engine, one needed the reach of an orangutan in order to accomplish the task. There was only a partial complement of cotter pins in the rigging. Closer inspection revealed that in several places the pulpit was screwed rather than through-bolted, and three of the screws poked through the gelcoat of the hull. As Doug was to remark partway up the Ditch, it looked as though it had been built on a Friday afternoon.

Finally, contrary to assurances, the certificate of ownership was not aboard. Word on the water had been that the Coast Guard was cracking down on drug smuggling and a rash of thefts of yachts and should we be stopped without the proper papers but with three licenses aboard, we could conceivably end up having our licenses suspended. After a dinner of cold chicken eaten by the street lamp on the bulkhead, I was ready to get back on the oldest aircraft in the western hemisphere and go back home.

A telephone call to the owner the next day produced more assurances but little tangible. Interspersed between nagging phone calls we spent the next two days sorting, replacing cotter pins and taping over sharp projections, checking the machinery, filling the engine with lube oil, and buying flashlights, batteries, and groceries. In the evenings, we read the manuals.

While I scrubbed the gummy drippings of an overhanging tree off the nonskid and waited for Gary to return from the telephone, I heard a Splip! Splip! Splip! in the canal. Looking down, I saw a long barracuda pouncing upon a smaller silver fish. As I stared, the barracuda smashed its prey against the fiberglass hull and entrapped it long enough to take a large bite out of the silver side. The eternal metaphor of power winning over weakness, I thought. No justice, no compromise, only an impersonal devouring. I felt as though we were that little fish trying to extract honest treatment from the partner over two thousand miles of telephone wire.

We were proposing to make a coastal trip in what was essentially a tributary party boat. Although purportedly a sailboat, she was high and beamy, with room for three large cabins in her interior. The forward cabin contained not only a double bunk which formed a V in the bow compartment, but also had

259

enough room for an awkward padded pew under which were stowed the life preservers. It had a hanging locker which nestled beside the forward head. The after cabin, a large, boxy space with a double bunk that sprawled athwart the room, contained only one handrail which was located inconveniently beside a narrow doorjamb. The bunk was raised on a tall platform in front of a pair of giant mirrors that would have satisfied even the most creative sexual fantasies. The galley, which ran along the starboard side of the engine compartment, contained the single useful luxury on the vessel, and the only thing aboard that provided uninterrupted service, a refrigerator with a small freezing compartment.

To port of the engine compartment were two narrow bunks stacked in a passageway between the main salon and the after head. It was here that we rigged up a crib of sorts for Josh, banked by the overhead cushion which was braced vertically in place by the two salon easy chairs. The main salon, a broad, open room without a grabrail, was a charming living room but a dismal sailboat cabin that converted to an obstacle course in rough weather. We removed the chairs, set without fasteners on the varnished deck, but the table and low partition between the galley sink and the main floor which was two steps above everything else acted as a hurdle.

Additionally, Gary and I were the only ones aboard who had sailed anything like this before. Doug and Kathy's sailing experience had been confined predominantly to Doug's Hobie Cat which he launched in the Hatteras surf. Nonetheless, when Doug and Kathy arrived, we shared a shrimp dinner in the cockpit, watching Josh explore the lockers while we ate, and pretended that this was indeed a vacation, while Gary prayed for the arrival of the owner's certificate. A pink slip came in the mail the next morning, not unequivocal proof, but enough of a compromise coupled with the pressing work schedules of the men, to push us off that afternoon. High tide took us skimming over the shallow coral reefs until we passed the last channel mark and bounded into the cerulean waters of the Straits of Florida.

While I fried the steaks, Doug set up his fishing line and Gary leaned against the coaming, steering casually with one hand as Joshua played in the spokes of the wheel. Kathy sat in the cockpit, feet braced against the starboard edge of the seat, looking back over the warm glow of the afternoon sun as it framed Doug's shoulders at the stern. As I turned the steaks, the smell of frying grease wafting up in my face in the narrow passageway of the galley, I began to realize I had not bargained for a tender stomach. Largely free of morning sickness, I had given little thought to any change afloat and it was not until the aroma of steaks slowly took on the odor of dead meat that I began to worry. The wind had picked up gradually, reaching the predicted eighteen knots and slowly surpassing it as the sun crept lower toward the horizon. The tubby sailboat began to bob awkwardly in the relatively gentle surf until I stuck my head out of the companionway to suck in some fresh air.

"What's the matter, Babe? You okay?" Gary asked, seeing my ashen complexion.

"Trade places with me, please," I replied without explanation.

"Sure."

Amiably, he climbed below and took the spatula while I crawled behind the wheel. Doug sat in the inflated life raft which occupied the entire afterdeck, his feet on the rail watching the trailing line.

"When I put Josh to bed, I can take the wheel if you'll tell me what to do," Kathy offered, eager to learn.

"You got it," I smiled as I drank in gulps of fresh air. "Gary can explain it all to you—greased wedges, up-drafts, God only knows what else," I said, raising my voice for Gary's benefit.

"Are you bitchin' about me again?" he growled benevolently.

"Yes, Dear."

"Greased wedges?" Kathy murmured, perplexed.

"I'm teasing. It's the principle by which the thing moves through the water so I'm told, but you don't need to know it to sail. Gary really is a good teacher."

She smiled, dark eyes sparkling.

"I want to learn."

"Whoa!" Doug shouted, scrambling for a better footing in the raft. "I got one. Feels like a whale!"

The nylon line ran free, sending out nearly the entire reel before throwing on the catch.

"*Wow!*" he cried, bringing all heads around to the stern again. "It's a whale! Watch it jump again! Look! Look! I think it's a dolphin!"

For two hours, Doug and Gary took turns fighting the fish toward the stern, reeling and playing the line carefully in hopes of keeping the fifty-pound test line from snapping.

"I think he's beginning to wear out!" Gary puffed over his shoulder. "I know I am!"

While I stayed at the helm, Kathy fed Josh, holding him in her lap, feet braced to keep from sliding off the seat in the increasing heel. After putting Josh to bed in his makeshift crib, she relieved me of the helm and set about learning to steer a compass course while I tried to take pictures of the fish as they scrambled to haul it aboard.

Since we had no gaff hook, Gary searched the lazarette, finally emerging with a telescoping boat hook. As Doug reeled the dolphin to the stern, Gary leaned over the pulpit to jab the hook into the fish's bright gills.

"I've just about got it in," Gary cried over the sounds of the wind and water.

"Hold him, Gare! He's working' the hook out. He's free, you got him?" Doug shouted suddenly as together they tried to pull the enormous dolphin up over the stern pulpit onto the deck.

With the fish hook out of his mouth, the fish was only held by the boat hook, jammed awkwardly into the flapping gills. Seeing his imminent capture, the fish began to thrash in an effort to release himself. In a swift motion, Gary levered the fish up even with the rail, jamming the hook farther into the gills. He held it there, all fifty pounds, puffing for a second while fish and man summoned their last burst of strength. The dolphin moved first, wriggling off the hook bit by bit.

"He's gettin' away!" Doug cried.

With a roar, Gary swung the huge dolphin over his head and landed him sprawling half out of the raft. When the fish saw his last hope of freedom, he tried to slither over the side, but Doug stumbled overtop Gary to grab the fish's tail and drag him back into the high-sided raft. The three of them lay there, gasping. It was done.

"God! He's huge!" Gary panted, pulling himself out of the tangle.

He and Doug surveyed their catch with satisfaction, watching as the life drained away and with it the dolphin's jubilant iridescent colors. Doug and I filleted steaks from the bones in the waning glow of sunset. I sliced, fighting my stomach, until between us, Doug and I reduced the fish to a head and the frame, stuffing white slabs of flesh into the freezing compartment of the refrigerator, and finally casting the bones overboard to be finished by another predator. With the fish dispatched, Doug, Kathy, and Gary dove into the steak dinner while I chewed unhappily on a peanut butter cookie.

The boat's plastic hull shook with each wave, reeling under the thundering blows. The four of us, now in foul weather gear, hung onto the cockpit, listening to things below rattle against their bins and occasionally fly across the compartments. As the motion grew worse, Kathy went below to climb in the bunk with Josh, protecting him from the debris now sliding around the cabin. Doug, Gary, and I stayed on deck.

When the waves began crashing onto the foredeck and housetop and cascading into the cockpit, we folded the bimini top against the house, strapping it into place. The wind had increased to about thirty-five knots and by this time I was heaving over the side every fifteen minutes, sprawled across the coaming with one arm hooked around the life rail. As the night wore on, it became evident that, under sail alone, we were sliding sideways at an alarming rate and Gary decided to turn on the engine. Unable to locate any information about fuel consumption or tank capacity, we had dipped the tanks before we left, and for what little the information was worth, knew we had almost full tanks. Gary went below and turned on the engine while Doug stood by the helm. When he came back up, I replaced Doug behind the wheel while the two of them checked the rigging and the lights. Frighteningly, Gary found that the jolting had disconnected the running lights, and we were now pounding through the heavily traveled waters of the Straits of Florida without any indication to other vessels that we existed. Knowing all too well how difficult it could be to distinguish the flickering lights of a small vessel as it alternately disappeared and resurfaced in rough seas, Gary tried to fix the lights. Reduced to jiggling and praying without success, he finally strapped a flashlight to the pulpit.

The engine, struggling to push the broad, high-sided yacht against the force of the winds, spluttered as the propeller rose and dipped erratically. The gauges at the foot of the steering pedestal began to creep toward the overheat mark. The genoa, the only headsail, was a roller-reefing arrangement, managed by a line which ran from the pivoting headstay to a winch in the cockpit. It enabled the crew to take several turns on the headstay from the safety of the cockpit, wrapping the sail around the wire like a scroll. While Gary took the helm from me, Doug and I started to crank the sail in, struggling with the force even on the large, double-geared winch. Gary eased the boat up toward the wind, throwing a luff long enough for us to take in some more sail then falling off again in order to keep from flopping over unexpectedly onto the other tack. As he headed the boat up again, we began to reef furiously, Doug bent over the winch with the heavy chrome handle while I tailed. It was an arduous job until suddenly a Pop! and the line spun more freely for a couple of minutes before stopping completely. We looked up to see a tear in the leech of the sail quickly working its way toward the stay until the genoa was two shredded pieces of dacron, flapping loudly across the deck.

"We've got to get it down!" Gary cried. "Nance, you take the helm while Doug and I go forward."

"For all our sakes, hold on!" I shouted after them as they crawled over the housetop.

Gary reached the mast, then unwrapped the halyard and tried to let it run free. Nothing happened.

"She's stuck. Doug, feed this out, and I'll try to pull it down!" he yelled over the shrieking equipment.

Doug scrambled to the mast and wrapped one arm around it, then held the halyard in his hand. As I saw Gary stumble toward the headstay, I was almost overwhelmed by fear. Finding anyone fallen overboard in this mess would be an impossibility. None of us wore life preservers and Gary was not a particularly strong swimmer in any case. I held the boat just off the wind and prayed. The sail made an effort to blind him, flapping its knotted lines in his face as he fought past it to grab the material just beside the slot and yank. Still nothing moved. When he fell to his knees, flailing around for a grip on the pulpit, my heart stopped.

"If you go overboard, you miserable so-and-so, I'll never forgive you," I said to the cockpit.

"Tie the halyard off really loose and come help me," Gary shouted to Doug.

Doing as he was ordered, Doug left several yards of slack on deck before cleating the line, then crawled forward to pull himself up beside Gary. With the added weight on the bow, the boat fishtailed and dove more determinedly into the waves, diminishing my already tenuous control on the steering. I fought against the swerving, trying to keep the sail from lashing their faces while I gagged into the flooded cockpit. The two of them stood, feet splayed out in an effort to balance while the deck plunged beneath them, and hauled on the sail. It remained stuck.

"It's no use. Come on back a minute and I'll get some stops," Gary shouted.

The two of them inched their way back to the cockpit long enough to arm themselves with some nylon webbing, then climbed forward again to fight the sail. As they reached the headstay and hung onto the pulpit, I thought for a second of all the missing fasteners we had found, and offered up another swift prayer for their safety. My heart sank when I saw Doug squat down so that Gary could climb onto his shoulders. Then, Doug struggled upright, pushing Gary partway up the headstay. Reaching as far above his head as possible, Gary began throwing hitches around the sail, gathering folds of it in his arms haphazardly until he had caught part of it in a series of knots like a parachute tangled in a tree. As he pulled the sail more and more closely into the stay, tying it with nylon stops, the noise began to diminish. Then Doug backed away from the headstay in order to let Gary down to the deck. He fell to his knees. My breath stopped and for one terrible moment, I was afraid they were both going over the side as they clawed for a hold. Still aboard, they righted themselves and finished tying the tatters of the sail into small billowing clouds that fought the restraints. After what felt like an hour of panic, the two of them slowly came hand over hand back to the cockpit. While Doug was sober-faced, Gary had returned with a triumphant grin on his features and stumbled to the wheel to kiss me swiftly.

"You okay?"

"Peachy," I whispered. "Hold this."

I fell over the coaming and heaved the accumulated stomach acid over the side before sitting up again and taking a deep breath. Gary reached out a hand and dragged me over the cockpit seat to his side, then put an arm around me as he steered.

"Doug, I want to get another fix and lie down if you would take it for a couple of hours," Gary said.

"Okay, just let me check Kathy and Josh first."

When they traded places, Doug sat behind the wheel, watching the black horizon for signs of another vessel and casting glances at the compass and the engine gauges which were holding steady just below overheat. While Gary fought his stomach long enough to take a Loran fix and check our location, I leaned back overboard, staring dully into the tiny flickers of phosphorescent light in the dark waters rushing by the hull. I could feel Doug pull on my jacket when I stopped gagging, hauling me back into the cockpit.

"You want a cookie?" I asked finally, dragging out a miraculously dry packet of peanut butter cookies that I had stashed in the winch box earlier that evening.

"No thanks," he grinned.

I leaned against him, munching on the crumbling cookie, trying not to drink in the salt spray that gushed over the side while I took in exhausted breaths.

"We gonna make it?" he asked, putting his arm around me as I began to weave with the motion of the boat, powerless to hold myself still.

"Hell, yes!"

"You and the baby gonna make it, Nance?" he persisted.

"Damn right!" I asserted, less than convinced.

We spent the next two hours huddled together behind the steering wheel. Every half-hour, I crawled to the side, hooked an arm over the life rail and heaved, expending the last dregs of energy. By the time Gary took his watch, I could do no more than sprawl on the cockpit seat with my head just under cover of the collapsed bimini top, oblivious to the chill water running down my neck. I spent the night and the next day prostrate on the soaked cushion wedged into the space with some equipment that Gary and Doug had laid over me to keep me from falling overboard.

The hours before we puttered into Miami harbor were a series of fleeting impressions: a grey, salt-sprayed day; Kathy's sitting huddled under the half-opened bimini top with Josh in her lap, trying to feed and entertain him while fighting her own seasickness; Gary's salt-encrusted face and beard, almost unrecognizable as he peered into my face and demanded that I make it. I had never before been so sick. The near-delirium of the previous twenty hours notwithstanding, once the waters calmed and the sun came out, I began to come round and by the time we entered the channel into Miami, I was able to sit up and take nourishment. Kathy, who had been fixing meals as well as taking care of Josh, came up from below and handed me a sandwich.

"Welcome back," she said with a smile.

"Thanks. Nice to be back."

Despite my seasickness and dehydration, neither the baby nor I seemed to have suffered any ill effects and once I had downed the tuna and a glass of milk, my strength began to return. After filling the fuel and water tanks, we docked at the municipal dock, a concrete bulkhead where a score of local fishermen gathered to jaw and drink beer until the wee hours.

Guessing that the genny halyard had jumped the sheave, Doug and I cranked Gary up the mast with a pocketful of tools and listened to him swear for half an hour while he worked the line free. Once we had finished stuffing the sail into a bag, we called a crew conference which produced a unanimous decision to spend the night in port, and a majority decision to make the next leg of the journey up the Inland Waterway. Gary, anxious to chop off the extra one hundred and fifty miles that the ride up the Ditch would entail, voted to go back outside and run up the coast, but, after a weather report confirmed that northeast winds of better than twenty-five knots would continue unabated, he was voted down. While more accustomed to autocratic rule than democracy, he accepted the vote with the warning that our fifty-eight-foot mast might ultimately make the decision for us.

The following morning before breakfast, we cast off and motored up the first stretch of the Inland Waterway. The first bridge proved no difficulty, but the second loomed as a barrier to our peaceful existence. Its midsection, a removable span that remained fixed except for the occasional attention of a large crane, claimed to have an overhead clearance of fifty-six feet. While we hung there, a fly caught between the spider web of the bridge and the giant frog of the ocean, a low-slung sailboat coasted up alongside. An elderly couple stood together in the cockpit.

"What's your clearance?" the man called.

"Fifty-eight feet plus antenna," Gary replied, cupping his hands to his mouth. "About fifty-eight, six. What are you?"

"Fifty-six."

We all stood on deck, staring at their mast.

"Would you watch us go through?" the man shouted again. "We'll get on the radio. Channel seventeen."

"Sure. Go ahead," Gary called back. "Nance, go down and get them on the radio."

Gary lined us up directly behind the other boat so we could better guess the distance between their mast and the bridge.

"Okay, you look good so far. Take it easy. Okay, a little more. Yeah. So far so good; it looks like about a foot over your mast from here."

"We're under!" the wife called triumphantly over the radio.

In another three minutes, they were in clear water on the opposite side of the bridge.

"Okay, we'll watch you go under."

"I don't know, Gary," Doug muttered, shaking his head, "They didn't look like they had two feet over their masthead to me."

"Me either," Gary agreed, squinting at the layout of the bridge. "What kind of water is there under the next span east?"

"Four feet according to the chart," I told him pointing out the spot.

"We draw four feet with the centerboard up," he mused outloud. "What do you think that looks like?" Gary persisted, pointing at the eastern span.

"Close."

"If we get under this and there's another shorter one farther up, we've got problems."

"Look, maybe we could put the mast on deck if we had to," I replied desperately, feeling the threat of a return to the ocean. "There are a dozen boat yards along here."

"Okay. What do y'all think? Does that span look two feet higher than the middle one?"

It did. Just.

"Okay, everybody on the port gunwale. Let's get her heeled over as much as we can toward the highest spot, and we'll just creep in and see how it goes. Keep your fingers crossed."

We radioed the sailboat that waited on the northern side of the bridge and told them what we proposed to do.

"We'll all be on deck so sing out loud and clear if it looks like we're not going to make it," I told her before climbing back on deck.

After putting Josh in a backpack she had brought, Kathy stood between two of the shrouds and hung over the side, while Doug and I did the same on either side of her. The bridge abutment was cement and as Gary eased the boat toward the westernmost side of the span, the three of us reached out hands to fend off the base. The boat was heeled slightly, shortening our clearance needs. Gary gave the throttle a spurt of power, then threw it into neutral and watched us drift toward the steel girder overhead. All eyes were on the masthead.

"What's it look like?" he cried.

"So far so good," I muttered, fascinated by the prospect of our mast coming into contact with the bridge.

"Joe says you look good," the woman shouted over the radio.

Gary touched the controls again and we edged into the gap.

"The antenna's going down," Doug said.

"Is it gonna break?"

"Don't know."

Thwack! The antenna, bent nearly double as it scraped under the first I-beam, sprung upright in the space between the first and second bridge supports.

"What do you think?" Gary wanted to know, motionless at the controls.

We held ourselves just off the bulkhead, walking along the rail as we kept several inches between the concrete and the teak trim of the boat.

"May as well keep going," Doug finally replied.

Gary touched the throttle forward again and then slipped it back to neutral.

Sproing! The antenna scraped by another beam and snapped back into place. Gary eased ahead.

"Now all we need is to run aground in here," he murmured.

Thwack! Thwack! Thwack! Thwack! Thwack! Thwack! Each time the antenna threatened to break and each time it came back for another blow. "You've made it! You're through!" our spotter cheered over the radio. Our exhilaration was only slightly dampened by the knowledge that if we found a lower bridge between this one and the next outlet to the ocean, we were stuck.

While the journey was a twenty-four-hour work day fraught with headaches, periodic breakdowns, and little sleep, it was made easier by the knowledge that we could be in the ocean noisily breaking to pieces in a northeast sea instead of motoring up the relatively calm waters of the Intercoastal Waterway. That knowledge coupled with the company of friends and beautiful scenery helped to alleviate some of the frustration. Setting up the grill which attached to a bracket in

270

the stern, we roasted dolphin fillets over the coals while puttering through marsh reeds that waved like liquid gold in the waning light. Pelicans flew past, making their perpetual crash landings in the ripples of our wake.

Josh often entertained himself by cranking one or the other of the winches, gleefully watching birds swoop by, and identifying "Boats!" and "Birds!" in a delighted voice. A constant breeze blew warm over the decks, a reminder of the winds that had chased us inside to plow past piling after piling, marking off our slow advance on the strip charts.

Low on cash and without credit cards, we stopped in St. Augustine to phone the partner, and ask for an advance on the fuel money owed us. The man was unavailable, call back in an hour. An hour later he was out. My suspicions notwithstanding, Gary cranked up the engine and we cast off, three of us staring wistfully behind at the still-unfamiliar but enticing town. Gary, determined to finish the job before he and Doug were due back at work, ignored our protests and passed under the next bridge, jaw set and blue eyes on the continuous string of markers which poked up between the marshlands.

Kathy was exhausted. Not only was she spending thirteen hours a day with Josh, feeding, changing, washing, supervising, entertaining, but she was using what free time she had learning to read charts, spot markers, and steer in an effort to be a fully functioning member of the crew.

We looked for every opportunity to add a little zest to an arduous plod, however littered with scenic beauty. Fortunately, we all relished simply being out of doors and the uninterruptedly clear weather. Our shared meal of supper was one bright spot in the day as we chatted over a glass of wine while drinking in the scents of the salt marshes and listening to the cries of the birds.

As Gary and I watched Kathy and Josh, we began to understand the energy involved in full-time motherhood, let alone working outside the home as well. I drew my knees up to my growing belly, hoping that the radical change would not destroy our marriage. Child-rearing and supporting that home looked frighteningly like full-time work apart from each other.

"Don't worry, Nance. After you've got 'em, you can't imagine your life without 'em," Doug assured me one afternoon.

The shaft bearing had sporadically worked its way loose, freed by a pair of ill-fitted set-screws that refused to stay in place. Gary had stopped at a marina in Georgia and stockpiled replacement screws but the time lost at each replacement had accumulated to a day and a half by the time we puttered into Norfolk harbor. Zombie-like, we had stood watches, passing familiar spots in the dark with the dazed recognition of somnambulists until we had finally tied to a pier in Norfolk to let off the Browns. Pressed by time and exhaustion, they planned to take a bus home while Gary and I took the boat the last one hundred and sixty miles up Chesapeake Bay.

A stiff northerly breeze had kicked up five-foot waves that considerably slowed our forward motion in that broad-sided tub. Without the genoa, we were forced to reach across the wind, advancing us by what felt like inches in hours. Gary and I traded two- or three-hour watches, each trying to give the other some time to sleep. The days were closing in on Gary. He had been ordered to report back to work on Wednesday.

The wind had died at dawn on Tuesday and we chugged with sails down, passing the lines of crab pots strung along the shores. As I passed the entrance buoy to the Choptank River, the engine died. By now, knowing the sound of the engine when it was running out of fuel, and the process by which one switched fuel tanks, I rushed below, only in time to hear the last cough before it stopped. We drifted for a few minutes while I raised the two sails, but, on a glassy surface, we were forced to drop anchor to keep from being pulled back down the bay by the ebbing current. It was then that we discovered that the engine manufacturer had a peculiarly sadistic sense of humour.

"This is unbelievable!" Gary shouted, waving the engine manual at me. "They tell you how easy this damned thing is to operate, but they give you instructions for restarting it that would stump a three-armed baboon! Look at this! I have to hold this down, this lever here, then hold down the fuel valve over there," he said, pointing.

272

"Where?"

"Come here."

He stood up and led me to the other side of the open engine compartment where a lever stuck off the engine a good eight feet from the first lever.

"You hold down that one over there, then this one at the same time, and *then* you push the button on the panel. *That* I might be able to do with my toe, but there is no way I could get it all at the same time!"

"Sure doesn't look like it," I agreed.

Too numb to worry, I poured a glass of iced tea and made two sandwiches, then curled up on the bunk behind Gary who was crouched over the port side of the engine again.

"Here, have a sandwich. It'll make you feel better. Then we'll try to restart the monster."

"How could you do it if you had to go the rest of the way alone?"

"Don't know," I replied with an unconcern born of exhaustion.

"I've got to call the office and see if they still want me," he decided, glancing at his watch. "I don't know what we'll do if they tell me to come in in the morning."

I knew what we would do. We would manage it. Somehow, we would get ourselves organized so that all our obligations would be met, regardless of how draining it would be. I sat back, sipping iced tea while I listened to the radio telephone call.

A reprieve! Instead of getting on in the morning in Philadelphia, the personnel department told him to call in again in two days. Although it was the beginning of an uncertainty in employment that has haunted us since, we were both relieved, and stretched out to eat before tackling the engine.

In the end, it was Gary who took the boat the last leg alone while I drove to the bank, paid the bills, and did the wash. On Wednesday evening, two weeks after we had set out, we were tying the boat up at Georgetown Yacht Basin. Gary locked it, climbed onto the dock and together we went home and fell into bed. The next morning, we plodded back down to clear up.

Along with the receipts for the fuel and spare parts, flashlights and batteries, we gave the partner a list of thirty-two items which, by our estimation, should have been under manufacturer's warranty. The mainsheet padeye, screwed through one layer of fiberglass rather than through-bolted, had pulled out of the deck, wiring had been incomplete, fasteners were missing, and others were insufficient. After spending the entire day scrubbing, washing out the sheets, and packing our own gear, we contacted the partner. According to our contract, we were due payment within the week. The partner flatly refused. Cajoling, appealing to his honesty, his integrity, and his sense of fair play availed us nothing. Only when he received our lawsuit notification did we receive a check. When the smoke cleared, it had been a gruelling, expensive experience. I felt as though I deserved a long rest.

It was not to be.

SIXTEEN

WHILE I was stirring up the last of the previous summer's frozen zucchini, the phone rang. It was Dennis Berg. For years, Chris Berg's brother had owned and run the *Quaker*, a tug built in 1903. Dennis now owned two boats and a barge, and chartered another barge in his gradually expanding business, Eastern Shore Marine. As I cooked dinner, I listened to the conversation.

"I'd really like to do it, but I'm afraid I'm already committed. Yeah. But Nance has her license. She could go for you," Gary said.

My stomach fluttered nervously. Although I knew the only way to gain experience was to work, I wondered why life continuously served up things in feast or famine inequity. The idea of leaving in two days' time for an eighteen- to twenty-day stint alone on a tug with a crew of complete strangers, particularly in my condition, shook me, yet it was with relief heavily tinged with indignation that I gleaned Dennis's answer. Thanks but no thanks. The next evening, he called again. I presumed he had tried everyone else on his list and was forced to resort to me. With my heart in my throat, I accepted the job. Gary, little aware of how frightened I felt, heartily congratulated me, wrapping me in a long bear hug.

"That's great! Super! You'll be fine!" he told me enthusiastically. "You know Butch. He's running as captain now, and the other guys are all right, I'm sure. I know a couple of the fellows he's got working for him. Butch is okay though, I know."

At the end of a silent drive to Baltimore to meet the tug the following morning, we ground over the broken concrete and dusty flotsam of a quay, stopping before a deep pothole in the gravel. The *Blue Star*, which had been running steadily between Havre de Grace and Salisbury with loads of gravel, sat tied to a dock by her nose, the quirky currents in the slip wafting her stern gently back and forth. About eighty feet long, pitted with large blotches on her house, *Blue Star* looked as though she had spent considerable time in a war zone. I sat in the car for a moment, staring at the boat.

"You okay?" Gary asked, looking at me with mild concern.

"Yeah, I think so," I replied, not daring to look him in the eye.

If he guessed my doubts over what greeting the crew would give me, he was unaware of how much my pregnancy now figured in my anxiety. It was beginning to tire me more than I would have liked to admit, and the thought of decking with what I could see were heavy nylon lines occupied much of my thoughts.

"It'll be okay. It just takes a little time to get used to it," he said softly, patting my knee.

Easy for you, I thought.

The dark hulk of a barge, bloody but unbowed after a series of engagements with various crane buckets, sat at the bulkhead farther toward the channel. Sucking in a deep breath, I opened the car door.

"Okay, here I go."

Gary climbed out of the other side of the car, and, laden with clothes, binoculars, flashlight, and foul weather gear, we traipsed over the debris and climbed over *Blue Star*'s bow. The tug was shut down.

Butch, lanky and friendly, met us on the foredeck and stuck out a hand. After showing us where to stow my gear in the mate's cabin at the foot of the inside steps from the wheelhouse, he gave us a brief tour of the tug, ending up in the wheelhouse.

"We haven't got any electric steering," he told us cheerfully. "They're workin' on it down there now, but I don't think it'll be back before she goes."

Great! I smiled at his airy acceptance of it but realized that his carefree attitude was probably due to a perpetual string of malfunctions. Without electric steering, maneuvering would be like trying to parallel park a woolly mammoth. The tons of water swirling round a large rudder offered not only powerful resistance to a turn, but added a dimension of unpredictability as well, occasionally catching the rudder midway in a turn and swinging it well past the helmsman's anticipated stopping point. It was an unrelieved test of sheer brawn. Fleetingly, I wondered if the whole thing was a colossal mistake. When Butch left Gary and me in the wheelhouse, I began to cry.

Gary quickly put his arm around my shoulders and whispered: "You can do it, Nance. Don't worry, you'll be fine. You can do it."

He kissed me and to keep me from breaking down completely, scampered down the ladder, waved goodbye, and jumped in the car. My last link to the outside world broken, I sat alone, brooding on the commitment I had made so quickly. Trying to settle my nerves, I went through the chart table, pulling out the few charts I would need to get from Baltimore up to Susquehanna Flats to the gravel quarry at Havre de Grace. Leafing through the charts, I was thankful that Gary had suggested I bring my own set. The table in which the charts were stored was small, necessitating folding rather than rolling them. Tattered and outdated, they had gaps where the folds had been recreased too many times, obliterating marks, place names, depths. Courses had been charted in ink, then erased imperfectly, then redrawn. Butch may not have needed the charts intact, having run the Chesapeake for many years, but I did, and went below to unpack and dredge up the brand-new book of charts I had bought that morning.

Finally, having put off confronting the crew as long as possible, I ambled down the deck to where Butch sat in the shade outside the galley, sipping a glass of lemonade. My fears about the crew were to prove groundless. The other two men, both fairly close to me in age, welcomed me aboard in a casually open manner, chatted for a while, exchanging the usual banter of broken machinery, trips, other experiences, and then returned to the black hole they insisted on calling the engine room.

Tinkering with the steering had proved fruitless. The worn contacts were pronounced too corroded to connect so a couple of hours later, Butch and I stood on either side of the wheel, hauling the tug around to make up in pushing gear and work our way out of the slip. Once we had eased into the main channel, Butch dismissed me to go below. Gratefully, I descended the steps to my cabin and collapsed on the bunk in my clothes.

After what seemed like only moments, I heard the rap of knuckles on the plywood door and a man's unfamiliar voice call into the small square screen to wake me for the afternoon watch. Groggily, I wandered down to the galley for a sandwich and stuffed it in my pocket before ascending the steps to relieve Butch.

As at ease as in his own living room, Butch leaned back in a chair, his feet propped up on the radiator. Chatty by nature, he offered to stay up with me to take the tow through the shallow Susquehanna Flats. Glad of the initial support, I pulled out my charts and began to tick off the buoys as they slid past. Instead of hoarding his experience, he shared with me the bits of knowledge he had accumulated over the years. Running his hand along a curve of channel that swept from Turkey Point toward the turn below Fishing Battery, he indicated the wide hook of channel, telling me where to overtake or meet another tow without running either of us aground.

As I looked out the starboard window, I could see the island and the bridges beyond, their outlines filmy in the veil of summer haze, and thought of the first time I had seen them from a tug. It had seemed to me that moonlit night that they were strings of diamonds and rubies laid on a bolt of velvet. This time, I was without Gary; the romance and beauty were gone, but the exhilaration was still there.

"Start to make your turn about here," Butch advised, breaking into my reverie. "It's easier with one barge. The last guy who brought both up here together ran 'em hard aground over there," he continued, pointing out the port window.

278

"Didn't even make the turn at all. Denny had to hire another tug to have 'em pulled off."

He chuckled. While Butch talked, I hauled the wheel around to make the eighty-degree turn at Locust Point, then set up for the approach to the triangle of buoys off the yacht yard at Havre de Grace. He pointed to the chart in front of me.

"You see that can?"

I looked at his finger, then squinted through my glasses to bring the black mark into focus.

"Yeah."

"When you have to, you can cut it by about ten feet inside the triangle. It's about ten feet deep. Something that's handy to know sometimes."

"Thanks. I'll remember."

He took the helm from me to take the barge and tug through the narrow opening of the railroad bridge. I remembered coming in the opposite direction with the tunnel section bound for Washington, D.C., years ago now. It seemed recent.

Denny's other tug waited at the bulkhead beside a barge which was being loaded with gravel. Until I saw his face framed by a curly bush of hair, I had not known Bob Atwater was running as mate with Chris Schlegel as captain. I had thought Denny was still running on the *Quaker*. Originally, Dennis had spent the better part of his life aboard her, running as many as three hundred out of three hundred and sixty-five days while his wife, Janet, stayed at home, managing the shoreside operation and raising their children. It was a tough life. Now, I learned, he had come ashore to a great degree and spent considerable time managing the company with frequent trips to Salisbury to work on the dilapidated equipment.

After we tied up beside the *Quaker*, I climbed the ladder to the small wheelhouse where Chris and Bob sat talking. The familiar faces brought back memories of my first job aboard a tug, and I began to feel more at home. We left Havre de Grace with the two barges made up end to end in pushing gear ahead of the *Quaker*. Butch and Chris had agreed to go down the bay in tandem with *Quaker* acting as steering and *Blue Star* adding her power tied up alongside the after barge. Once *Quaker* took the barges through the railroad bridge alone, we made up about two-thirds of the way forward on the after barge, tying three lines to the cleats on the barge's deck, at bow, quarter, and stern. Then we settled down to watch the bay slide past, sitting in the wheelhouse and staring at the broad vista of the Chesapeake.

Bob and I were on watch at one A.M. when we began to see the glimmering lights of sailboats darting back and forth across the bay between the Magothy and Love Point. Like ghosts, the sails would materialize silently, flutter across our bow on a tack, and glide back into the darkness. As we churned closer to the bridge, they became more and more bold, appearing out of nowhere to come straight for the tow. Bob's voice came over the radio, a casual drawl I had come to enjoy as much for the easygoing attitude it represented as for the fun I had shared with him over the years.

"Nance, does it seem like there's a lot of sailboats out here tonight?" he asked. "I see one guy over there who's tryin' to cream himself on the barge."

"Yeah. I see him. It sure seems like a lot tonight, particularly for this hour. Whoops, here comes one. He's tacked right across our path."

"Where?"

"Starboard. You might not be able to see him past us."

"Oh, yeah. I got him now. Looks like he's going over again."

"Yeah."

"Listen, don't be afraid to blow your horn," he told me.

He had almost read my mind. Reluctant to do anything that would attract attention, I had only recently stopped trembling each time I picked up the radio. It was not until the sixth trip from Philadelphia to Baltimore that the C&D Canal dispatcher acknowledged my request for passage through the canal before the fifth call to him, thinking, perhaps, that it was an overly conscientious yacht owner. In commercial radio traffic, a female voice stood out. Having mastered my diffidence over broadcasting, I was now faced with overcoming a reluctance to blow a horn that would alert everyone clear to Easton of my presence.

"What the hell is this, Nance?" Bob's voice came over the radio.

"I don't know. Seems like an awful lot, doesn't it? I can't remember when the Potapskut Overnight runs. My brother sometimes races in it but I haven't talked with him for a while."

"Got in mind runnin' down family?" Bob chuckled.

Another voice broke into our conversation.

"The two vessels in the middle of the sailboat race, where exactly are you?"

"Tug *Quaker* here, pushing two barges about four miles above the Bay Bridge," Bob answered.

"Yeah, I see. Is it pretty thick up there? I've got a container ship coming up at Bloody Point. Should I slow her down?"

"Couldn't hurt. There are about thirty out here scootin' around."

"Well, thank you for that. Here comes summer!"

"Amen!"

We signed off and threaded our way through the apparitions, only once having to warn off a particularly careless or daring sailor as he raced toward our oncoming bow. Once below the bridge, the sailboats thinned to an occasional romantic out for an all-night sail. Since our main function was to act as a pair of eyes for the blind spot the *Blue Star* created for the *Quaker*, Butch had lashed the wheel in place, leaving the center button, which controls the disposition of the steering, set all the way out on manual. With a piece of nylon, he had taken several turns around the radiator and then the wheel, holding it just right of amidships to compensate for the angle we had on the tow. Stiff from sitting, I stood and squeezed through the space between the chair and steering wheel in order to peer out of the starboard window. As I brushed past the wheel, the rudder suddenly swung hard over to port. The *Blue Star* jammed her nose against the barge, straining at her lines in an attempt to submerge. The stern line groaned as it was pulled taut by the weight of the tug against it. Frantically, I clawed at the lashing trying to free the wheel and right the tug. Unable to understand what had sent her hard over, I reasoned that perhaps one of the corroded contacts had suddenly come to life in

281

the engine room, giving the steering a different command. The stern line snapped, freeing the tug to slew around precariously, taking water over the rail as she worked her way down. Without knife or sharp edge, I tore at the nylon line that held the wheel, frightened that another minute would see the rest of the lines pop and trip us completely. I had heard of more than one crew that had been killed that way. The deckhand, puzzled but less concerned than I, appeared on deck.

"Nancy?"

In desperation, I wrestled the line free, frantically spinning the slack helm. The tug still fought to submerge herself, straining against the quarter and bow lines. Bob's voice came over the radio, seemingly casual.

"You okay up there, Nance?"

Too busy to answer, I searched for the reason the helm would not respond and then realized that, in all likelihood, I had grazed the steering button just enough to pop it out of manual position and into the nebulous spot which let the rudder swing freely. Grasping the button in both hands, I yanked it back out, then tried the helm again. She answered! As the tug righted, I breathed more easily. I leaned out of the window to call to the deckhand.

"Can you find another line or maybe tie that one back together to get our stern hooked up again?"

"Yeah, I'll try."

"Good. I'll give you a hand up here when you're ready."

Puzzled, but willing to follow as much of the instruction as he understood, he wandered down the deck and soon had the other eye of the long nylon line on the barge cleat and was draping it over the narrowing gap between the vessels, ready to secure the stern again. While he made up the line, I picked up the radio microphone.

"Yeah, everything's okay up here, Robert," I called cheerily, trying to disguise the panic I had felt only a moment before.

"Yeah. Okay!"

Once the deckhand had tied the frayed end of the stern line around the towing bitts, I settled down to tick off the last few hours of my watch, struggling to keep my eyes open as the blackness faded to grey and then the sun peered over the Eastern Shore.

As we negotiated the sharp curves of the Wicomico River, we used the *Blue Star* as a misplaced bow thruster, adding a little forward push to get us around a left-hand curve, hauling back on the single bow line dropped over a cleat on the barge in order to bring the tow around a right-hand turn. As we passed Koppers creosote plant, working our way around the ninety-degree bend, we stirred up a caldron of mud where we had rubbed over the marshy beach. Although it was midafternoon, halfway through my watch, Butch had decided to take the wheel. The long tow was barely scraping past the outer reaches of the turns, nosing the fronds of grass that stuck up through the water. As the turns tightened farther upriver, the length of the tow threatened to wedge the *Quaker* and barges in one of the hairpin bends.

"I think maybe next time we ought to break 'em apart, Butch," Chris said, referring to the cumbersome length of the two-barge tow.

"Aw, don't you like all this excitement?" Butch replied with a chuckle.

"We're gonna have to squeeze you against that point to get around this one," Chris answered.

"Well, don't moosh me."

We had come out of the turn before Koppers, clearing the twiggy pier that jutted into the river, and were aimed for the next bend. In the center of the upcoming turn, a dock with a small covered shed at the end thumbed its nose at the numerous tows that traveled between the Chesapeake and Salisbury. The owner, ensconced in a lawn chair, appeared the very picture of satisfaction while he surveyed his domain. Ducks paddled amidst the reeds, heron and gulls wheeled overhead, and the brown river lay like a placid snake sunning herself under a bright blue sky.

The throb of the propellers reverberated off the riverbed, their motion bringing up swirls of waste oil and creosote which shimmered darkly in our wake. Accustomed, perhaps, to seeing a turn begun a safer distance from the small speedboat which hung from the rafters of his shed, or responding to a warning note in his psyche, the owner rose from the comfort of his chair to saunter protectively toward his pier. The barges continued forward, aimed for his dock. The man moved closer to his pier.

"Back her down, Butch," Chris's voice came over the radio.

"Roger."

Blue Star was sandwiched in between the barges and the hairy finger of shore which poked into the curve. As Butch spoke, *Blue Star* nudged aground. Instead of stopping with us, the barge slid past, gracefully ducking under the bow line by which we were leashed to her, moving easily into freedom. As I saw the single eye begin to lift off the barge's cleat, I scrambled to the foredeck. The deckhand had jumped to the barge, ready to catch the line's eye on the next cleat while I threw off the wraps on the forward bitt. Frantically, I paid out slack until the deckhand caught another cleat, then I struggled to secure the line again while it burned through my hands. The deckhand returned to help, pawing to get enough coils of line around the steel bitts to stop its escape. Finally, we got two wraps, and stood back for a second, flinging on another and then another until the line held. Once we had hitched ourselves to the barge again, we jumped back, waiting for the force of the moving barge to stretch and snap the line.

Chris had thrown *Quaker* into reverse in an effort to stop the inexorable movement of the tow. The tug shuddered hard against the push cables, rattling and groaning as she fought her bonds. The pier owner, in clear anticipation of a crash, had backed partway up his lawn again. Having mentally relinquished his dock, he stood now in fear of this monster eating its way up his lawn to consume the porch.

Our resecured bow line stretched thin, slipping on the bitts with loud snaps and pops. The barge pulled away from the *Blue Star*, leaving her still stranded on the shoal point, then suddenly, the tug moved. She halted, then moved again, and she was floating freely again, yanked off the ground by the barges. Butch pushed the throttle down, backing hard. All eyes were on the narrowing distance between the bow of the tow

284

and the brittle dock. Perceptibly, the barges slowed, then stopped. They were less than ten feet from the pier. No one moved for a second. Finally, convinced the danger was past, the owner returned to his lawn chair.

"He probably thought we were going to buy him a new dock," Bob said over the radio with a touch of amusement.

"Not today!" Butch returned, relief washing over his features as he collected his composure.

The rest of the ride to Salisbury was uneventful, a mosaic of spring color which washed over the houses and hollows along shore. Pristine lawns manicured and blotched with bright gardens were civilized havens cut in surrounding swamps.

The crew change at Salisbury brought a hostile new face. The engineer got off and in his place a young man came aboard, tattooed to the nines, with a suspiciously sleepy-eyed look who was distinctly unhappy to see a woman in the wheelhouse. He made his displeasure known in numerous barbed asides, obscenities, and a goading banter while I tried to maneuver. Ignoring his subtle assault produced nothing but an increase. Finally, in Havre de Grace, he pushed a step too far. We sat under the gravel chute, ready to pivot the barge around against two half-collapsed dolphins. It was not a difficult maneuver, but one I wished supervised by the captain who was at the time on the telephone. Standing on the foredeck within full hearing of the dock crew, the engineer leaned back and demanded that I begin the shift immediately.

"Look, all you gotta do is catch a line and swing her around. Can't you even do that?"

"He'll be back in five minutes," I said curtly. "I'd feel better if he were here to consult when I did this."

"You're keepin' everybody waitin'! Can't you even do that on your own? What's your problem? All you got to do is catch a line up there and swing the barge around."

Fully aware of my inexperience, threatened by his challenge, and knowing it was foolish to allow someone who had never worked inside a wheelhouse to instruct me, I nonetheless felt as though unqualified acquiescence on my part would have sealed my fate. What would Gary do, I wondered, having watched him ridden by jealous deckhands who were convinced that "book-learnin'" could not match "knowin'." He wouldn't let himself be pushed, that much I knew.

"Well?" he persisted. "Are you gonna keep everybody waitin' all day?"

My rising anger overcoming my timidity, I leaned out of the window and looked down on his head.

"Okay. Get me a bow and a spring and we'll do this," I said.

"You don't need to do that. Just go up there and I'll get a line in the middle," he retorted.

"You listen. If we're going to do this, we're going to do it my way. Now, what's it going to be?"

"Well, we'll wait if you're gonna be like that!"

To my surprise, the confrontation brought his needling to a halt.

Having established a niche for myself with the resident crew, news of the crew change came as a disappointment. It gradually became a time to dread when Butch and the engineer began working on me, amusing themselves by describing the replacement as a cross between the Abominable Snowman and the Texas Ax Murderer. As we passd through the final bridge toward Havre de Grace, the engineer and Butch sat in the wheelhouse while I brought the tow slowly toward the dolphins just east of the loading dock.

"Yeah. Hook's something," Butch chuckled, shaking his head.

"Hook?"

"That's the name they call him."

"Why?" I asked, wondering how a man with only one hand could deck.

"'Cause that's his name," the engineer replied with open-eyed innocence.

"He looks like a grizzly bear," Butch went on jovially.

"Yeah, but it's not so much what he looks like as what he's *done*," the engineer murmured.

"What's he done?"

"Well, we can't prove nuthin' but rumor is that he's a convicted ax murderer, out west somewhere, and he got off

286

with an insanity plea. Then he skipped the state and's been layin' low around here."

"*Ax murderer?*"

"Well, of course we can't prove anything, but we don't let him cook, you know, with the knives and stuff. I keep clear of him when he decks too. He's kinda unpredictable."

"Oh."

"But he's okay, though," Butch interjected with a serious look. "So far's I know he's never hurt a lady."

"Well, that's nice."

"Yeah, but if I was you, I'd mind my P's and Q's," the engineer said.

"Yes."

I had at the back of my mind a notion that they were kidding me. I could not imagine anyone with a conscience leaving a woman alone on a tug with a person as crazy as they described, but then again, I asked to be here. I was hardly their responsibility. We had tied against the dolphins while waiting for the loading chute to clear, and it was at about noon that Preston and Hook trudged down the deck, duffle bags slung over their shoulders.

"Is that Hook behind?" I asked Butch as I watched the two of them negotiate the cleats on the narrow decking outside the barge's high coaming.

"Yep, that's ol' Hook."

Perhaps they had not been teasing. A thick, kinky bush of hair met an equally thick black beard, effectively obscuring all but the man's eyes. A hulking presence, he walked hunched under the weight of his duffle bag, glancing up at the wheel-house as he stumped along behind Preston.

Gary had worked with Preston before and assured me he would accept me without a problem. As I watched him stride square-shouldered and determined up the ladder, I wondered. Introductions were subdued as we eyed each other. It was not until Butch left that I felt completely vulnerable. On watch, I was trapped and sat while Preston unpacked his gear in the captain's cabin just behind the wheelhouse.

"What have you done before this?" Preston asked while he

yanked open drawers and flung things around the cabin with an intensity I found alarming.

"Well, not a lot. I haven't done enough maneuvering to suit me. I still feel uncomfortable with it, but I want to learn."

"Well, anything you want to do or try, just let me know. You'll never learn until you do it."

"True enough," I muttered.

I had heard such reassuring words before only to discover that the captain had no intention of allowing me to learn. Trying to bring a barge to a dock in Baltimore, a straightforward opportunity to shift without the added complications of current and obstructions, I had repeatedly had the wheel taken from me and my questions about the procedure answered with stony silence.

It was not until evening that the single barge was loaded and we were headed out. Preston had turned the barge around and left me in the wheelhouse while he went down to help Hook with making up in pushing gear. Then he allowed me to take the tow away from the dolphins while he sat in the chair, making little notes in the log. Although it was Preston's watch, I stood behind the wheel, guiding the tow toward the broad opening of the first bridge.

"You wouldn't mind holding it for me for a few minutes while I get this done?" Preston muttered.

"No, of course not."

As we approached the first railroad bridge, a broad opening between cement pylons, Preston looked up casually.

"Just set yourself up for this, point for the middle, and the rest will follow, okay?"

"Yeah, fine," I said softly, exhilarated at having a chance to take it through the bridges for the first time.

I could feel him checking, looking up periodically without a word as we passed under the first bridge.

"Listen, I'm not quite done, you don't mind?"

"No, I don't mind."

The second bridge was an even broader gap and we went through its span effortlessly.

"Do you want to take it through the next one?" he asked gently.

288

"Well, if you trust me to. Yeah, I'd like to try."

"Okay," he stood up behind me. "Just aim for the center and keep your eyes on the way the barge shifts until you get it inside the fenders. Once you've got the needle threaded, you're pretty much set and you can put the rudder amidships and put the juice to her."

"O-kay!"

I slowed the engine and stood behind the wheel staring squarely out of the window at the tiny space between two blocks of cement that protected the base of the bridge from miscalculations. Little by little, I edged the tow forward, watching the sides of the barge as we slid toward the concrete slabs.

"Okay, you look pretty good, come a little port since the thing's not quite square to the channel, and then you've got it inside."

I swung the helm briefly to port then back and watched the tow respond to the gentle sideways motion.

"Okay, you look fine. You're inside, now give it a little more juice."

Obediently, I pushed the throttle down until I heard the engine answer in a deeper bass, and kept my eyes on the stone sides of the bridge as we passed through unscathed.

"You did it. There you go," Preston said once I had cleared the fenders. "Now you've got to swing the thing around like crazy to get it round the turn."

I did as I was told, whipping the tow just past the small black can that marked the outside of the shoal triangle off Havre de Grace, and then lined the tow up for the straight run down the buoys to the eastern turn.

"Wow! Thanks a lot!" I crowed, finally able to let out my breath.

"No problem," he said amusedly.

"Gee, I like this!"

"Yeah."

Hook was an equally happy surprise. When he joined me in the wee hours of the following morning as I guided the tow down the bay toward Hooper Straits, I had a sudden flash of apprehension. It was only several minutes into a conversation that I realized Butch and the engineer had been royally ribbing me, and that Hook was anything but the wild man he looked. Soft-spoken and gentle, he told me about how he and his wife, Beth, had run a home for the mentally handicapped, taking them on camping trips, teaching them the basic skills needed to survive the mundane technicalities of life. This was his first introduction to the water and he obviously loved it. With enthusiasm, he described his other trips, the things he had learned, and the kindnesses shown him by some of the other members of the crew. Listening to him, I was reminded of Harry. He possessed the same gentleness and exuberance for the adventure of life, and the same friendly willingness to work.

It was fortunate that the crew was so pleasant because virtually everything mechanical and electrical that could malfunction, did. For a time, the only bilge pump was a portable gasoline model that was hauled between tug and barge to keep each afloat. The radar, which worked well in clear weather and broad daylight, fainted at dusk and fog. The depthsounder was one of the few instruments that plodded faithfully along, helping to pinpoint location in haze by matching its estimations to those on the charts.

Aware of the equipment's eccentricities, Preston adjured me to keep track of our speed and location by dead reckoning, checking the buoys we passed, and plotting our course unceasingly. This not only gave me much-needed practice with a necessary skill, but ensured him an uninterrupted night's sleep when everything electronic in the wheelhouse gave out on me.

Preston's easygoing reassurances went a long way toward building my confidence. His evening litany, "If you need me, don't hesitate to call," only stirred a latent pride in being able to manage on my own.

The trip was a magical time for me, filled with the excitement of accomplishment, made all the sweeter by the nagging thought that it was all too soon to end. The nonstop run between Havre de Grace and Salisbury became a familiar melody, accompanied by the ever-changing harmony of quirky radar, unreliable steering, and radios that faded in and out. As I ran past the friendly faces of Hooper's Island Light, Bloody

Point Light, Tolchester, and Turkey Point, I began to feel more a part of this special world, less an outsider.

One moonless night as I ran up the line of flashing buoys from Tolchester past Poole's Island looking for the quick-flashing turning mark, I suddenly realized something felt wrong. We had gone too far. Pulling back on the throttle, I coasted along, scanning the black horizon for the light. Nothing. Farther ahead, I saw the running lights of two vessels downbound, one a ship coming from the canal, the other, a nameless tug pulling a barge.

"*Henry M* to *Blue Star*," an easygoing voice came over the radio.

The *Henry M* was a tug out of Baltimore that was running perpetually between Havre de Grace and Hart Island with a bargeload of rock. We had crossed paths often in our shuttles and passed the time of day over the radio. It was the captain of the *Henry M* who had advised me when and where to overtake him in the narrow channel from Locust Point past the Fishing Battery in the Susquehanna Flats. Although he was a faceless voice on the radio, I knew him as a generous man, knowledgeable and confident enough to share his experience.

"*Blue Star* back to *Henry M*."

"Yeah, Cap. Go on over to channel six," the voice said casually.

"Roger, switching to six."

"*Blue Star*, you're off the channel, Babe. You're in real shallow water there. You see me over here?"

"Is that you comin' down in front of that ship?"

"That's me. Turn and split the distance between where we are now and you'll be okay."

"Bless you, *Henry M*."

With anonymous tact, he had saved me from an acute embarrassment. It was then that I felt initiated into the club of commercial tugboating, helped by another whose memories included his own youthful inexperience, and whose advice was offered as simply as an outstretched hand. It was a gesture I have never properly thanked though always appreciated.

At the end of three weeks, my pregnancy still a secret, I

went home. I had lost forty pounds since leaving the *Progress*, and all my work clothes hung on me with unisex abandon. But despite the camouflage, I knew my days aboard tugs were numbered. Every attempt to throw a deck line or haul on the hawser announced itself uncomfortably, and soon, common sense would win over stubbornness. Gary had been gone for two weeks by the time I got home, and expected to be away for another three before coming home for a day and then meeting a sailboat in Newport to race to Bermuda. Since we had spent so much time together, the time apart was now more difficult, so when Freddie Carter telephoned to ask Gary to make a trip on the *Nanticoke*, a sister to the *Progress*, I volunteered.

"Listen, he's gone as far as I know until he's due to race. What's the trip?" I asked.

"It's just a run to Norfolk for a LASH tow. Shouldn't take more than four days or so," he replied.

"I'll go."

Freddie paused.

"Uh, well, yeah, Nance," he stammered.

Hearing the reluctance, I backed off.

"Look, I've got the license to run as your mate, so if you get stuck for someone, I can do it. And I'm only an hour from Wilmington."

"Yeah, okay, thanks, Nance. I'll let you know if we need you. Thanks."

Although he had spontaneously offered to sign a recommendation for my license, comfortable with the idea of a woman mate, he was less easygoing about the actual fact of one aboard a tug without a husband in evidence. However, pressed for time and crew, he returned the call a half an hour later and by that evening, I was unpacking groceries in the *Nanticoke*'s galley. Freddie's wife, Huldy, had agreed to come as cook, a compromise that assuaged Fred's sensibilities.

Happy to be working rather than lying at home watching my belly grow, I had not considered the possibility that Gary's and my paths would cross. It was when I came up to relieve Freddie at midnight that he told me we had passed the *Patriot* in the C&D Canal, and he had spoken to Gary.

"He wants you to call him on eighty-eight."

"Thanks."

When Freddie closed the door to the captain's cabin, I took the microphone off the overhead and switched the radio to channel eighty-eight.

"Tug *Nanticoke* to *Patriot*."

"*Patriot* back to *Nanticoke*. Hey, Babe, how about you!" Gary's voice came through the speaker.

"Where're you headed?" I asked, suddenly yearning to touch him in the darkness of the wheelhouse.

"We're going down to the anchorage and then I'm getting off."

"You're kidding! When will you be home?"

"Tomorrow probably."

"For how long?"

"Five days."

"And then you go up to Newport."

"Right."

"I don't get off here for four or five days."

"Freddie told me."

Resentment at the forces pulling us apart overwhelmed me. On different boats going in opposite directions, we talked until our voices were drowned by the gritty interference of the land.

As I rounded Thimble Shoal Light at the entrance to Hampton Roads, I saw the *Progress* in the distance, plowing out of the harbor towing an unrecognizable object welded to a flat barge.

"Tug *Nanticoke* to *Progress*."

Doug's voice came on the line.

"My *Gawd*, Nance, is that you?"

"Yeah. Hey, Doug. What're you doin' up?"

"What are you doin' out here? Aren't you too far gone to run any more? Don't they know you're pregnant?"

"Not until this minute. I guess everyone south of Wolf Trap knows now," I replied.

If the crew of the *Michael Keen* had heard the conversation, they gave no indication. Scotty was now captain and met us at Newport News to make up the LASH tow. We worked in the

293

sun, laughing over the same old stories and catching up on one another's lives. That evening, weathered in with the tow, I called Gary from the guano-covered dock. It was a nice reversal, a taste for each of what the other experienced while apart, but the trade was short-lived. When I got home, Gary had gone again, this time to race to Bermuda and then return in time to get on yet another tug. Alone, puttering around the garden, I had ample time to brood over a woman's lot. Hungry for adventure, yet unable to leave the raising of our child to someone else, I worried over how I would manage full-time motherhood and returning to work.

Several weeks later, Denny called, this time for me. I had arrived! He needed a mate for three or four days on the *Quaker*, and I drove to the gravel pit at Havre de Grace to trade places with Preston. Halfway down the bay, the electric steering went out. Unlike the *Blue Star* which boasted a wheel about four feet in diameter, the *Quaker* had a shining brass wheel the size of a fifty-seven Ford Fairlane's, making manual steering even more of a battle of wills. Although my belly was by no means large, getting a knee to my chest to put a foot in the high spokes for extra leverage was no simple task.

Denny and Preston met us off the mouth of the Wicomico in Preston's runabout to tinker with the wiring below in an effort to give us steering for the sharp turns of the river. While the thought was appreciated the trip proved fruitless and Butch and I stood on either side of the small wheel, yanking it around the bends to a chorus of grunts and groans.

Having confided to Preston that I was pregnant and could not deck any longer, he smiled.

"I thought so. But listen, if you can't do the job you were hired to do, all of it, you owe it to the man to tell him."

I knew he was right, and so when Denny asked me if I could stay through the weekend to take the barge to Seaford then make a trip to Norfolk and back, I confessed, feeling oddly as though I had been caught with my hand in the cookie jar.

"Denny, I'd be glad to stay on the extra time, but there's something you should know," I gulped and turned my back to Butch and Preston who were waiting to use the telephone. "I'm pregnant and I can't really deck any more."

There was a silence on the other end of the line for a few seconds.

"Well," he sighed, "don't strain yourself."

Relieved at his response, but knowing that should anything happen, it would be my responsibility, I continued.

"I don't think I can deck at all, but I'll do my best to make it up in other ways, whatever I can, cooking, shopping, cleaning."

"Well," he drawled, "we've had some old men who can *never* deck."

I dropped the phone onto the cradle and sucked in a long, sweet breath.

The next morning we left for Seaford to collect the barge. It was to be my last run for Denny. The weather cloyed, one of the syrupy days of August on the Chesapeake. Nightfall was a blessing. We had run up the Nanticoke River to collect the barge, a hulk with peeled-back coaming reminiscent of the foil on a baked potato. The river currents redistribute the channel each season, making navigation difficult for anyone unaccustomed to feeling her way along the bottom.

At quarter to twelve, I dragged myself up the ladder to the wheelhouse, a ham sandwich in the pocket of my shorts and a glass of iced tea in my hand. My arms were a mass of welts where the mosquitoes had feasted and I felt groggy from the heat.

"I'll stay up and help you get into Tangier Sound," Butch told me.

"I appreciate it, Butch, but I remember how it goes from here on, I think," I replied, both more confident now, and wanting to prove that I was not a liability in captain's overtime.

"No, that's okay. It's a little tricky."

He sat up with me, chatting amiably until we reached the junction buoy at the Nanticoke and Wicomico rivers. After detailing possible pitfalls in the sound, Butch went to bed, leaving me alone. The new deckhand, Pat, an intelligent, quiet man, periodically poked his head in the window for a word or two while standing in the zephyr created by our forward motion.

The steamy August day had faded into an equally steamy night. Without the radar, I was dependent on running from buoy to buoy with the doubtful aid of an eccentric compass.

When Pat came up at two, he found me prancing nervously around the wheelhouse, binoculars to my eyes, flashlight in hand as I tried to match the configuration of the chart to what I could make out through the lenses. I handed him the binoculars.

"Can you see a four-second red flasher down about there?" I said, pointing into the dim glow of the moonlight.

He put the glasses to his eyes and moved them deliberately over the horizon in an arc.

"I'm pretty sure we're here," I said, pointing to a spot under the glare of a flashlight. "It's so hazy I lost the range behind us about fifteen minutes ago. I should be seeing that flasher by now."

Pat looked at the chart, then put the glasses to his eyes again.

"Maybe it's out," he remarked. "Looks like there's one out on Deal Island."

"Yeah. Problem is, I'm counting on this buoy. It's my turning mark."

"Aren't you afraid this kind of thing will be bad for your baby?" he asked, handing the binoculars through the open window.

"You have children of your own?" I smiled.

"A little girl. She just went back to live with her mother," he replied laconically.

"I'm sorry. Is she far away?"

"Too far. Illinois."

"How old is she?"

"Three. Aren't you worried that all this pressure on you is going to affect your baby?" he repeated with concern.

I shook my head, touched at his tenderness.

"I really don't think so. I can't stand not to work, not to be here. It would be far worse for the baby if I were home fuming about being alone, gaining too much weight, resenting being cooped up. I really do believe that, Pat. I need to keep busy doing something I love for as long as I can."

Unconvinced, he let the subject drop.

"Want anything from below?"

"No, thanks."

"See you later then."

The light of the rising moon was filtered through a veil that obscured the buoys more than one mile distant, leaving me without reference point. It was like swinging from tree to tree, forsaking one grip before obtaining another. Looking over the compass, I could see only one buoy. The angle felt wrong. Slowing the tug, I began to reassess my position from all points as best I could. The last mark had been out and the one before it dim, and without radar I could not see whether we lined up on them or had taken, as my instinct told me, a right-hand curve. The breeze, however soft, had begun to shift direction slightly and I was in a hole with only one flashing red light visible. There should have been two. After a few moments when I did not speed up, Pat climbed the ladder to stand beside the open window.

"Take these, Patrick, and see if you can make out two buoys. There should be one about sixty degrees from the other," I said, handing him the binoculars and hoping he could see through them better without having to readjust for spectacles.

"All I see is the one," he said pointing to the buoy off our starboard bow.

"Doesn't feel right."

I had stopped the tug completely by now and hoped that Butch would not awaken.

"I see it!" he said suddenly.

"Thank God! Where?"

He put out an arm, letting me sight down its length, then gave me the binoculars.

"That's got to be it. Light's out. I'll make for it slowly until I see the next one. Thanks a million."

"S'pose the next one's out?"

"Keep a good thought."

Having had the chance to run down Tangier Sound completely cold gave me a new sense of accomplishment, an exhilaration in my growing ability. The buoy Pat had spotted was indeed the turning mark, and as we approached it, I could see the next buoy appear in sequence, calming my pounding heart. Although the night was sticky, the moon had climbed high overhead and raised the dim outlines of the grass-fringed shore. Nowhere else, I thought, could I experience such beauty. The day had dawned by the time Butch relieved me and I lay down in my clothes and fell asleep.

As we rounded Old Point, a summer squall blew up, rolling in the rich, blue-black clouds of warning before hosing us down with a shower. We all sat in the wheelhouse, enjoying the delicious relief from the sweaty heat of the past several days. As I wandered below to lie down, I watched the storm chase off across the bay. It felt glorious.

After leaving the barge at a dock in Norfolk, we headed home light tug. The storm had cleared out the sticky heat and when I came up on watch at midnight, a bright moon was rising over the bay, casting the dark hulls of passing ships in relief against the shore. Although I had several tight-throated moments where I could not identify quick-flashing current buoys that were unmarked on the chart, we passed into Tangier Sound without incident to enjoy a quiet, starry night. Like the poem "Jemima," when it is good it is very, very good, and this night was one of the best. Nature was dressed in an indigo satin gown, spangled with the diamonds, rubies, and emeralds of the buoy lights and crowned with a tiara of stars. A fresh breeze blew offshore, a fragrant reminder of the lush summer crops just past their prime that stretched for miles on the other side of the salt marshes. The feeling of being there, of being alone with the elements, drinking in the sensual pleasure of the soft air, the scents of land and water, is to me unlike any other. It is a feeling of utter peace and contentment. I did not let myself think that it was in all probability the last time I would have that pleasure for a long time. Right then, it was perfect.

S E V E N T E E N

AFTER THE trip to Norfolk on the *Quaker*, I decided that discretion and common sense dictated my coming ashore. While it was a free decision, I had no peace with it, throwing myself without enthusiasm into childbirth classes and gardening. I yearned to work again, to be out on the water. I missed the thrill of accomplishment, the companionship, and the change of routine. I missed the satisfaction of seeing my own name on a paycheck, of knowing that my services were valuable enough to command pay.

When Jack called, I was ripe for a job.

"We've got a tunnel section to take from Port Deposit to Baltimore," he said on the telephone. "Can Gary run as mate?"

"No, he's gone but I can."

"Fine. Be at Wilmington at six tomorrow morning."

"There's one problem, Jack. I'm pregnant," I told him timorously.

"Congratulations."

At that point he had five children with another on the way and was understandably casual about the whole thing.

"No, Jack. I'm really pregnant. I mean I can't deck at all."

"Just how pregnant are you?" he asked suspiciously.

"Seven and a half months."

"Holy Cow! Can you even get into the wheelhouse? It's the *Mercury*."

The upper wheelhouse on the *Mercury*, an old 1898 steam tug converted to diesel, was about the size of a roomy telephone booth. Inside, a large chair bolted to the center between the two steering tillers took up most of the available space, leaving enough room to squeeze in the door and sit down, with standing room only for a visitor.

"No problem."

"Fine. See you at six."

By the time I arrived at the yard, the other three were there, leaning against their cars and sipping coffee from cardboard cups. Although I had done a tow with two of the men three months before, they were unaware until I stepped out of the Honda that I was going to have a baby. As I walked over to them, carrying a small overnight bag and draped in one of Gary's oversized shirts, all eyes were on my belly. Bill, the engineer who had been on board in July when Gary and I helped to bring a large crane to Philadelphia, was the first one to recover.

"When's it due, Nance?"

"Second or third week in November."

I thought of the conversation I had had with the childbirth class instructor the night before when I told her why I would miss the next class.

"Do you think you can get to help within an hour?"

I had thought of the age of the tug, the temperamental radios dependent on ancient wiring, the vagaries of nature.

"I don't know."

"It's something to think about."

It was indeed. I had not escaped being dropped from a helicopter onto the deck of a supply boat in the Mexican Gulf only to be air-lifted off a tug in the midst of labor. Even so, the job was a straightforward one that Gary and I had done before and one which required little either in heavy decking or navigating.

The tunnel section was an identical piece to the one *Progress* had taken through the railroad bridge seven years before en route to Washington, D.C., and just another in a series that were being delivered to Baltimore Harbor for its cross-harbor tunnel. The point tug for the tow sidled up to us shortly after we had climbed aboard the *Mercury* which sat at a bulkhead at Wylie's shipyard in Port Deposit. The crew, whom Gary and I had seen on a duplicate job several months before, betrayed no surprise at my obviously advanced condition, but hailed us cheerfully before running around to one end of the section to pick it up on the hawser bridles.

The captain left me alone in the wheelhouse and joined Bill and Charlie on deck to struggle with the weight of the lengthened pushing cables as they made up to the tunnel section. Seated at the controls, I felt guilty performing the painless chore of moving the old tug from one side to the other. Had I not been pregnant, I knew it would have been me on deck with Bill and Charlie, and the captain sitting happily at the controls. Once made up in pushing gear, we cast off and the other tug pulled the tunnel section away from the dock, cautiously at first, then, as we cleared the shore, faster. Sitting in the wheelhouse, staring at the wall of rusted, unpainted steel, I was glad to have this last job. It was not glamorous, or even inspiring. It was just a piece of work that needed doing and needed a full crew to do it. Our contribution to the tow was both power and rudder, but we were completely at the command of the lead tug. Without eyes, our movements were directed at every step by the captain or mate of the forward tug. Going through the tight gap of the railroad bridge was, for us, simply a matter of responding to orders over the radio.

"Five degrees right rudder."

"Five degrees right."

"'Midships."

"'Midships."

"Give me a little astern with the rudder amidships."

"Stern power with rudder amidship."

Once we had cleared the bridge, the orders were few, an occasional warning to keep an eye out for a buoy that would slide past particularly closely, or an assist on a bend. Most of the chatter between the tugs was about family, home, hobbies, as well as comments on the numerous conversations among well-heeled pleasure boaters.

"Hey, Nancy! Did you hear that menu that lady was reelin' off? Turkey and tarragon mayonnaise, wine, salad. Maybe we should take a detour!"

"John, you could lead me to Canada and I wouldn't know

the difference until I started seeing whales."

He chuckled.

"Kinda gotcha back there, haven't we?"

"At your beck and call."

As I watched the bubbles float past our hull in the still, murky water of a hot Chesapeake day, I knitted listlessly and longed for a life I feared I was leaving forever.

"Hey, Nancy! Did you hear that guy? They found a body in the harbor with a bag over its head and cement feet. Sounds like an execution, doesn't it?"

"Maybe we should just go to Canada instead. They must need a tunnel section."

"Yeah, I got ya. Pretty grisley, isn't it?"

"Yeah, yuk!"

It was not until we had put the tow to dock, following the careful instructions of both John, the captain, who had stayed in the wheelhouse, and his mate who wandered along the dock, relaying information and instructions over a hand radio, that I wished I had brought a camera. Over the years, I had found a camera to be a problem, something that was in the way while working when all the best pictures could be had, or forgotten when at leisure. But when I stepped out onto the wheelhouse steps in full view of the dock crew who had lined up to watch the lady in the wheelhouse, their expressions were worth capturing on film.

Four men in rolled-sleeved T-shirts had jostled each other the entire time we were putting the section to the bulkhead, pointing occasionally to where I stood beside the captain, and punching each other in the ribs like schoolboys. But when I opened the door and stepped outside to check the distance between the tug and the bulkhead, their mouths dropped open and to a man they stood staring at my figure, transfixed. The mate who stood on the dock with the radio in hand cast an amused smirk at the men before waving goodbye.

The job finished, we sailed light tug for Wilmington, the weather giving me a gracious farewell. A quiet, clear night with stars cast overhead like myriad strings of Christmas lights faded into a rosy dawn. The reeds onshore, salt clinging to the stems, smelled like fresh grain and were bronzed in the glow of the sun rising over the marshes. As we passed through the swing bridge before turning into the creek where Compass Marine was located, the pungent odor of creosote surrounded me, drowning out all other smells until we had emerged into the muddy swamp on the other side. Then it was done.

Two months later, Matthew entered our lives. Although I love motherhood and cannot bring myself to leave Matt for uncertain days or weeks at a time, I feel as though half of my life is missing. We keep hoping, and planning. We know the chances of accepting all the Robsons are slim. Still, we try, we think, we search. We have been told before that things are impossible. Ultimately, nothing that is right is impossible.

anchor-pulling tug. A tug used to hoist anchors which secure oil rigs in place. Such tugs may also tow the rigs to their locations.

barge-chaser. A slang term for a man who oversees arrival, loading, and departure of his company's barges. The barge-chasers work with the marine insurance surveyors setting up a tow to the insurer's satisfaction, retrieving new cables, and tightening guy wires and fasteners which hold a cargo to a flat deck barge. Other times, they oversee the loading of various cargos—grain, fertilizer, scrap metal, etc. The men run errands, bring extra LASH straps for a tow, double-check conditions of the barges, and obligingly ferry tug crews to and from airports for crew change.

bitt. A strong, short, upright post fastened to the deck, usually found in pairs. On *Progress*, there were four sets of quarter bitts, i.e., bitts affixed to the forward or after quarters of the vessel's deck. A line can be wrapped in figure eights around the post of the bitt and then under the horn, which, on these quarter bitts, is a downward-pointing tongue affixed below the level of the gunwale.

bitts, towing. The freestanding bitts on the stern which are welded to the deck close to the deckhouse. They straddle the centerline of the vessel beside the capstan which allows an easy lead through the bitts to the capstan drum. It is to these bitts that the hawser is secured during towing.

bollard. An upright post or bitt, usually metal, which is often shaped like a fire hydrant, ranging in size from knee-high to waist-high, and affixed to a dock or barge around which mooring or towing lines are thrown. They can accommodate the thick deck lines of vessels as large as oil tankers.

bone in her teeth. An expression used to denote a frothing white bow wave.

bridles. The pair of cables which are shackled to the end of the hawser and are used to attach the hawser to the barge when towing. On *Progress*, the cable is one inch in diameter and has a large loop spliced into

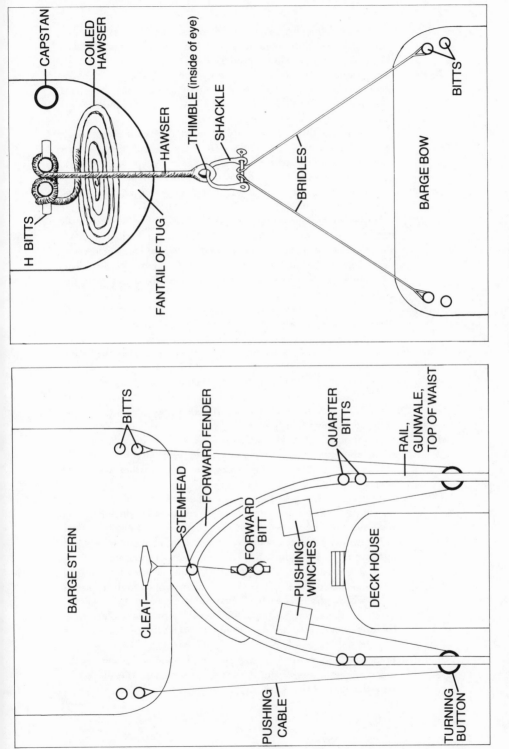

Tug in towing position.

Tug in pushing position.

one end which is dropped onto the barge's bitt, and a smaller eye with a thimble in the opposite end through which it is shackled to the spliced eye of the nylon rope hawser.

Buffalo china. Generically, thick, heavy-duty china. It is often used for plates, cups, saucers, and bowls not only on tugs, but in various institutional cafeterias where the place settings get hard wear.

C&D. Chesapeake and Delaware Canal.

capstan. A large vertical drum, revolving on a spindle, which acts as a winch by which the hawser is pulled in. On *Progress*, it is operated by a control on deck just above the machine but is powered by an electric motor which is switched on below in the engine room.

chain plate. On sailing vessels, a metal plate fastened vertically to the hull for securing the lower ends of the standing rigging—the shrouds, for example, that support the mast. When I used it in reference to a barge, I really mean a piece of angle-iron (an L-shaped metal strapping). One side is welded to the deck of a flat barge. The other side sticks up at right angles. Holes are drilled in the upright side to accommodate the wires and chains which secure the cargo to the deck of the barge.

deck. To deck is to heave lines to dock, to help make up to a barge, to pull hawser, in short, to do any of the work on deck as distintict from work in the engine room or wheelhouse.

Ditch. Slang term for the Intercoastal Waterway (ICW), also called the Inland Waterway.

dog. A swiveling lever used to clamp or secure some object, as a cabin door. On *Progress*, there were four on each door, one at each rounded corner. To turn these levers into the secure position is *to dog* the door, clamping it tightly shut.

dolphin. A cluster of pilings, held together by several wraps of cable (wire), to which something the size of a tug and barge or larger can tie. The cluster is designed for strength where the weight of the vessel would snap a single piling.

DPC. An acronym for Defense Plant Corporation which built a series of one-design tugs during World War II. The tugs, of which *Progress* was one, became known as DPC's. They are each eighty-six feet long, twenty-four feet wide, with a draft of about ten feet, and approximately forty-three feet off the water to the antennas. Originally designed to carry ten- to eleven-man crews, they had two bunks in each of the five lower cabins and one bunk in the captain's cabin which adjoins the wheelhouse on the boat or upper deck. On *Progress*, three of the original bunks had been removed, one from the engineer's cabin and two from a cabin on the port side which became a spare gear locker.

fantail. The deck of the stern of the tug. As seen from above facing aft, the usual configuration of the tug's stern is similar to the shape of a partially opened lady's fan.

forepeak. The forward compartment in any vessel, it takes its name from the fact that it is formed into the pointed bow of the vessel. On *Progress*, the forepeak is a room located beneath the foredeck and accessible through a trapdoor in the galley or, when necessary, through a large, removable plate bolted to the foredeck.

full bore. A slang expression also used in many places other than the maritime to denote going full blast, wide open, hammer down, as fast as the machine will go.

fuzzy bills. Tiny, gnatlike insects.

genoa. Genoa jib, also called genny. It is a large foresail used on racing and cruising sailboats.

hawser. Any heavy line or cable used for mooring or towing. Here it is used to mean specifically the line used to attach the tug to the barge when towing. The laid nylon line on *Progress* is eight inches in circumference, and twelve hundred feet long. When stored, it is coiled onto a wooden rack which holds the coil off the deck so that water will drain through.

H-bitts. A pair of bitts connected by a cross member, forming an H.

Inland Waterway. The Intercoastal Waterway, the Ditch.

LASH. An acronym for Lighter Aboard SHip. It is a specific type of barge designed to be hauled from the water and loaded with its cargo intact aboard a ship for transport, whereas most other barges have their cargos in holds of some kind and unload at terminals or onto vessels, then return empty for another load.

light tug. A tug running alone without a tow.

Loran. An electronic LOng RAnge Navigation system. A shipboard receiver translates the time difference between the receipt of pairs of radio signals into numbers that relate to coordinates, or hyperbolic gridlines on a chart, identifying the exact location of the vessel.

making up. A term used to denote attaching the tug to a barge, either in the pushing position (with the cables) or alongside.

monkey fist. A ball-like knot used to encase a weight at the end of a heaving line. Sometimes the term is used to denote the heaving line itself.

on the hip. A term used to denote attaching the tug to the side of the barge either to port or starboard, or being so attached.

pushing cables. The pair of wire cables which are used to hold the barge tight against the bow of the tug when the tug is in pushing position. The wires are one inch in diameter with eyes or loops made into the ends that are dropped onto the bitts of the barge. The bitter ends of the pushing cables are then led down the sides of the tug, outboard, through the turning buttons, then up the deck forward to the drums of the pushing winches which, on *Progress*, are welded to the foredeck. It is by these winches that the cables are pulled taut.

307

pushing winch. A winch is a machine or engine used for hoisting or heaving. The pushing winches on *Progress* are two horizontally mounted cylinders or drums about twelve inches in diameter around which the pushing cables are wound. Each winch drum is attached to gears which are turned manually by a large wheel mounted on the inboard side. The entire drum gear mechanism is housed inside a metal boxlike casing intended to keep lines, cables, and unwary deckhands out of the grinding teeth of the gears.

reef. To reef is to reduce the sail area on a sailboat, which helps somewhat to right the boat in a heavy wind, retaining the sail's stabilizing effects as well as its drive without taking the sail down altogether.

Roaring Forties. The rough passage of water between forty degrees and fifty degrees south latitude.

scupper. A hole for carrying off water from the deck. On *Progress*, the scuppers are cut in the waist (the metal sides of the tug attached to the deck) at deck level on each side, fore and aft, and are about the size of a bread box.

soft line. Any pliant line as distinct from a wire cable.

steering quadrant. A large, metal quarter-circle (quadrant) attached horizontally to the top of the rudder post. The steering cables are attached to the quadrant and thus control the rudder.

stemhead. The post which sits atop the extreme bow of the tug.

Stokes litter. A type of form-fitting metal stretcher which cradles a person and which can be safely lowered and raised by helicopter.

towing bitts. *See* bitts, towing.

turning buttons. Fixed metal sheaves or pulleys about the size of a large frying pan. They are positioned in slots in the waist, approximately amidships, one on each side, and act as bending points for the pushing cables, *q.v.*

winch. *See* pushing winch.